*New York Times v. Sullivan*

# LANDMARK LAW CASES

## AMERICAN SOCIETY

Peter Charles Hoffer

N. E. H. Hull

*Series Editors*

RECENT TITLES IN THE SERIES:

*Murder in Mississippi*, Howard Ball

*The Detroit School Busing Case*, Joyce A. Baugh

*Sexual Harassment and the Law*, Augustus B. Cochran III

*The DeShaney Case*, Lynne Curry

*The Battle over School Prayer*, Bruce J. Dierenfield

*Nazi Saboteurs on Trial*, Louis Fisher

*Little Rock on Trial*, Tony A. Freyer

*One Man Out: Curt Flood versus Baseball*, Robert M. Goldman

*The Free Press Crisis of 1800*, Peter Charles Hoffe

*The Treason Trials of Aaron Burr*, Peter Charles Hoffer

Griswold v. Connecticut, John W. Johnson

M'Culloch v. Maryland, Mark R. Killenbeck

*The Slaughterhouse Cases, Abridged Edition*,
Ronald M. Labbé and Jonathan Lurie

Mapp v. Ohio, Carolyn N. Long

Dred Scott *and the Politics of Slavery*, Earl M. Maltz

*The Snail Darter Case*, Kenneth M. Murchison

*Animal Sacrifice and Religious Freedom*, David M. O'Brien

*Capital Punishment on Trial*, David M. Oshinsky

*The Michigan Affirmative Action Cases*, Barbara A. Perry

*The Sodomy Cases*, David A. J. Richards

*The Supreme Court and Tribal Gaming*, Ralph A. Rossum

*The* Insular Cases *and the Emergence of American Empire*,
Bartholomew H. Sparrow

San Antonio v. Rodriguez *and the Pursuit of Equal Education*, Paul Sracic

Mendez v. Westminster, Philippa Strum

*The Confederacy on Trial*, Mark A. Weitz

*The Times and Trials of Anne Hutchinson*, Michael P. Winship

*The Miracle Case*, Laura Wittern-Keller and Raymond J. Haberski, Jr.

*The Zoning of America*: Euclid v. Ambler, Michael Allan Wolf

*The Battle for the Black Ballot*, Charles L. Zelden

For a complete list of titles in the series go to www.kansaspress.ku.edu.

KERMIT L. HALL AND
MELVIN I. UROFSKY

# New York Times v. Sullivan

## Civil Rights, Libel Law,

## and the Free Press

UNIVERSITY PRESS OF KANSAS

Published by the University Press of Kansas (Lawrence, Kansas 66045), which was
organized by the Kansas Board of Regents and is operated and funded by Emporia
State University, Fort Hays State University, Kansas State University, Pittsburg State
University, the University of Kansas, and Wichita State University

Library of Congress Cataloging-in-Publication Data

Hall, Kermit.
New York Times v. Sullivan : civil rights, libel law, and the free press /
Kermit L. Hall and Melvin I. Urofsky.
p. cm. — (Landmark law cases & American society)
Includes bibliographical references and index.
ISBN 978-0-7006-1802-6 (cloth : alk. paper)
ISBN 978-0-7006-1803-3 (pbk. : alk. paper)
1. New York Times Company — Trials, litigation, etc. 2. Sullivan, L. B. — Trials,
litigation, etc. 3. Trials (Libel) — Alabama — Montgomery. 4. Freedom of the press —
United States. 5. Libel and slander — United States. I. Urofsky, Melvin I. II. Title.
KF228.N4H35 2011
342.7308'53--dc22
2011014246

British Library Cataloguing-in-Publication Data is available.

Printed in the United States of America

10 9 8 7 6 5 4 3 2 1

The paper used in this publication is recycled and contains 30 percent postconsumer
waste. It is acid free and meets the minimum requirements of the American National
Standard for Permanence of Paper for Printed Library Materials Z39.48-1992.

*For Phyllis*

# CONTENTS

Editors' Preface  *ix*

Introduction  *1*

1. A Place in Time  *5*

2. "Lies, Lies, Lies"  *28*

3. Trial by Jury  *45*

4. "Let 'em See the Dogs Work"  *69*

5. The Road to the Alabama Supreme Court  *83*

6. A New Game Plan  *100*

7. Briefing the Court  *119*

8. "May It Please the Court"  *138*

9. "Uninhibited, Robust, and Wide-Open"  *160*

10. Libel Law after *Sullivan*  *182*

11. Coda: Civility and Reputation  *201*

Chronology  *207*

Bibliographical Essay  *209*

Index  *215*

# EDITORS' PREFACE

One usually associates southern honor with duels in antebellum days, gentlemen settling reputed libel and slander cases with pistols or swords instead of lawsuits. While all but the Magnolias of the Old South might have disappeared by the beginning of the 1960s, the honor of white southern officials was very much at stake as they confronted the civil rights movement. They grew increasingly agitated over the national media's coverage of events in their communities, especially as images such as those of a sneering overweight police chief overseeing police dogs snarling at youthful marchers or the abusive arrest of unresisting picketers became a staple of the nightly news. Such images, in their opinion, greatly distorted their overall conduct during this troubling time.

When the *New York Times* published a full-page advertisement that accused the governor of Alabama and others in office of wantonly and willfully mistreating Martin Luther King and other civil rights activists, southern honor (and the prospect of bankrupting the civil rights movement in the South) induced Montgomery, Alabama, public safety commissioner L. B. Sullivan and others to file suit for defamation. Alabama trial and appeals courts in short compass agreed that under Alabama law the *Times* had defamed the plaintiffs. Harsh words and material errors of fact in the ad (even though it was not written by *Times* staff) were defamatory, and the *Times* was ordered to pay half a million dollars in damages. In a companion case, four of the members of the Southern Christian Leadership Conference, all ministers, were also sued for having allowed their names to be listed as endorsees of the ad's contents. They, too, were socked with stiff damage awards, even though they had not actually approved of their inclusion in the ad as endorsees and, in fact, had not known anything about the ad until after it was published.

In 1964, after a stellar array of legal talent argued the issues before the high court, a unanimous Court announced a decision that profoundly altered the landscape of defamation law. At stake was more than the monetary awards or even the crushing blow the suit would have delivered to the civil rights movement. If the plaintiffs were allowed to enjoy their victory, freedom of the press would be the biggest loser. For political opinion, including criticism of the conduct of those in office, is the foundation of all other political rights. Silence the opposition in the press, and who can denounce tyranny? Thus the case lay both in the realm of civil rights law and in the First Amendment's freedom of the press guarantee. As Justice William Brennan wrote for a unanimous Court, "Thus we consider this case against the background of a profound national commitment to the principle that debate on public issues should be uninhibited, robust, and wide-open, and that it may well include vehement, caustic, and sometimes unpleasantly sharp attacks on government and public officials."

But Brennan was not done. He introduced a new First Amendment test. "The constitutional guarantees require, we think, a federal rule that prohibits a public official from recovering damages for a defamatory falsehood relating to his official conduct unless he proves that the statement was made with 'actual malice' — that is, with knowledge that it was false or with reckless disregard of whether it was false or not." Even if the advertisement was derogatory and it contained some errors of fact, "neither factual error nor defamatory content suffices to remove the constitutional shield from criticism of official conduct." For "a rule compelling the critic of official conduct to guarantee the truth of all his factual assertions — and to do so on pain of libel judgments virtually unlimited in amount — leads to a . . . 'self-censorship' " that would chill all political opinion.

The bare-bones description above cannot begin to capture the high drama of *New York Times v. Sullivan* as it unfolded. Fortunately, the case has here found two of the foremost students of American constitutional history to tell its story, Melvin Urofsky and the late Kermit Hall. Hall began the work and Urofsky finished it, but their collaboration is seamless and altogether convincing. It moves swiftly and surely from the editorial offices of the *Times* in New York City to the street corners of Montgomery, Alabama, from a trial court in the Alabama capitol to the Marble Palace in Washington, D.C., bringing to life the lawyers and their clients, the human faces behind the law. It is a masterwork by two masters of the craft of history.

# Introduction

When I entered the field of American constitutional and legal history in the early 1980s, Kermit Hall was an established figure, respected both for his monographs and for the important reference works he edited. More important, as I soon learned, his unfailing generosity and sense of humor made him one of the best-liked scholars in the country. Although five years younger than I, he was the senior and took me under his wing. Before long we were cooperating on a variety of projects, he writing for me and I doing the same for his volumes. I was teaching in Sicily when I opened my e-mail on August 14, 2006, to learn of Kermit's tragic death the day before while on vacation. No one seemed able to believe it, and for the next few weeks people posted their stories about the Kermit Hall they knew. All were stories of friendship, of mentoring, of kindness, and of humor. They all said he would be missed, and he still is.

Kermit had been working for many years on a study of *New York Times v. Sullivan* (1964), but he kept getting promoted into increasingly more demanding administrative positions, until he became the seventeenth president of the State University of New York at Albany. Administrative work is not conducive to scholarship, and I would often tease Kermit as to why he wanted to give up being a respected and productive scholar for administrative work, a thankless task at best. But he had his reasons, and insisted he would do the book.

After Anthony Lewis published his study of the case, I asked Kermit if he was going to continue, and he said yes, he had a different take on the case. Where Lewis had emphasized *New York Times* as a First Amendment decision championing freedom of the press, Kermit saw it as involving civil rights and southern legal culture as much as, if not more so than, the press. I, too, saw the issue primarily in terms of the civil rights movement of the 1950s and 1960s, and would have liked the opportunity to see how Kermit would have explicated it. I have no doubts it would have been brilliantly done.

About six months after Kermit's death, my friend Michael Briggs of the University Press of Kansas approached me, and said that Kermit had had a contract with the Press for the book. He thought that much of the book had already been written, and wondered whether I would be interested in finishing it. After I said I would be glad to do it as a memorial for Kermit, Michael went to Phyllis Hall, who graciously seconded the idea.

As it turned out, Kermit had done a lot of research, but he had written only two articles, and I have used those as parts of chapters 1, 2, and 11. Since I had a general idea from these articles what Kermit wanted to do, I decided to take the basic assumption that we both shared about the importance of civil rights in the case, and go from there. I had to trust that since Kermit had been very complimentary of some of my earlier work, this was not a radical departure from the general approach he would have taken.

In the pages that follow there are several threads that run throughout the book. One is the civil rights movement, and the great struggle for African American equality. The Warren Court had no choice but to take *New York Times v. Sullivan* on appeal, since its decisions beginning with *Brown v. Board of Education* (1954) had helped create the climate in which a civil rights group's running a political advertisement in the *New York Times* led to a libel suit in Montgomery, Alabama, with enormous punitive damages.

Another thread is the hostile interaction between an established way of life that took for granted the lower social position as well as inferiority of black Americans and the demand by people of color that they be treated with dignity and be given what the Constitution had promised, the equal protection of the laws. Much of this story played out and was shaped by the cultural milieu of Montgomery in the late 1950s. Here it is worthwhile to quote from an article that Kermit wrote:

> Let me be clear that my point is not that muzzling the leadership of the civil rights movement through libel law was either a *good* or a *wise* strategy on the part of southern segregationists. Nor do I intend this as a paean either to southern racism or the section's

alleged gentility. Such an argument would stand the region's history so completely on its head as to beggar reality. Nonetheless, I do believe that viewing *Sullivan* from the perspective of the southern, white elite can help to cast in sharper relief the implications of Brennan's opinion, not just for the civil movement (as important as that was) but for our understanding of the competing vision of public discourse that informed the moderate segregationist position in the first place.

As we both understood, "moderate segregationist position" did not mean support of integration or granting African Americans the rights they demanded; rather, it meant opposition to violence and control of the political system by those lower-class white elements that the elite despised.

As Justice Brennan noted, although Alabama had used its libel law as a form of sedition act, legal protection against defamation is an essential part of any civilized society that sees itself as operating under the rule of law. Libel law — or to be more precise, the way that law was used — may have been the villain of this story, but the laws of Alabama were like those of most states. In fact, with the exceptions carved out in *Sullivan* and its progeny, the libel laws of this country are not much different than they were fifty years ago.

Finally, this book does not in any way discount the importance of a free press in a democracy, or deny that this case is seen by many scholars as the beginning of modern Press Clause jurisprudence. The Court, however, never intended its opinion to be a blank check for defamation, and inherent in Justice Brennan's opinion is the assumption that a free press will also act as a responsible agency.

I am indebted to my good friend Michael Briggs, the editor in chief at the University of Kansas Press, for suggesting that I do this work, and for making the arrangements with the estate of Kermit Hall to make it happen. Peter Hoffer and Natalie Hull once again invited me to contribute a work to the Landmark Case Series, and both made valuable comments on the original manuscript. Tony Freyer of the University of Alabama Law School and Steven Lawson of Rutgers University also made helpful suggestions. Carol Kennedy is an author's dream of a copy editor, as is Larisa Martin the ideal production editor. Susan Schott, the assistant director of the Press, is someone I always want working on a book of mine. My thanks to all of them for helping to make this a better book; I, of course, am alone responsible for remaining faults.

The book is dedicated, as I am sure Kermit would have wanted, to Phyllis, and I am also grateful to her for the opportunity to honor Kermit.

CHAPTER I

# A Place in Time

Montgomery, Alabama, in 1960 was just beginning to experience the effects of the revolution wrought by the air conditioner on the South's economy, politics, and social order. Sun Belt cities such as Montgomery beckoned businesses from the chill winds, high wages, and organized labor of the North, but new money and new people – outsiders – posed a Hobbesian choice to the city's established white political leadership: either it could accept economic growth and in so doing threaten the traditional social and political order, or it could seek to sustain that order at the risk of further economic erosion. Montgomery had been the first capital of the Confederacy, the place where Jefferson Davis took the oath as its president, an important commercial center in the cotton culture of the Black Belt, and, in the mid-twentieth century, the decayed but proud relation of industrialized and unionized Birmingham to the north. The white social ethos of Alabama's state capital exuded deference to one's betters and a paternalistic scheme of race relations that purchased social harmony through segregation. By 1960, however, the pressures for change threatened these social and political arrangements, battered as they were by a new, populist form of municipal politics, in which fear of racial change and outside influences became the controlling issues, and by an increasingly aggressive civil rights movement that demanded a place for blacks in determining the course of the city's fate.

During most of the first half of the twentieth century, William A. Gunter Jr. dominated Montgomery politics. He served as mayor from 1910 to 1915 and from 1919 to his death in 1940. Gunter was a charismatic figure, an Episcopalian, a patrician, and the descendant of a family of wealthy antebellum planters. To secure his political hold over the upper classes in the friends-and-neighbors politics of the city, Gunter had bested the Hill family, whose most famous member was

United States Senator Lister Hill. Gunter secured his victory when voters installed a city commission form of government, one that divided duties between three commissioners, the most important of which was the commissioner of public safety. With the Hills eliminated, the only significant threat to Gunter's political rule came from lower-class whites, many of whom were associated with the Ku Klux Klan, followers of the Anti-Saloon League, who condemned Gunter's disapproval of prohibition, and fundamentalist Baptists and Methodists, who chaffed at Gunter's easygoing and tolerant lifestyle. Gunter retained influence through a shrewd distribution of city patronage, a willingness during the Great Depression to provide city jobs to hundreds of persons (even at the cost of running up a debt that frightened fiscal conservatives), and the unwavering support of the *Montgomery Advertiser*, the city's influential morning newspaper, and its editor, Grover C. Hall Sr. At each turn, the *Advertiser* sustained Gunter, especially in his constant attack on the Klan.

After Gunter's death in 1940, the political machine he had crafted gradually fell into disrepair, and no leader emerged with either Gunter's personal appeal or his political skills. Even Gunter's leadership would have been sorely tested had he lived by the potent mix of demographic and economic changes that his successors in office proved so unsuccessful in mastering. While Gunter was mayor, for example, the proportion of whites to blacks in the city remained stable, with about 61 percent white and 39 percent black. Migration patterns associated with World War II altered this relationship; whites moved from rural to urban Alabama and blacks to northern industrial cities. By 1960, Montgomery's population of 134,000 was some 28,000 greater than a decade before, with almost all of that growth coming among lower-middle-class whites. In that year about 65 percent of the population was white and 35 percent black.

The new white voters owed little to the old Gunter machine. Moreover, as was true of most Sun Belt cities, Montgomery became more segregated, by both race and wealth. Developers in the late 1940s and 1950s began dozens of new housing developments in the city targeted to specific income groups. These projects increasingly concentrated the white lower middle class on the east side of the city, with the upper-class enclaves primarily in the southern sections, in neighborhoods such as Cloverdale. The black population, on the other hand, remained where it had been – principally on the north side of the city.

These demographic changes eroded the network of personal acquaintances and family alliances upon which Gunter's machine depended. The new mixture of voters added an unknown element of uncertainty to the political process. As the behavior of the electorate grew more unstable, the ability of politicians to conduct business as usual diminished as well. Moreover, the institution of civil service reform in 1949 denied Gunter's successors in city hall the all-important patronage base upon which the mayor had previously rested his power. With no favors to give, the machine had increasing difficulty binding the voters. The surging ranks of lower-middle-class whites were susceptible to appeals from politicians who played heavily on what had historically been the silent issue in city politics: race.

The ranks of black voters in Montgomery actually increased during the 1950s, even though the black population grew at a slower rate and became a smaller percentage of the total population. The U. S. Supreme Court's decision in *Smith v. Allright* (1944) granted blacks throughout the South the right to participate in the previously all-white Democratic primary. The justices concluded that the historic exclusion of blacks from primary elections was a form of "state action" prohibited by the Fourteenth and Fifteenth Amendments. Following the decision, the ranks of black voters slowly rose. By 1960, about 10 percent of the city's 25,000 registered voters were black, up from only 3.5 percent in 1950. Even though small in number, black voters were nonetheless important. The increasingly sharp divisions in the white electorate between the rivals from the east and south sides of the city heightened black voters' influence in municipal elections.

For a brief period in the 1950s, control of the black vote became one of the chief objects of Montgomery politics. In 1953, David Birmingham successfully campaigned to fill an unexpired term on the City Commission by combining black voters with east-side segregationists resentful over the domination of the white business and professional classes from the south side. Once in office, Birmingham set about rewarding his black supporters, calling for the integration of the city's police force and public parks, something that the two other commissioners, both machine supporters, reluctantly embraced. Only two weeks before the Supreme Court handed down its decision in *Brown v. Board of Education* in 1954, the Montgomery City Council voted to hire its first black policeman. This policy stirred a backlash among east-side segregationists, who felt betrayed – by Birmingham and by the machine.

At the same time, black leaders boldly pressed their new political advantage. High on the list of their demands was the adoption by the city council of the so-called Mobile Plan for seating on public buses. The Mobile plan appealed to Montgomery blacks because under it drivers, unlike in Montgomery, were not required to unseat black passengers. Instead, whites took seats at the front; blacks took seats in the back. The line separating them shifted back and forth; no person was ever required to give up his or her seat.

Birmingham's coalition proved short-lived, as it collapsed under the weight of a white population unprepared for either the Mobile Plan or significant black political participation. The initial result was the election in 1955 of Clyde Sellers, a termite exterminator, former Highway Patrol director, and ardent segregationist, to replace Birmingham as police commissioner. Sellers campaigned against Birmingham by opposing the Mobile Plan and any further concessions to the increasingly active Montgomery black community.

Sellers's victory alerted black leaders that they would have to seek change outside the Commission in order to make the city's public transportation system better accommodate black needs. When Rosa Parks boarded the Cleveland Avenue bus of the Montgomery City Lines at City Square on December 1, 1955, she took a seat in a white section. A few stops later the bus driver ordered her to surrender her place in favor of a white rider. She refused; within days the Montgomery bus boycott began.

The bus boycott thoroughly polarized Montgomery. Blacks immediately organized the Montgomery Improvement Association (MIA) to run the boycott and named 26-year-old Martin Luther King Jr. its president. Joining King on the group's board were his close friend Ralph David Abernathy and Solomon S. Seay Sr., another black minister. The MIA quickly recognized that direct action alone would not win the day; its executive board, after some delay in the hope that compromise might ensue, decided to follow the recommendation of its attorney, Fred Gray. On February 1, 1956, two days after King's home was bombed by unknown persons, Gray filed a lawsuit in federal district court seeking an end to bus segregation.

Not the least of the many lessons of the boycott was the recourse by all of those involved in it to the law. Local state courts, of course, had never been friendly forums for blacks, let alone for blacks engaged in civil rights protest. Hence Gray sought the protection of federal courts. The white business community and the white segregationists associated with Sellers turned instead to the local state courts, where their influence was greatest and their understanding of the law most likely to be appreciated. Sellers successfully pressed for the indictment of the boycott leaders under the Alabama Anti-Boycott Act of 1921. On February 21, 1956, the Montgomery County grand jury returned indictments against eighty-nine blacks, twenty-four of whom were ministers, for the misdemeanor of conspiring to boycott a lawful business.

The boycott was especially embarrassing for the fading Gunter machine. It eroded some of the machine's most cherished assumptions about the nature of the social order at the same time that political influence slipped into the hands of persons the machine had historically disdained – white, populist, race-baiting, lower-class, religious fundamentalists. With the collapse of the machine went the traditional vehicle for distributing political power, conducting public debate, and adjusting race relations. This institutional dislocation fueled tension in the white community between moderates seeking accommodation and ardent segregationists, and it also heightened the already frayed relationships between lower-class whites and blacks.

Aggressive northern news media flocked to cover the boycott, and their presence made the events surrounding it all the more galling to moderate white leaders. What the northern press reported was not the paternalism and civility ostensibly associated with the Gunter machine's relations with the black community, but the ugly violence of the Klan and the lower-middle-class segregationists. The increasing attention paid by the northern press to the boycott spurred the segregationists to press for victory over black agitators, while white moderates from the city's south side searched for a compromise, all the while damning the interference of the northern liberal press. But the impetus for the boycott – the black community's growing sense of rage at decades of discrimination – would not be dampened, and the boycott continued until the MIA prevailed in court.

On November 13, 1956, the United States Supreme Court in *Gayle v. Browder* mandated that the city stop enforcing segregation on the buses. The decision was a stunning victory for the MIA, and it offered a means by which white moderates might bring about accommodation based on the rule of law. It was, moreover, a significant blow to ardent segregationists, who were already fuming over the interference of the federal courts in the day-to-day lives of the South following the Supreme Court's decision in *Brown*.

The segregationists responded to this legal defeat by turning to extralegal institutions. The largest organization in Montgomery by early 1958 was the White Citizens Council, which demanded whites' absolute subservience to the segregationist line and which had its strength on the city's east side. When a group of white women in 1958 organized a series of weekly interracial prayer meetings at a black Roman Catholic hospital, the Council singled them out for public ridicule. In November, under threats that their husbands' businesses would be destroyed, most of the white women publicly recanted their racially moderate beliefs, though one of them, librarian Juliette Morgan, committed suicide after repeated harassment and threats to her husband's business.

In early 1960, therefore, a regime of total segregation seemed within the grasp of east-side political forces at the same time that the leaders of the once formidable Gunter machine, who disdained this new political force, wanted to set the public record straight—they and not the Klan embodied the South's real traditions. The demagogic exploitation of race, they asserted, violated the machine's tradition of political deference based on class, paternalism toward blacks, and habits and manners of civility in public discourse.

The lower-middle-class segregationists were scoring impressive political and legal victories, in both the state and Montgomery. Former attorney general John Patterson in 1958 won election to the Alabama governor's mansion by conducting a political campaign of unalloyed racism that handed George C. Wallace a surprising defeat. In the wake of Patterson's victory, Wallace declared that he would "never be out-niggered again." Patterson also won an order from Circuit Judge Walter Burgwyn Jones, who would later preside over the trial phase of *Sullivan*, that outlawed the NAACP in Alabama. Finally, Montgomery city officials in January 1959 made clear that they were not going to retreat from their hard line, ordering that all thirteen city parks and the city zoo be sold as a way of evading a federal court order mandating their integration.

In March 1959, segregationist power surfaced again in the municipal elections. Earl James, another east-side leader, won the mayor's post over incumbent William A. "Tacky" Gayle, a machine supporter, the scion of a distinguished Alabama family, and generally a moderate on the race issue. James had successfully charged Gayle with being soft on the segregation issue because he had lost the bus boycott. An even more portentous political event for segregationists was the election of Lester Bruce (L. B.) Sullivan over incumbent segregationist police commissioner Clyde Sellers.

L. B. Sullivan was born in Records, Kentucky, on March 5, 1921, to Henry and Pauline Sullivan. His father was a farmer and county sheriff; his mother was a school teacher. Sullivan grew up in Vanceburg, Kentucky, and after graduation from high school worked with his brother in a construction business. In 1941 he entered the Army Air Force and, following his father's example in law enforcement, joined the military police, where he rose to the rank of sergeant while stationed at Maxwell Field in Montgomery. Following the war, Sullivan remained in Montgomery, where he raised a family of three children and held several different jobs. He worked briefly as a routeman for the Colonial Bread Company, and in 1947 he joined the local office of the federal Office of Price Administration. Sullivan gradually made helpful political connections, attaching himself to the rising political fortunes of Gordon Persons. In 1947 Sullivan was chosen by the Alabama Public Service Commission to be first inspector and then chief inspector of field activities. In 1951 then Governor Persons appointed Sullivan director of public safety for Alabama, a position he held until 1955.

In 1954 Sullivan enjoyed considerable public notice for his role in cleaning up Phenix City, Alabama, a small town immediately across the Chattahoochee River from Columbus, Georgia, and the Fort Benning military reservation. Phenix City had earned the title of "the most corrupt city in America." Its problems were mostly economic; it was the poor relation of prosperous Columbus, which benefited directly from the army's massive presence. Phenix City, positioned as it was on the wrong side of the river, derived only the indirect consequences of the U. S. Army's presence – gambling, prostitution, illegal liquor sales, and loan sharking. The good times rolled in Phenix City until Albert Patterson, a crusading Democratic candidate for attorney general of Alabama who lived there, vowed in his 1954 campaign to wipe out organized crime. During the evening of June 18, an assailant shot Patterson twice in the mouth as he sat in his car near his office in Phenix City. John Patterson, the son of the slain candidate, undertook the prosecution of the assassin and the vice syndicate that had for years run the city. He was joined by Sullivan, who headed the state police, and Walter Burgwyn Jones, a long-serving circuit judge from Montgomery County. The three conducted a highly successful cleanup campaign, and that experience forged a bond among them that carried over into Montgomery.

Sullivan left his post as director of public safety a year later, returning temporarily to private life. From 1955 to 1957 he worked as a consultant for the International Association of Chiefs of Police, attended the Federal Bureau of Investigation Police Academy, and graduated from the Northwestern University Traffic Institute. In the latter year he became director of safety and worked in sales for the P. C. White Truck Line.

Sullivan spun through his personal life a web of politically useful contacts among the middle and lower middle classes of the city's east side. He was an active club worker, holding membership in the Alcazar Shrine, the American Legion, the Elks, the Eagles, and the Andrew Jackson Lodge of the Masonic Order. His religious fundamentalism complemented and reinforced his racism; he was at once a Baptist and a member of the Ku Klux Klan. In his 1959 campaign against Clyde Sellers, Sullivan promised voters "the continuation of Southern traditions and customs," at the same time that he also declared his intention to promote "industrial growth and development for our city, county, and state." White moderates like Gayle distrusted Sullivan and his political ambitions. He was "smooth, polished, relatively sophisticated for Montgomery. He had read a few books." He was also pragmatic and opportunistic, qualities that he demonstrated in his campaign against Sellers.

Sullivan succeeded in painting the ardent segregationist Sellers as weak on the race issue and public order. During the summer of 1958,

Martin Luther King Jr.'s closest associate and friend, the Reverend Ralph D. Abernathy, had an affair with one of his female parishioners. On August 29 the women's husband, Edward Davis, who had been studying at Indiana University, attacked Abernathy in the basement of the minister's office, with first a hatchet and then a gun. The minister fled from his church into the street, where fortuitously two Montgomery police officers took Davis into custody. When King arrived at the courthouse to aid Abernathy, Montgomery police, already ruffled by the bizarre behavior of both Davis and Abernathy, arrested King for loitering. He was convicted and fined ten dollars. Police Commissioner Clyde Sellers, however, decided to pay King's fine rather than have him jailed as a martyr. In the 1959 commission race, Sullivan effectively exploited this incident, charging Police Commissioner Sellers with using "kid gloves to handle social agitators."

Once in office Sullivan implemented reform of the police department designed to fulfill his campaign pledge to undertake "fair and impartial enforcement of laws." The new commissioner reorganized internal police operations, created neighborhood patrols, developed outreach programs through the police department for the city's youth, and established a police reserve "composed of people from all walks of life." Calvin Whitesell testified to Sullivan's commitment to enforce the law inside and outside the police department:

> Sullivan was the first commissioner that I knew who kept his own records of arrests by police. Way back in those days every policeman that made an arrest for resisting arrest, [Sullivan] kept his own file on it, because this is the way the policemen in those days used to batter defendants. They would say the suspect was resisting arrest, hit him with a club or whatever—a flashlight. Sullivan watched for those [false arrests and police brutality], and if a guy got three of those, when he got three of those in quick order, he got called on the carpet. . . . And we got rid of some people. He would either run them off the force or put them in another area where they couldn't be involved in arrests.

Unfortunately for Sullivan, his reforms coincided with a growing level of civil rights disturbances in the Alabama capital that placed great pressure on the police force and on his leadership.

Sullivan's first major crisis occurred in February 1960, when the sit-in movement reached Montgomery. At 4 PM on February first of that year, the first black sit-in began at the F. W. Woolworth lunch counter in Greensboro, North Carolina. Within days the protest spread through the rest of the South, moving to Charlotte, Raleigh, then Rockhill, North Carolina, and on to Orangeburg, South Carolina, and Nashville, Tennessee. The movement was unique, and in its novelty lay a source of profound concern for the white South. In the sit-ins, young blacks took an aggressive role that captured the attention of the national media, including the *New York Times*, whose editors dispatched, as they had done during the bus boycott, additional correspondents to cover breaking civil rights developments.

On February 25, thirty-five students from all-black Alabama State College sought service at the snack bar in the basement of the Montgomery County Courthouse. The students were rebuffed and arrested. The following day Governor John Patterson, who was the ex officio chairman of the State Board of Education, demanded the expulsion of the students. On February 27, most of the eight hundred students at Alabama State marched to the state capitol to protest Patterson's actions. Governor Patterson and Commissioner Sullivan decided to apply unofficially sanctioned force and intimidation against the students. While state and Montgomery police stood idly by, Klansmen wielding baseball bats waded into the group of black students. The attack went unpunished, even though the *Montgomery Advertiser* ran pictures of the incident, with several of the mob clearly identified. The *Advertiser*'s editor, Grover Hall Jr., condemned the attack and rebuked Sullivan for failing to bring it to a halt and to seek arrests against those who had perpetrated it. At the same time, the extremist press praised the incident. The Montgomery *Home News* observed that "the crisp crack of a hickory bat on a Negro head snapped the people out of their apathy into the realization that the steady, cold siege against their way of life was now breaking out in . . . obviously Communist-inspired racial strife." It served, the editor said, as "a signal for the white Christian race to stand up and be counted."

These events formed the immediate background of the *Sullivan* case. Segregationists controlled the White Citizens Council and the police force; they used both to cow white moderates and black civil rights protestors. The political culture of Montgomery associated with the Gunter machine – its values of paternalism, deference, and civility – was in disarray. Its once influential leaders not only were driven from office but suffered the ironic fate of being attacked at home by segregationists while being held up to national ridicule by some parts of the northern press that equated all white citizens of Montgomery as bigots. Such a characterization distressed the traditional white leadership class because it projected on them values that they associated with their lower-middle-class east-side opponents. Taken together, lower-class segregationists and northern journalists threatened to rob the once powerful leaders of the Gunter machine of not just their political fortunes but their sacred honor. The civic culture of Montgomery, as a result, was already under considerable stress when a full-page ad, titled "Heed Their Rising Voices," appeared in the March 29, 1960, issue of the *New York Times*.

State authorities in the South had mounted a full-scale legal attack on the nascent civil rights movement, seeking to outlaw such organizations as the NAACP and discredit individual leaders. In Alabama, for example, Governor John Patterson in early 1960 directed state revenue authorities to charge Martin Luther King Jr. with tax evasion and perjury in completing his Alabama state income tax returns. The charges against King, who had already moved his ministry from the Dexter Street Church in Montgomery to his father's church in Atlanta, Georgia, specified that he had diverted money raised for the Southern Christian Leadership Conference (SCLC) into his own pockets without ever reporting it as income. King had founded the group of southern black ministers as a vehicle for pressing his desegregation initiatives specifically and social change in the South generally.

Prominent northern civil rights leaders made a virtue out of the necessity of raising money to defend King. Bayard Rustin, a political and civil rights organizer in New York City, founded the "Committee to Defend Martin Luther King and the Struggle for Freedom in the South" and served as it executive director. Rustin had worked with the Congress of Racial Equality (CORE) in the 1940s, and had advised King on the doctrine of nonviolence during the bus boycott. The chairman of the committee was A. Philip Randolph, a pioneer in the black civil rights movement and the president of the Sleeping Car

Porters Union, and the board included such notable figures as the Reverend Harry Emerson Fosdick and labor leader Morris Iushewitz. At Rustin's prodding the committee determined to bring attention to King's plight through a full-page ad in the *New York Times* that would also call attention to the sit-in movement generally and events in Montgomery specifically.

Rustin selected John Murray, a tall, thin white man of great style and humor to create the ad. A writer by trade, Murray was the son of a prominent Irish-Catholic family, whose history included ancestors who had strongly supported the abolition of slavery before the Civil War. A 1948 graduate of Yale University, Murray's credits included everything from off-Broadway plays to training films on sexual hygiene for the United States Army. The ad was principally Murray's work, although he had modest assistance from two other New York writers, William Branch and John Killens. The ad was based on an earlier memorandum prepared by Rustin that outlined the sit-in movement and stressed how events at the Alabama state capitol might be exploited for fundraising purposes. The memo also listed the names of more than two dozen prominent entertainers, theologians, and educators. Murray attempted to "project it [the ad] in the most appealing forum" – "to rev it up a little bit to get money."

Late in the afternoon of March 23, 1960, Murray entered the second-floor offices of the national advertising department of the *Times* on West 43rd Street in New York City. The writer presented two items to Gershon T. Aronson, a twenty-five-year veteran of selling advertising space for the newspaper. The first item was Murray's typewritten manuscript of the advertisement, now headed "Heed Their Rising Voices"; the second was a letter from Randolph. The latter requested the *Times* to run the advertisement and vouched for the authenticity of the persons who endorsed it.

Aronson immediately sent the ad forward to the *Times*'s Advertisers Services Department to consult about the size and style of the type arrangement. The ad itself was laid out by the Union Advertising Agency, a respected New York City firm that served as an intermediary between newspapers and advertisers.

As a matter of standard operating procedure, Aronson also had a copy of the typescript of the ad sent to the Advertising Acceptability Department. There D. Vincent Redding, a six-year employee of the

*Times* and manager of the department, was responsible for screening the acceptability of all advertisements before they were published. This particular kind of editorial ad had to conform to the *Times*'s Advertising Acceptability Standards contained in a small booklet. Redding read and approved the ad based mostly on the fact that it "was endorsed by a number of people who are well known and whose reputation I had no reason to question." He made no attempt to check, as the guidelines required, the accuracy of the most powerful assertions contained in the ad. His approval signaled the newspaper's Production Department to proceed to publication.

After Redding had given his endorsement but before the ad could go to press, Bayard Rustin changed his mind. He decided that Murray's version lacked sufficient appeal. Rustin on March 28 asked Murray and the two other writers to attend a meeting in his office, but only Murray was available. Rustin informed the writer that the ad lacked sufficient emotional appeal, so much so that the civil rights leader worried that it would not generate enough of a response to cover the $4,552 charged by the *Times* to run it. After an extended discussion, Rustin pulled open a file drawer from which he took a list of black ministers associated with the SCLC. Rustin and Murray then proceeded to alter the approved proof, inserting two new items. The first was a single sentence that read "We in the South who are struggling daily for dignity and freedom warmly endorse this appeal." The second was a list of twenty new names, including four Alabama ministers: Ralph D. Abernathy and Solomon S. Seay Sr. of Montgomery, Fred L. Shuttlesworth of Birmingham, and Joseph E. Lowery of Mobile.

Murray cautioned Rustin not to use the ministers' names as endorsees without first seeking their approval, but the civil rights organizer replied that there was insufficient time to do so since the ad was scheduled to run the following day. Rustin also insisted that since SCLC was King's organization in the first place, there was no need to consult with the individual ministers. Hubris and impatience prevailed; Rustin had the ad altered. Since the business day was over by the time the ad was rewritten, Rustin called his personal contact at the Union Advertising Agency to obtain a promise that the ad would be promptly revised the following morning and sent to the *Times* immediately. Vincent Redding, having already given his approval based on the Randolph letter, never knew of Rustin's changes, nor did the twenty new endorsees whom Rustin added. On March 29, 1960 the full-page advertisement appeared on page 25.

Murray had taken the ad's heading, "Heed Their Rising Voices," from an editorial printed in the *Times* ten days earlier. Like so much else in the case of *New York Times v. Sullivan*, the choice had an ironic twist. Its author was Turner Catledge, the newspaper's managing executive editor since 1951 and a native of a farm near New Prospect, Mississippi, who, like the paper's publisher, Adolph Ochs, had moved north to pursue a career in journalism. Catledge grew up in a South dominated by separate but equal, a custom that he had embraced until joining the staff of the *Tunica Times* in 1922. In the course of his duties with that small weekly Mississippi paper, Catledge wrote a series of articles denouncing the Ku Klux Klan. "I thought very little about the plight of blacks," Catledge wrote years later, but "I realized that they [Supreme Court decisions outlawing segregation] were right, that segregation in public institutions and facilities cannot be tolerated." Catledge was determined that the *Times* should play a vital role in what he described as the "Great Revolution" — the series of events involving race relations that flowed from the Supreme Court's controversial decisions in *Brown v. Board of Education*. Catledge's own experience with race relations in Mississippi motivated him to ensure that the *Times* adequately covered the story of the budding civil rights movement there, including detailed reporting on the Montgomery bus boycott. Catledge and Ochs also recognized that because of the *Times*'s status as the nation's newspaper of record, such coverage was essential and, given the paper's readership, economically sound.

The *Times* covered the civil rights movement in the South through several correspondents, the most notable of whom was Atlanta-based Claude Sitton, and stringers in all of the major cities, including Montgomery and Birmingham, Alabama. The sit-in movement quickly captured the attention of the *Times*, whose editors dispatched Sitton and other correspondents to cover the breaking news throughout the South.

The editorial that Catledge penned for the March 19 edition also reflected the newspaper's policy of supporting the strategy of peaceful civil disobedience adopted by King during the Montgomery bus boycott and of urging Congress to enact civil rights legislation. The full sentence from which the advertisement's heading was taken read: "Let Congress heed their rising voice, for they will be heard."

The first four of the ten paragraphs of the advertisement dealt specifically with the sit-in movement that Sullivan had sought to squelch. Appealing to the Constitution and the Bill of Rights, Murray's words recited how "thousands of Southern Negro students . . . engaged in widespread non-violent demonstrations . . . had boldly stepped forth as the protagonists of democracy." The third paragraph dealt specifically with events in Montgomery. It reported that eight hundred students from Alabama State College had marched to the state capitol and on its steps had sung "My Country, 'Tis of Thee," after which their student leaders were expelled. Moreover, the third paragraph also claimed that "truckloads of police armed with shotguns and tear-gas" then "ringed the Alabama State College campus." When the students protested these actions by refusing to reregister for classes, the ad continued, "their dining hall was padlocked in an attempt to starve them into submission."

The fifth and sixth paragraphs focused on the plight of Martin Luther King Jr., identifying what the ad called "Southern violators of the Constitution" who were determined to destroy King and to answer his "peaceful protests with intimidation and violence." The sixth paragraph in particular claimed that these "Southern violators" had "bombed his home almost killing his wife and child," that they had "assaulted his person," and that they had "arrested him seven times — for 'speeding,' 'loitering,' and similar 'offenses.'" The grand design of these "Southern violators" was to "behead this affirmative movement, and thus to demoralize Negro Americans and to weaken their will to struggle." The remaining four paragraphs pleaded for not just moral support "but material help so urgently needed by those who are taking the risks, facing jail, and even death in a glorious re-affirmation of our Constitution and its Bill of Rights."

Below these paragraphs were two blocks of endorsements. The first contained sixty-four names, including such prominent figures as Eleanor Roosevelt, Norman Thomas, Marlon Brando, Harry Belafonte, Sidney Poitier, Shelley Winters, Van Heflin, Nat Hentoff, Eartha Kitt, Nat King Cole, and Frank Sinatra. A second block listed the SCLC ministers, including the four from Alabama. To the right was a coupon to be clipped and returned with a contribution.

# The New York Times.

> **"** *The growing movement of peaceful mass demonstrations by Negroes is something new in the South, something understandable. ... Let Congress heed their rising voices, for they will be heard.* **"**
>
> —*New York Times editorial*
> *Saturday, March 19, 1960*

# Heed Their Rising Voices

As the whole world knows by now, thousands of Southern Negro students are engaged in widespread non-violent demonstrations in positive affirmation of the right to live in human dignity as guaranteed by the U. S. Constitution and the Bill of Rights. In their efforts to uphold these guarantees, they are being met by an unprecedented wave of terror by those who would deny and negate that document which the whole world looks upon as setting the pattern for modern freedom....

In Orangeburg, South Carolina, when 400 students peacefully sought to buy doughnuts and coffee at lunch counters in the business district, they were forcibly ejected, tear-gassed, soaked to the skin in freezing weather with fire hoses, arrested en masse and herded into an open barbed-wire stockade to stand for hours in the bitter cold.

In Montgomery, Alabama, after students sang "My Country, 'Tis of Thee" on the State Capitol steps, their leaders were expelled from school, and truckloads of police armed with shotguns and tear-gas ringed the Alabama State College Campus. When the entire student body protested to state authorities by refusing to re-register, their dining hall was padlocked in an attempt to starve them into submission.

In Tallahassee, Atlanta, Nashville, Savannah, Greensboro, Memphis, Richmond, Charlotte, and a host of other cities in the South, young American teen-agers, in face of the entire weight of official state apparatus and police power, have boldly stepped forth as protagonists of democracy. Their courage and amazing restraint have inspired millions and given a new dignity to the cause of freedom.

Small wonder that the Southern violators of the Constitution fear this new, non-violent brand of freedom fighter . . . even as they fear the upwelling right-to-vote movement. Small wonder that they are determined to destroy the one man who, more than any other, symbolizes the new spirit now sweeping the South—the Rev. Dr. Martin Luther King, Jr., world-famous leader of the Montgomery Bus Protest. For it is his doctrine of non-violence which has inspired and guided the students in their widening wave of sit-ins; and it is this same Dr. King who founded and is president of the Southern Christian Leadership Conference—the organization which is spearheading the surging right-to-vote movement. Under Dr. King's direction the Leadership Conference conducts Student Workshops and Seminars in the philosophy and technique of non-violent resistance.

Again and again the Southern violators have answered Dr. King's peaceful protests with intimidation and violence. They have bombed his home almost killing his wife and child. They have assaulted his person. They have arrested him seven times—for "speeding," "loitering" and similar "offenses." And now they have charged him with "perjury"—a felony under which they could imprison him for ten years. Obviously, their real purpose is to remove him physically as the leader to whom the students and millions

of others—look for guidance and support, and thereby to intimidate *all* leaders who may rise in the South. Their strategy is to behead this affirmative movement, and thus to demoralize Negro Americans and weaken their will to struggle. The defense of Martin Luther King, spiritual leader of the student sit-in movement, clearly, therefore, is an integral part of the total struggle for freedom in the South.

Decent-minded Americans cannot help but applaud the creative daring of the students and the quiet heroism of Dr. King. But this is one of those moments in the stormy history of Freedom when men and women of good will must do more than applaud the rising-to-glory of others. The America whose good name hangs in the balance before a watchful world, the America whose heritage of Liberty these Southern Upholders of the Constitution are defending, is our America as well as theirs . . .

We must heed their rising voices—yes—but we must aid our own.

We must extend ourselves above and beyond moral support and render the material help so urgently needed by those who are taking the risks, facing jail, and even death in a glorious re-affirmation of our Constitution and its Bill of Rights.

We urge you to join hands with our fellow Americans in the South by supporting, with your dollars, this Combined Appeal for all three needs—the defense of Martin Luther King—the support of the embattled students—and the struggle for the right-to-vote.

## Your Help Is Urgently Needed ... NOW !!

Stella Adler
Raymond Pace Alexander
Shelly Appleton
Harry Van Arsdale
Harry Belafonte
Julie Belafonte
Dr. Algernon Black
Marc Blitzstein
William Bowe
William Branch
Marlon Brando
Mrs. Ralph Bunche
Diahann Carroll
Dr. Alan Knight Chalmers

Joseph Cohen
Richard Coe
Nat King Cole
Cheryl Crawford
Dorothy Dandridge
Ossie Davis
Sammy Davis, Jr.
Ruby Dee
Harry Dolly
Scotty Ecklund
Dr. Philip Elliott
Dr. Harry Emerson Fosdick

Anthony Franciosa
Mathew Guinan
Lorraine Hansberry
Rev. Donald Harrington
Nat Hentoff
James Hicks
Mary Hinkson
Van Heflin
Langston Hughes
Morris Iushewitz
Mahalia Jackson
Paul Jennings
Mordecai Johnson
John Killens

Eartha Kitt
Rabbi Edward Klein
Hope Lange
John Lewis
Viveca Lindfors
David Livingston
William Michaelson
Carl Murphy
Don Murray
John Murray
A. J. Muste
Frederick O'Neal
Peter Orlov
L. Joseph Overton

Albert P. Palmer
Clarence Pickett
Shad Polier
Sidney Poitier
Michael Prelsker
A. Philip Randolph
John Raitt
Elmer Rice
Cleveland Robinson
Jackie Robinson
Mrs. Eleanor Roosevelt
Bayard Rustin
Robert Ryan
Maureen Stapleton

Frank Silvera
Louis Simon
Hope Stevens
David Sullivan
Julian Sons
George Tabori
Rev. Gardner C. Taylor
Norman Thomas
Kenneth Tynan
Charles White
Shelley Winters
Max Youngstein

*We in the south who are struggling daily for dignity and freedom warmly endorse this appeal*

Rev. Ralph D. Abernathy
(Montgomery, Ala.)

Rev. Fred L. Shuttlesworth
(Birmingham, Ala.)

Rev. Kelley Miller Smith
(Nashville, Tenn.)

Rev. W. A. Dennis
(Chattanooga, Tenn.)

Rev. C. K. Steele
(Tallahassee, Fla.)

Rev. Matthew D. McCollum
(Orangeburg, S. C.)

Rev. William Holmes Borders
(Atlanta, Ga.)

Rev. Douglas Moore
(Durham, N. C.)

Rev. Wyatt Tee Walker
(Petersburg, Va.)

Rev. Walter L. Hamilton
(Norfolk, Va.)

I. S. Levy
(Columbia, S. C.)

Rev. Martin Luther King, Sr.
(Atlanta, Ga.)

Rev. Henry C. Bunton
(Memphis, Tenn.)

Rev. S. S. Seay, Sr.
(Montgomery, Ala.)

Rev. Samuel W. Williams
(Atlanta, Ga.)

Rev. A. L. Davis
(New Orleans, La.)

Mrs. Katie E. Whickham
(New Orleans, La.)

Rev. W. H. Hall
(Hattiesburg, Miss.)

Rev. J. E. Lowery
(Mobile, Ala.)

Rev. T. J. Jemison
(Baton Rouge, La.)

**Please mail this coupon TODAY!**

---

Committee To Defend Martin Luther King
and
The Struggle For Freedom In The South
312 West 125th Street, New York 27, N. Y.
UNiversity 6-1700

I am enclosing my contribution of $............
for the work of the Committee.

Name ..............................
(PLEASE PRINT)

Address ..............................

City ............ Zone ...... State ......

☐ I want to help    ☐ Please send further information

*Please make checks payable to:*
**Committee To Defend Martin Luther King**

---

## COMMITTEE TO DEFEND MARTIN LUTHER KING AND THE STRUGGLE FOR FREEDOM IN THE SOUTH
312 West 125th Street, New York 27, N. Y. UNiversity 6-1700

*Chairmen:* A. Philip Randolph, Dr. Gardner C. Taylor; *Chairmen of Cultural Division:* Harry Belafonte, Sidney Poitier; *Treasurer:* Nat King Cole; *Executive Director:* Bayard Rustin; *Chairmen of Church Division:* Father George B. Ford, Rev. Harry Emerson Fosdick, Rev. Thomas Kilgore, Jr., Rabbi Edward E. Klein; *Chairmen of Labor Division:* Morris Iushewitz, Cleveland Robinson.

"Heed Their Rising Voices" was just what its creator John Murray said it was: a piece of propaganda designed to attract sympathy and money. It was an "editorial-type ad," one that pushed a particular point of view; it was neither news reporting nor an editorial. While Murray had considerable experience as a writer, "Heed Their Rising Voices" was his first effort at creating paid political advertising.

The committee's decision to place the ad in the *Times* stemmed directly from the paper's prestige and political sympathies. Founded by Henry Jarvis Raymond in 1851, the paper became the political organ of the Republican Party and the respectable, stable, and conservative antislavery groups that supported it before the Civil War. The *Times*'s chief competitor during these early years, Horace Greeley's *Tribune*, urged social reforms sufficiently radical, such as the abolition of slavery, that it alienated much of the middle- and upper-class market in New York City. Over the next century, Raymond's newspaper won great distinction by balancing a progressive view of many social issues with a dignified approach to reporting the news. During the first half of the twentieth century, the *Times* leadership had steadily built up the paper's reputation, garnering an impressive list of Pulitzer Prizes that in the process made it America's most influential daily newspaper. In placing the advertisement in the *Times*, the committee hoped it would receive national coverage.

The *Times*'s daily circulation was about 650,000, a number that doubled on Sundays. Most of these papers were sold, of course, in the New York City area and the northeast corridor stretching from Washington, D.C., to Boston. Elsewhere circulation dropped markedly, with most copies sold to libraries, educational institutions, and a few individuals. On an average day in Alabama, for example, the *Times* sold about 390 papers and about 2,500 on Sunday. Of the Alabama circulation, approximately 35 copies were distributed in Montgomery County.

These numbers leave no doubt that Rustin directed his ad not at the population of Dixie, but at the sympathetic, white, progressive, and intellectual leadership of the liberal North, where its non–New York City circulation was largest. The ad's invocation of "Southern violators" echoed prevailing stereotypes of the South as a racist, backward, and violent place. The ad named no individuals and it made no specific reference to any public officeholder, but it did offer a damaging picture of police forces in the South, who were quickly earning a well-deserved reputation for brutality in dealing with the nonviolent civil rights movement, and created a less than flattering impression of the public officials responsible for overseeing the police. Neither Murray nor Rustin expected that the ad would have any effect in the South.

Early in the week of April 3, 1960, William H. MacDonald, the assistant editor in charge of the editorial page of the *Montgomery Advertiser*, was rummaging through the "exchanges" on his desk. Exchanges were other newspapers, and MacDonald read them to find out what they considered newsworthy. The *New York Times* was one of the most important of these exchange papers because of its coverage of international events and foreign affairs. The editorial staff of the *Advertiser*, and its sister afternoon paper, the *Alabama Journal*, also read the *Times* for other matters, most especially the reporting and editorial commentary by the New York paper on what was then the most important issue in the region—the growing civil rights movement. Southern newspaper editors, such as MacDonald, viewed the *Times* with a mixture of awe and contempt. It was at once the epitome of the modern newspaper and the mouthpiece for the Northeastern liberal establishment. MacDonald read through the *Times* that day just as he had been doing for the previous twelve years, since he had come to work on the paper as a summer job between his law studies at the University of Alabama. A summer's job turned into a career, and MacDonald never returned to law school.

As MacDonald scanned the March 29 issue of the paper, his eye stopped on page 25, which contained an impressive full-page ad headlined "Heed Their Rising Voices." He read the ad and "kind of chuckled," thinking to himself that "it had some foundation it fact," but he "was not greatly distressed by it." He did show it to his immediate superior, Grover C. Hall Jr., the editor and vice president of the *Advertiser*. Hall gave it slight attention; he "sort of umphed" and walked on by.

A short time later, MacDonald broke from his duties and walked to the Capitol Book Company, a distance of about six blocks. The ad was still on his mind when, in the course of browsing through the book and magazine racks, he came upon Calvin Whitesell, the new city attorney for Montgomery. Whitesell was a youthful 31-year-old graduate of the University of Alabama Law School and aspiring political figure who had aligned himself with the new, strongly segregationist regime in City Hall, headed by L. B. Sullivan. MacDonald, in an offhanded fashion ("The same way you would ask: 'What did you think of the football game?'"), asked Whitesell if he had read the ad. Whitesell, who never read the *Times*, had not, but his political antenna immediately perked up. He asked MacDonald to see the ad; both men then walked the six or so blocks back to the *Advertiser* offices. There Whitesell quickly scanned the ad and then he took the paper back to his office, where he shared it with Sullivan and the two other city commissioners, Earl James and Franklin "Frank" Parks. A day later, Whitesell returned the paper to MacDonald, who then sent it on to other members of the editorial staff.

On April 4, Ray Jenkins, the city editor of the *Journal*, came across the ad as he worked his way through the March 29 issue of the *Times*. Jenkins was born and raised on a farm in south Georgia and then graduated from the Journalism School at the University of Alabama. His first job in 1954 was as a reporter for the *Columbus Ledger* in Columbus, Georgia. Jenkins was assigned to cover Phenix City, a city with which he established a "unique relationship . . . in that I participated in the vice by night and exposed it by day." Jenkins covered both the assassination of Attorney General Albert Patterson and the sensational trials that followed. The *Ledger* won the Pulitzer Prize in 1955, and Jenkins basked in the glow of his paper's success.

Four years later Jenkins moved his career forward another notch, this time joining the staff of the larger and more prestigious *Alabama Journal* at the behest of Grover Hall Jr. His first assignment as city editor on January 15, 1959, was to cover the inauguration of John Patterson, the son of the martyred attorney general.

Jenkins immediately grasped the newsworthiness of the ad. He understood that King was a figure at once revered and hated in Montgomery. The ad was bound to be of interest among both blacks and whites, with King's tax evasion and perjury trial set to begin in only a few weeks. Jenkins set about checking as many of the assertions as possible and then composed a seven-paragraph story on his typewriter. That story listed some of the signers of the advertisement and quoted parts of the text that dealt with assertions that the civil rights movement had been subjected to "an unprecedented wave of terror."

Jenkins then noted certain discrepancies in the ad and suggested that there might be others, although he was unable to confirm them in the time available. The one error that Jenkins noted was a statement that Negro student leaders from Alabama State College were expelled "after students sang 'My Country, 'Tis of Thee' on the State Capitol steps." Actually, Jenkins wrote, "the students were expelled for leading a sitdown strike at the courthouse grill."

Jenkins also reported that the ad had erred in another way. Its authors had claimed that "When the entire student body protested (the expulsion) to state authorities by refusing to reregister, their dining hall was padlocked in an attempt to starve them into submission." Jenkins informed his readers that officials at all-black Alabama State had said that "there is not a modicum of truth in the statement." These same officials assured him that "our registration for the spring quarter was only slightly below normal" and they "deny that the dining hall was padlocked." When Jenkins finished the story, he threw the newspaper in the wastebasket, since he was the last of the editorial staff to review the exchanges. Jenkins thought the advertisement more newsworthy than did MacDonald, but both journalists concluded that it was little more than another round in the sparring between King's civil rights followers and segregationist officials.

Much has been made of the role played by Jenkins in the events leading up to the lawsuit, perhaps too much so. MacDonald, of course, had already called the ad to the attention of the city attorney and Grover Hall before Jenkins's article appeared. Yet neither Jenkins nor MacDonald played a decisive role in the events that followed. Instead, that honor clearly belongs to Merton Roland Nachman, the attorney who eventually argued the case before the Supreme Court.

Nachman was 37 years old in 1960. After graduating from Harvard College and then the Law School, he returned to his home state of Alabama, serving as assistant attorney general from 1949 to 1954. Almost immediately, Nachman established himself as a successful advocate in a landmark decision in *Alabama Public Service Commission v. Southern Railway* (1951), in which the United States Supreme Court held that federal courts should ordinarily abstain from deciding constitutional claims when a state administrative proceeding has begun on the issue and it can be reviewed by state courts. Nachman's first victory came at age twenty-seven and with less than the three years required for admission to the Supreme Court bar. The Court waived the rule, although Justice Felix Frankfurter complained, "I don't know why we have these rules if we aren't going to enforce them." In 1954, Nachman entered private practice in Montgomery with Walter Knabe, a future city attorney for Montgomery, remaining there until 1959, when he joined the firm of Steiner, Crum, and Baker. The Steiner firm included among its clients the city's two newspapers, the *Advertiser* and the *Journal*.

In politics, Nachman was a moderate southern Democrat, who sought to distance himself from the excesses of the states' rights wing of the Democratic party in the South. He supported Harry Truman in 1948 against the insurgency of Senator Strom Thurmond and the Dixiecrats, and in 1956 he worked for several weeks in the Washington office of presidential candidate Adlai Stevenson. When Stevenson lost the election, Nachman returned to private practice.

Perhaps nowhere was Nachman's sense of tolerance more evident than in his decision in 1958 to represent Edward Davis, the assailant of Ralph Abernathy, in a civil suit for libel against Johnson Publishing Company. A criminal jury had acquitted Davis of charges of assault and attempted murder, but *Jet* magazine on September 18, 1958, published a patently false exposé of Davis. The magazine reported that the claims about the sexual liaison between Davis's wife and Reverend Abernathy were false and that Davis "was the pawn of persons seeking to embarrass Reverends Abernathy and King." The story went on to explain that Davis had been discharged from his teaching position in Greenville, Alabama, a small town just south of Montgomery, because he had sexual relations with his grade-school students. "It was an outrageous falsehood," Nachman declared, one that called out for help. Nachman took the case, along with Truman Hobbs, a future federal district court judge who played a critical role in desegregating public facilities in Alabama. They secured a judgment in Judge Walter B. Jones's circuit court in Montgomery of $67,000 in damages, which the Alabama Supreme Court subsequently reduced to $45,000 on appeal.

The year before Nachman had also represented three city commissioners—Gayle, Sellers, and Parks—in a $750,000 libel suit against *Ken* magazine, a pulp publication based in New York City. The magazine had run a feature story entitled "Kimono Girls Check in Again" that purported to expose rampant prostitution and gambling in Montgomery. During the Gunter era the after-hours life of the city had been tawdry, but following World War II city authorities had mounted an extensive anti-vice campaign. Such actions appealed to the fundamentalists among the east-siders and also presented to northern businesses thinking of investing in the city a sense of moral order and progressive efficiency, qualities that were particularly important in attracting business in the wake of the bus boycott. Nachman made quick work of the case in federal district court in Montgomery. He showed that the author of the essay had never visited Montgomery, that he had fabricated his lurid tales about the city's moral bankruptcy, and that the magazine had published them knowing that they were false. *Ken* settled the suit, paying $15,000 in damages to the commissioners and issuing a public apology.

By the spring of 1960 Nachman had established himself as the preeminent libel lawyer in Montgomery and one of the best in the state. He had fashioned political moderation, a keen intellect, and impressive lawyering skills into an increasingly successful law practice. Perhaps as a result of his years at Harvard, Nachman held a far more cosmopolitan vision of the world than did most of Montgomery's public officials. For Nachman one window on that world came from his daily reading of the *New York Times*, to which he subscribed.

Nachman discovered "Heed Their Rising Voices" at about the same time that MacDonald and Jenkins were reading their exchanges. Because of his experience as a libel lawyer, however, Nachman saw something far different than did the two journalists. He immediately recognized that the falsity of the statements in the ad might make them libelous per se under Alabama law. His success against *Ken* magazine was only the most recent manifestation of the common law rule in Alabama that persons making false libelous statement about public officials were subject to damages. "Heed Their Rising Voices," at least in Alabama, was no ordinary newspaper ad; it was an actionable insult.

More than the lawyer's mind was at work, however. Like many moderates, Nachman was frustrated by the excesses of the burgeoning civil rights movement and its white segregationist tormentors. (Like most moderates Nachman supported segregation; they were not "moderate integrationists.") The ad was not just wrong, it was mean-spirited, at least in Nachman's eyes, and it promised to do nothing but contribute even more to an already high level of misunderstanding and distrust. When Nachman opened the page to the ad, he was, in his own words, "outraged by it and knew that some of the things were absolutely false and some of the charges were grossly exaggerated to the point of bullshit." At that moment, Nachman became the prime moving force in what would become the lawsuit brought against the *Times*.

Nachman clipped the page from the newspaper and delivered it to the three city commissioners. He indicated to Police Commissioner Sullivan that, even though he was not directly named in the ad, there could be little doubt that he could bring an action against the *Times*. The ad cast aspersions on Sullivan because it attributed to the police force the lead complicity in bombing the home of Martin Luther King Jr., and more generally in fomenting a "police state terrorism." Nachman pointed out to Sullivan that the ad discredited his administration because it essentially concluded that his efforts to make the police force more progressive, better trained, more efficient, and more responsive to the citizenry had failed. Calvin Whitesell had almost simultaneously brought the ad to the commissioners' attention. In short, Nachman and Whitesell told the commissioners that, based on existing Alabama law, they could sue the *Times* for libel, and in doing so they were almost certain to win.

# CHAPTER 2

# "Lies, Lies, Lies"

The law of libel in Alabama and elsewhere in the United States in 1960 had its roots deep in Anglo-American law, and reflected values that had been unchanged for many years. The *Sullivan* case is about First Amendment law and civil rights, but it is also about how traditional society valued an individual's reputation. While many of the litigants saw the suit as a means of retaliating against northern newspapers that supported civil rights, they also believed that the *Times* had no understanding of southern mores. By focusing attention on African American agitation to the exclusion of everything else, the *Times* had, in their eyes, vilified traditions of decency and mutual respect that had always been the hallmark of southern society.

When William MacDonald had shown Grover Hall the advertisement, the editor had expressed little interest in it. But when the copy of Jenkins's story crossed his desk the afternoon of April 5, Hall reacted entirely differently. "Grover Hall read the story," Ray Jenkins reported years later, "and came running out there and wanted to see that ad. So I fished the thing out of the trash can and gave it to him." Hall had apparently not paid sufficient attention when talking to Mac-Donald; Jenkins's story, however, left little doubt in Hall's mind that something was amiss.

Grover Hall was a deeply complex figure, who attempted to walk a line between fidelity to the South he loved — and with it the system of racial control that made it so distinctive — and the emerging liberalism on race matters and economic development that ground against such ideas. Hall was a bachelor who reveled in his reputation as a dandy; a white newspaper editor who was not a knee-jerk segregationist; and a son who never quite lived up to his father's success in winning a Pulitzer Prize. The younger Hall had earned a reputation for professional reporting on civil rights matters, had once served on the national board of the American Civil Liberties Union, and had urged a moderate course during the bus boycott, opposing violence and showing some sympathy for the Mobile plan. Yet Hall was also a southerner and Alabamian. Like his father, he disdained lower-class white segregationists, such as L. B. Sullivan, whom he disliked, and the Klan because they mocked the South's historic position on the race issue. He viewed the *Times* as a model of modern newspaper report-ing, but he also believed that its editors and reporters had affronted his and his paper's honor by giving far too much attention to white extremists, which the *Advertiser* railed against, and discounting the South's ability to evolve gradual solutions to the race issue.

The contradictions in Hall's position had brought him under sub-stantial personal and professional pressure. His paper had lost adver-tising and subscription revenues as a result of its conciliatory position during the bus boycott. Hall attempted in 1957 to recoup his financial loss by dispatching reporters to investigate race relations in the heart of the liberal North. The so-called Ascalon series revealed racial injus-tices, discrimination, and de facto segregation in the big cities of the North. Hall was proud of his efforts; he believed he would win the Pulitzer Prize for investigative journalism in 1957. When he did not, he bitterly chalked up his failure to liberal northerners.

On April 7, 1960, Hall reacted directly to the ad. In a blistering edi-torial, written in the space of about forty minutes, Hall denounced the *Times* and the author of the ad, John Murray. Hall observed that "the Republic paid a dear price once for the hysteria and mendacity of abo-litionist agitators. The author of this ad is a lineal descendant of those abolitionists and the breed runs true." Hall took particular exception to those portions of the ad describing the behavior of the student pro-testors, the supposed response of Alabama State officials in, among other things, attempting to starve the students into submission, and the role of the police in dealing with the disturbances. "Lies, Lies, Lies," Hall stridently proclaimed, "and possibly willful ones on the part of the fund-raising novelist who wrote those lines to prey on the credulity, self-righteousness and misinformation of northern citizens."

A newspaper editor as egocentric and energetic as Hall should have wanted to enhance the right of the press to comment critically on public figures. Hall took the opposite position; he complained that the *Times* ad fostered a climate of disrespect for authority by holding the South up to national ridicule. Hence, in an attempt to protect the honor of his section and his class, an Alabama newspaper editor, and a liberal one at that, cast his journalistic fate with segregationists that he neither liked nor respected.

On April 9, Roland Nachman gave instructions to L. B. Sullivan, Earl James, and Frank Parks to write identical letters not only to the *Times* but to each of the four Alabama preachers, demanding that they prepare a full retraction. The latter were joined as parties in order to keep the litigation in the Alabama courts and to block removal to the potentially more sympathetic federal courts.

The events in Montgomery were given additional momentum by developments in Birmingham to the north. Turner Catledge had dispatched Harrison Salisbury, who had previously served in the prestigious post of Moscow correspondent, to investigate racial conditions in the South. Salisbury left on April 1, two days after "Heed Their Rising Voices" had appeared. As a foreign correspondent, he routinely "parachuted" into unfamiliar territory and then within days—sometimes hours—had to size up a complex situation and write stories that would be understandable to the *Times* readership. The South was in some ways just another foreign country. His first stop was Birmingham, where the sit-in movement was about to begin. Salisbury interviewed blacks and whites, and he concluded that something approaching a reign of terror existed. As the city's police commissioner told him, "Damn the law—down here we make our own law." In a two-part story that appeared on April 8 and 9, Salisbury described Birmingham as a city where telephones were tapped, mail was intercepted and opened, and the "eavesdropper, the informer, the spy have become a fact of life." No New Yorker, he declared,

> can readily measure the climate of Birmingham today. Whites and blacks still walk the same streets. But the streets, the water supply and the sewer system are about the only public facilities they share. Ball parks and taxicabs are segregated. So are libraries. A book featuring black rabbits and white rabbits was banned. A drive is on to forbid "Negro music" on "white" radio stations. Every channel of communication, every medium of mutual interest, every reasoned approach, every inch of middle ground has been fragmented by the emotional dynamite of racism, reinforced by the whip, the razor,

the gun, the bomb, the torch, the club, the knife, the mob, the police and many branches of the state's apparatus.

Salisbury dubbed Birmingham the "Johannesburg of America," words that particularly insulted the white leadership of the self-proclaimed "Magic City" of the South. The city's chief of police, Eugene "Bull" Connor, took exception to Salisbury's story, since it equated the behavior of the police there with the same state terror tactics that had characterized Hitler's Germany and that the "Heed Their Rising Voices" ad had attributed to law enforcement officials in Montgomery. As was true in Montgomery, the Birmingham press immediately attacked the *Times*. John Temple Graves, the editorial columnist for the *Birmingham News*, described Salisbury as a "tooth-and-claw hate . . . purveyor of prejudgment, malice and hate" and the *Times* as engaged in fomenting "hatred of the South, engendered by racial emotions" that amounted to "almost a total lie."

(The response would have been even more bitter if they had seen the paragraph that the New York editors had excised from Salisbury's story: "To one long accustomed to the sickening atmosphere of Moscow in the Stalin days, the aura of the community which once prided itself as the 'Magic City' of the South is only too familiar. To one who knew Hitler's storm troop Germany, it would seem even more familiar.")

Grover Hall in an April 17 editorial joined the Birmingham and Montgomery events. He denounced the *Times*'s writers as "abolitionist hellmouths" who propagated "the big lie" about the city's racial conditions and said that in doing so they were "misleading the United States and much of the civilized world." Hall charged the *Times* with "dereliction and emotionalism," and observed that "it seems incredible that men of honor could be challenged by a famous Southern newspaper to check the facts and ignore that challenge."

Although there is no evidence to suggest any direct coordination, there was nonetheless an almost simultaneous movement in the two cities to bring lawsuits against the *Times*. On April 19, at Nachman's direction, the three commissioners — Sullivan, James, and Parks — individually filed suits in the Montgomery County Circuit Court against the *Times* and the four ministers, seeking damages of $500,000 against each of the defendants. On May 6, the three city commissioners of

Birmingham — Connor, James Morgan, and J. T. Waggoner — filed suit for libel against the *Times* and against Harrison Salisbury. (In addition, a grand jury indicted Salisbury on forty-two counts of criminal libel, and if he were brought to trial, he would have faced the possibility of twenty-one years in jail and $21,000 in fines.) Each plaintiff asked damages of $500,000, a total of $3,000,000 from the commissioners of the two cities alone, an amount of nearly $22 million in current value. On May 31, the three city commissioners of the town of Bessemer, an industrial enclave where Birmingham's steel mills were located, filed identical libel suits, seeking another $1,500,000. On July 20, 1960, a Birmingham city detective named Joe Lindsey brought a similar action asking for $150,000.

To this total must be added two other suits. The first of these was brought on May 30 by Governor Patterson for $1,000,000. The previous day an all-white jury had found King not guilty of violating Alabama income tax laws. Patterson on May 9 had written to the *Times* demanding, as had Sullivan, Parks, and James, that the newspaper retract the ad. Patterson claimed that he had been specifically maligned because in his capacity as governor he also served as "ex-officio chairman of the State Board of Education." Attorney General MacDonald Gallion urged this course of action on the governor, as did the members of the Board of Education.

A week later the *Times* retracted the ad, and in a story headlined "Times Retracts Statement in Ad," explained that the copy had been received "in the regular course of business from and paid by a recognized advertising agency in behalf of a group which included among its subscribers well-known citizens. The publication of an advertisement does not constitute a factual news report by The Times nor does it reflect the judgment or the opinion of the editors of the Times." Upon receiving complaints, the paper had launched its own investigation into the actual facts, and was retracting two paragraphs of which Governor Patterson had complained. The *Times* had never intended to suggest misconduct on the part of any public official, and "to the extent that anyone can fairly conclude from the statements in the advertisement that any such charge was made, The New York Times hereby apologizes to the Honorable John Patterson therefore."

That same day, May 16, Orvil Dryfoos, the president of the *Times*, wrote to Governor Patterson and apologized. He enclosed a copy of the page with the retraction story, and repeated that "to the extent that anyone could fairly conclude from the advertisement that any charge was made against you, The New York Times apologizes." In all likelihood Dryfoos and the editors thought this a tempest in a teapot, since the factual errors were minor. They did not realize that under Alabama law any error could be fatal to the defendant in a libel case. They also did not realize that under Alabama law the plaintiff could demand an apology, on the assumption that in some instances that would be enough to assuage honor and end the matter. But although the person who made the allegation had to be given the chance to apologize — in order for him or her to understand that an insult had occurred — the person who claimed to have been maligned could still proceed with a libel suit.

Patterson did nothing for two weeks, waiting until King's trial ended. When the all-white jury acquitted the civil rights leader, Patterson filed his own suit, not only against the *Times* and the four ministers, but against King as well. Finally, Clyde Sellers, a former commissioner who had overseen the police, also brought suit against the *Times* and the four ministers. Together, therefore, by early June 1960, the *New York Times* and the four ministers faced suits amounting to $3,000,000 in Montgomery. In addition, the *Times* had another $3,150,000 in damages in Birmingham. Given the state of libel law in Alabama and elsewhere at this time, the paper appeared to have little chance in court.

The laws of defamation have their roots deep in English feudal society, and grew out of an attempt to prevent violence. If one lord of the realm impugned the reputation of another, the result would often be a fight to the death as the insulted baron defended his honor by the sword. To remove questions of reputation from the tilting field to the courts, *De Scandalis Magnatum* was promulgated in 1275. Reenacted and expanded several times, the law made it a crime to slander the peers of the realm. Such falsehoods threatened "great peril and mischief . . . to all the realm, and quick subversion and destruction of the said realm." In an era when personal bonds rather than a powerful state held society together, an attack on the good name of one feudal lord constituted an assault on the basis of society.

Then in 1606 Sir Edward Coke prosecuted the case of *De Libellis Famosis* in the secret court of the Star Chamber, in which a publisher of poems had made fun of two archbishops of Canterbury. The case set out the standard that a person may libel another person by harming their reputation, even by saying things that are true, and whether the object of the libel is a public or a private person, or even whether he be dead or alive (one of the archbishops in this case was, in fact, dead at the time of the scurrilous poem). The punishment for libel might be fine, imprisonment, or cutting off the ears of the offender.

Libel, according to Coke, deserved a severe punishment, because in addition to the harm it did to the victim's reputation, "it inciteth all those of the same family, kindred, or society to revenge, and so may be the cause of quarrels and breach of the peace, and may be the cause of shedding blood, and of great inconvenience." To accuse one of the King's ministers of corruption — even if true — was a great offense, since it called into question the integrity of the state.

Although the Long Parliament abolished the Star Chamber in 1641, Coke's report of the case shaped the law of defamation for more than three and a half centuries. In essence libel (a written defamation) or slander (a spoken accusation) fell into four broad categories — *blasphemy*, a libel against religion or the church; *obscenity*, a libel against the moral norms of society; *private libel*, the defamation of an individual; and *seditious libel*, any political comment that had the tendency to lower public estimation of the government, its officers, and the law.

Blasphemous libel went hand in hand with laws establishing an official church and outlawing heresy, and eventually faded as religion, even in states such as Great Britain that still have an established church, became more of a private matter. Nonetheless, blasphemy laws — specifically aimed against defamation of Christianity — remained on the books in England and Wales until quite recently. The last person actually jailed for blasphemy in the United Kingdom was John William Gott in 1921, and the last successful prosecution occurred in 1977. In 2008 Parliament abolished the law entirely.

In the United States one can still find some state codes with blasphemy laws dating from colonial times, but they are unenforced. The last known conviction for that offense was of the atheist Charles Lee Smith, who rented a storefront in Little Rock, Arkansas, in 1928 and put a sign in the window reading "Evolution is True. The Bible's a Lie.

God's a Ghost." In 1952 the Supreme Court, in *Joseph Burstyn v. Wilson*, held the New York blasphemy law unconstitutional as a prior restraint on speech, and declared that "it is not the business of government to suppress real or imagined attacks upon a particular religious doctrine, whether they appear in publications, speeches, or motion pictures."

Obscenity laws, unlike blasphemy, are still very much alive and on the books in both the United Kingdom and the United States. The Obscene Publications Acts of 1959 and 1964 attempt to define the legal bounds of obscenity in England and Wales, although in the last several decades the most prominent prosecutions have resulted in either the Crown dropping the charges or the defendants gaining a not guilty verdict. For example, in 1960 the court found the publisher of D. H. Lawrence's *Lady Chatterley's Lover* not guilty of obscenity, and in 1984 the government dropped the charges against *Gay's the Word*.

American courts for many years used the *Hicklin* test to determine whether a publication was obscene. Derived from the 1868 British case of *Regina v. Hicklin*, it rested on how the most erotic passages would affect particularly susceptible persons, such as teenage boys. Beginning with *Roth v. United States* in 1957, the Supreme Court has wrestled on and off with how to square the enforcement of social norms with the First Amendment command that there shall be no law abridging freedom of speech. Justice William O. Douglas in particular believed that the First Amendment meant exactly what it said — *no* restrictions — and he also argued that the government should not play the role of censor.

A majority of the Court, however, has held that communities have a right to proscribe material they find offensive, providing that the articles failed the test announced in *Miller v. California*, namely, that they lack "serious artistic, literary, political, or scientific value." The result is that there is no single national standard for obscenity, and what may be considered obscene in one jurisdiction (a small southern town) may not be so in another (Los Angeles). Efforts by Congress to deal with obscenity on the Internet have so far proved fruitless, both in terms of successful prosecutions and in meeting the First Amendment requirements as interpreted by the Court. Perhaps the confusion is best summed up in Justice Potter Stewart's famous comment over what constitutes obscenity: "I shall not today attempt further to define the kinds of material I understand to be embraced . . . but I know it when I see it."

Seditious libel is considered by many civil libertarians to be the most dangerous kind, since it gives the government the power to punish its critics. In a democratic society, this means choking off political discourse that the state finds uncomfortable, and seditious libel played a large role when the Supreme Court heard the *Times* case.

Under the cloud of a possible war with France, Congress in 1798 passed a Sedition Act, modeled on English precedents. Despite the First Amendment, the law forbade writing, publishing, or speaking anything of "a false, scandalous and malicious writing . . . against the government of the United States, or either house of the Congress of the United States, or the President of the United States."

The Sedition Act had only a little to do with fear of internal rebellion and everything to do with silencing the Jeffersonian Republican opponents of the Federalist administration. In the next two years the government, with the aid of stacked juries and relentless judges, secured fifteen indictments against Republicans, and ten cases resulted in convictions despite the absurdly trivial nature of the allegedly seditious comments. Matthew Lyon, a Republican congressman from Vermont, languished four months in jail for ridiculing President John Adams's "continual grasp for power" and "unbounded thirst for ridiculous pomp, foolish adulation, and selfish avarice."

None of the convictions under the law ever came up on appeal to the Supreme Court, so it would be well over a century until the high court, after World War I, dealt with how the restraints on supposedly seditious speech squared with the First Amendment's guaranty of free expression. (The two major laws, the Espionage Act of 1917 and the Sedition Act of 1918, both borrowed heavily from the earlier statute.)

In *Schenck v. United States* (1919), the Court unanimously upheld the conviction of Charles Schenck, the secretary of the Philadelphia Socialist Party, who had called conscription unconstitutional and urged draftees to resist induction. Oliver Wendell Holmes Jr. spoke for the Court, and his opinion reflected what had been the standard meaning of "free" speech since the eighteenth century—while government could not impose prior restraints on speech or publication, it could afterward punish those who violated the law. In wartime, Holmes declared, Congress had the power to proscribe those types of speech that would create "a clear and present danger that they will bring about the substantive evils that Congress has a right to prevent." The "clear and present danger" test became the starting point for all subsequent speech cases for the next half-century, and not until 1969 did the Court finally do away with the crime of seditious libel completely in *Brandenburg v. Ohio.*

With this background in mind, we can now turn to the last of the four libels.


Private libel, the defamation of an individual, and his or her recourse under law, is an area of tort law that is still very much alive today, even though somewhat circumscribed following the Supreme Court rulings in *Sullivan* and its progeny. As in 1960, much of the law of defamation is the creature of state tort law that is a descendant of centuries of haphazard and often baffling evolution. This common law process continues, as states make adjustments to both constitutional limits and new technologies, such as the Internet.

Reputation has always been an important consideration in society. The value of a "good name" can be seen in Shakespeare's *Othello*, when Iago says to the Moor:

> Good name in man and woman, dear my lord,
> Is the immediate jewel of their souls;
> Who steals my purse steals trash; 'tis something, nothing;
> T'was mine, 'tis his, and has been slave to thousands;
> But he filches from me my good name
> Robs me of that which not enriches him
> And makes me poor indeed.

The fact that it is the villain, Iago, who deceitfully declaims these words does not detract from the intrinsic message — reputation matters.

In the Middle Ages, punishment for slander could be terrible indeed. The Laws of Alfred the Great, compiled about 880 AD, held that "if anyone is guilty of public slander, and it is proved against him, it is to be compensated with no lighter penalty than the cutting off of his tongue." By the thirteenth century recourse had been moved to the ecclesiastical courts, which treated slander as a spiritual offense, a sin that required appropriate penance. The sinner was wrapped in a white shroud and, holding a lighted candle, knelt in public acknowledging that he had born false witness and begging the pardon of God and the injured party. After the English Reformation, jurisdiction moved to common law courts. But as several scholars have noted, by then the die was cast. The law of defamation would forever be "a forest of complexities, overgrown with anomalies, inconsistencies, and perverse rigidities . . . a veritable fog of fictions, inferences, and presumptions."

Following the precedent set in secret Star Chamber prosecutions, the first order of business was to determine whether a defamatory statement had been made, and then whether the defendant had in fact been the person who disseminated the slander. In common law prosecutions for libel, judges ruled on the first question, known as "the law of the case," that is, whether publication, either orally or through print, was libelous; a jury decided the "facts of the case," whether the defendant was the culprit. In all defamation suits, there had to be evidence that a third party had either heard or seen the libel. If A directly accused B of cheating at cards, for example, that did not constitute a libel; if, however, A publicly told C that B was a cheat, that did. A private letter from A to C, however, did not qualify.

The end of feudalism and the rise of a mercantile society in England did not decrease the importance of a good name, because commercial relations often relied on a merchant's reputation. If Mr. Brown promised that he would pay £100 for a shipment of grain and gave you his hand as assurance, his good name would be enough to secure the contract. If, however, Mr. Smith had a reputation for going back on his word, a handshake would rarely be enough. For merchants like Mr. Brown, a good name meant a great deal. In terms of the law, courts did not look so much on actual personal injury—the notion of emotional damage was still in the future—but on damage to reputation and how that injury might affect the plaintiff's relationships with other people.

But what actually constitutes defamation? The answer is—a lot. In a well-known definition, the New York Court of Appeals—summing up the older ideas embedded in Anglo-American law—cited any statements that "tend to expose one to public hatred, shame, obloquy, contumely, odium, contempt, ridicule, aversion, ostracism, degradation, or disgrace, or to induce an evil opinion of one in the minds of right-thinking persons, and to deprive one of their confidence and friendly intercourse in society" (*Kimmerle v. N.Y. Evening Journal* [1933]). One might think that only false statements would be defamatory, but at common law the truth of the allegation mattered less than that it had been made; the writer or speaker's intent and accuracy were irrelevant. This was especially true in cases of criminal libel, in which the government prosecuted a person for comments made about an official.

The English law of defamation crossed the Atlantic to the colonies, and according to some scholars, private suits took up a good part of the business of local colonial courts. Many colonists, even if not wealthy or part of the upper classes, valued their reputation, and women as well as men often resorted to the courts when their honor was impugned. To call a woman a poor manager of her household or to imply that she had loose morals was an insult that could not be tolerated. Records of such private suits indicate that in seventeenth-century America courts had less interest in awarding monetary damages — since few defendants had great means — than in possibly restoring the *status quo ante*, to minimize hostility through an apology and restore social harmony.

If the object of defamation turned out to be a public official, then he could resort to the state for a criminal prosecution. Kai Erikson's study of "wayward Puritans" shows that prosecutions for contempt of authority constituted a large part of the Essex County, Massachusetts, courts in the late seventeenth century. Here again, truth mattered not; the court wanted to know only if the statement had been libelous, and whether the defendant had made it. Above all else, society valued and wanted to protect the reputation of its leaders, in the belief that any lessening of their status could lead to the disintegration of the social and political order.

At that time a group of writers living outside London, dubbed the "country" faction, began attacking the politics as well as the legal and philosophic views of the court, which many of them viewed as corrupt. These writers included Whigs such as John Trenchard and Thomas Gordon as well as Tories such as Viscount Bolingbroke. The *Cato Letters* of Trenchard and Gordon especially appealed to Americans, and grew out of increasing malaise in England following the collapse of the crown-chartered South Sea Company as well as the growing influence of commercial activity. The country writers took scant comfort that England had already begun to enjoy one of its most prosperous eras, since in their eyes the economic growth of the nation corrupted both society and politics.

The *Letters* not only reflected this gloomy view, but also set out a libertarian position on freedom of expression. Trenchard and Gordon valued free expression not only as a way to enhance knowledge, but also as a means to prevent change. Ironically, they saw England as the freest country on God's earth, and its constitutional system as the best in the world, so therefore any change could only be for the worse, leading to tyranny. Free expression would permit the citizenry to discover corruption and fight it, thus maintaining free institutions. "Freedom of Speech," according to Cato, "is the great Bulwark of Liberty; they prosper and die together." The *Letters* also included essays on the law of libel, challenging the orthodox view that mere critical statement constituted a libel; publication of the truth could never be libelous. James Alexander published several of Cato's essays in John Peter Zenger's *Weekly Journal*, adding his own commentary and explanations.

Eventually the notion of truth as a defense became embedded in American and later in English law, as did the idea that a jury would decide both if a statement was libelous and whether the defendant had made it. In the more than two centuries before the *Sullivan* case, common law decisions developed an elaborate system of rules that would allow truth as a defense yet still protect the reputations of private as well as public individuals.


The common law of libel is far more than the awarding of monetary damages for malicious lies that do harm to a person's reputation. To reach that step, or to avoid it in the case where the alleged defamation was true, courts established a number of tests and assumptions. To begin with, defamatory statements were presumed to be false. In some ways we can trace this back to the old English notion that it mattered not whether a statement was true or false, since in both instances it harmed a person's reputation. In a trial, therefore, the burden of proof is not upon the plaintiff to prove the statement false, but upon the defendant to prove it true. Truth, however, is not always easy to establish. It is one thing to show that on a particular date a certain event took place—on the morning of September 11, 2001, terrorists commandeered four commercial air flights, and crashed two of the planes into the World Trade Center in New York, and a third into the Pentagon outside of Washington, D.C., killing nearly 3,000 people. This statement is factual, and one can with objective certainty ascertain the time, date, the damages to the buildings, and the number of casualties. Once we get into why al-Qaeda launched the attacks, the mentality of the nineteen hijackers, the impact of the attack on the United States, and many other issues related to the event, we start dealing with subjective matters that are open to interpretation. What is "truth" for one person may not be so clear to another.

To take another example, Tom Smith charges that the mayor of Smallville has engaged in cronyism, arranging it so that his close friends get city contracts for construction, maintenance, and other services. To "prove" this, Smith lists the names of the businesses that have received city contracts, and shows that the biggest recipients are companies whose owners all belong to the same fraternal lodge as the mayor or play poker with him on Wednesday evenings or were groomsmen at his wedding. The "fact" that these men are the mayor's friends can be easily established, but does that make the awarding of city contracts to them a matter of "cronyism," which smacks of corruption? In a small town it would not be surprising for the mayor and leading businessmen to be friends. Is there any evidence that any contract was awarded improperly, in that it violated city and state regulations? Is there anything to show that the contractual obligations are not being fulfilled, that potholes are not being repaired, or that sprinkler systems have not been properly installed in the schools? Were the mayor to sue Tom Smith, the court would hold the statement as presumably false, and Smith would have a very difficult time proving otherwise.

A second rule involved intent. In criminal law, an essential element of most crimes is intent: the person knew or should have known that a particular act violated the law, and she or he went ahead and did it anyway. In libel law, it did not matter whether the statement resulted from malice, ignorance, negligence, or just plain misfortune. One published at one's peril, and as far as the law went, one presumed malice—an evil intention—from the simple fact of publication.

Thirdly, the aggrieved party did not have to show any actual injury to his or her reputation, since this too was inferred from the publication. Nor did the plaintiff have to prove any particular monetary damage; he or she could claim almost any amount, and it would be up to the jury's discretion how much in general damages would be awarded.

These "galloping" presumptions, as one scholar called them, gave a clear advantage to the plaintiff, who started out not having to prove the allegations were false, not having to prove malice on the part of the alleged defamer, and not having to show actual harm to reputation. In addition, although most states made libel a tort, for the past eight centuries the actual definition of defamation has always had a fluid quality about it, easily shaped to meet the needs and prejudices of local communities. In the middle of the nineteenth century Lord Chancellor Lyndhurst declared that "I have never yet seen nor been able myself to hit upon any thing like a definition of libel which possessed those requisites of a logical definition." This, of course, left an enormous burden of proof on the part of the defendant, who not only had to prove the truth of all the statements, but also had to confront the elastic boundaries of what constituted a libel. Moreover, in order to utilize truth as a defense, the publisher of serious criticism had to ensure the absolute accuracy of everything said; one factual error, no matter how inadvertent or minor, destroyed the claim of truth.

There is some evidence that in the North use of libel law to protect one's reputation may have been on the wane in the mid-twentieth century. The noted First Amendment scholar Zechariah Chafee wrote just after World War II that "a libeled American prefers to vindicate himself by steadily pushing forward his career and not by hiring a lawyer to talk in a courtroom." David Riesman, an astute observer of contemporary American society, seemed to suggest that there was something almost un-American in pursuing a libel suit. He compared European societies, where feudal notions of personal reputation still survived, to America's capitalist society, where reputation was only an asset, "good will," and had little intrinsic value otherwise. But as many commentators have noted, the South before the civil rights era retained many aspects of a feudal society, and in 1960 personal reputation did matter to the citizens of Montgomery.

The "galloping presumptions," which prevailed not just in Alabama but in almost every state in the nation, clearly had a chilling effect on free speech, and the common law recognized this. It offset at least some of the severity with so-called privileges, including fair comment for literary criticism (one could not sue a critic for panning a book or play), speeches by legislators on the floor of the assembly (tracking the privilege given to Congress in Article I, Section 6, of the Constitution), reprinting these speeches or other official records, and fair comment on public officials or candidates for public office. This last "privilege" varied from state to state. A majority of states distinguished between fact (the mayor is now in his second term) and opinion (the mayor has not governed the city well), but protected opinion only so far as the factual basis of the opinion was accurate. Here again the burden of proof for accuracy lay with the publisher of the statement, who would lose the privilege if any of his statements proved factually incorrect. A few states were more speech protective, and allowed the privilege even if there were minor errors made either through inadvertence or in the good-faith belief that they were correct. Alabama took the stricter view.

Finally, as the Alabama Supreme Court noted:

> Where the words published tend to injure a person libeled by them in his reputation, profession, trade, or business, or charge him with an indictable offense, or tend to bring the individual into public contempt, they are libelous *per se*. The publication is not to be measured by its effects when subjected to critical analysis of a trained legal mind, but must be construed and determined by its natural and probable effect upon the mind of the average lay reader.

Given this very broad — and quite common — definition, it was hard to see how the *New York Times* could win this case.

When a writer interviewed those parties still alive in Montgomery in the 1990s, they insisted that all of the lawsuits arose independently. Perhaps, but Montgomery in the 1960s was still a small community, one in which ties of family, friends, neighborhoods, and clubs bound persons together. Lawsuits, moreover, often make for strange bedfellows. Grover Hall and Roland Nachman held L. B. Sullivan and the other city commissioners in contempt for their race demagoguery and their connections to lower-class whites on the east side. Yet they all shared a common disdain for an implacable northern press and an active black civil rights movement.

The stakes were high for all concerned. The plaintiffs saw not only their own honor and dignity impugned, but that of the region as a whole. The suit, Hall proclaimed in an *Advertiser* editorial of May 22, 1960, promised that "the recent checkmating of the *Times* in Alabama will impose a restraint upon other publications." For the management of the *Times*, the lawsuits represented a threat to the paper's balance sheet and, ever more important, a chilling of its coverage of the civil rights movement. Only an infinitesimal portion of the Alabama public would have ever read the ad had not Ray Jenkins and Grover Hall decided to report it. Nachman and others, however, were not worried about the *Times* changing minds in Alabama; they worried, instead, about the fate of their reputations in the North. Besides, Nachman was certain that the law was on his side and that he would make short work of the *Times* in the trial to follow.

# CHAPTER 3

# Trial by Jury

It is important to keep the civil rights context in mind, and to recognize that L. B. Sullivan and the other commissioners wanted to punish the *Times* and, through a victory in court yielding large damages, to stop the *Times* and other northern media from reporting what they considered a biased and unfair view of events in the South. Roland Nachman later claimed that it had not been his intention to punish the paper for its civil rights position; he had seen it from the start as a simple matter of libel. That may be true, but there can be little doubt that for the plaintiffs, the black defendants, the majority of people in the South, and certainly for the *Times*, this case had the simple goal of punishing those who supported civil rights.

In terms of the law, the *Times* stood on shaky ground. It had failed to do its usual job of fact-checking, and had taken the advertisement as it was, relying on the reputation of the men who submitted it. There were factual errors, and even if the ad did not mention Sullivan and the others by name, readers could infer that the men in charge of public safety and government in Montgomery had perpetrated violence on African Americans who sought nothing more than their basic rights. We may think Alabama law unduly harsh in how it defined libel, but it was no more so than that of most states in the Union, including those in the North. In fact, when the Alabama Supreme Court reviewed the case, it relied not only on prior Alabama decisions, but on identical rulings in other jurisdictions. Moreover, the strategy to hit the *Times* in its wallet and thus deter other northern press had a sound basis in law. "Punishment by way of damages in a libel action is intended not alone to punish the wrongdoer," the Alabama Supreme Court noted, "but as a deterrent to others similarly minded," and it cited numerous cases to support this proposition. The *Times* availed itself of good legal talent, but despite the demurrals and objections and procedural issues they raised, the law was clearly on Sullivan's side.

Louis Loeb was a partner in the prestigious New York law firm of Lord, Day, and Lord, but he essentially had only one client—the *New York Times*. He came up from Wall Street every day to the paper's office on Times Square, where he was available if any editor or reporter had questions, and he counted Arthur Hays Sulzberger, the *Times* publisher, as a personal friend. Loeb had been in large part responsible for the paper's legal policy of never settling a libel suit, lest it encourage nuisance suits—attacks with little basis in law or fact but a hope that the paper would pay just to have the plaintiff go away. Over the years the newspaper had lost very few jury trials, and then for modest damages. Loeb realized immediately that this case would be different. The plaintiffs were asking for very large sums of money, the trial would be in an Alabama court before a southern judge and jury, and the paper's coverage of the civil rights movement had not made it popular in the South.

Loeb first had to find an Alabama lawyer to represent the *Times*. A cultured man who friends said resembled a theatrical British colonel, Loeb knew New York law, and had done well defending the *Times* in its home state. But this case would be tried in Montgomery; the paper needed someone who was familiar with Alabama's rules on libel and courtroom procedure and who would not be seen as an outsider. Lord, Day, like most large New York firms, had correspondents—lawyers and firms in other parts of the country who would handle local matters. Loeb tried his two regular correspondent firms, one in Montgomery and the other in Birmingham, and neither would take the case. He finally found T. Eric Embry, a lawyer with a maverick firm in Birmingham that had defended a large number of African Americans charged with various crimes.

By this time the northern press in general and the *Times* in particular had become so hated in Alabama that when Loeb flew down to Birmingham, Embry got him a room in a motel outside Birmingham under an assumed name. After Loeb assured himself that Embry could do the job, the paper brought Embry and his partner, Roderick Beddow, up to New York not only to meet with the lawyers, but to make them familiar with how the *Times* functioned. They wanted the two men from Alabama to know what went into getting out the paper every day, what reporters, editors, pressmen, and others did. In addition, the *Times* management made it clear to Embry and Beddow that they did not care what it cost to defend the case – but they would not voluntarily settle. Privately Loeb and others at the *Times* had already figured out that they would probably lose in the trial, and that their only hope for salvation would be an appeal to the United States Supreme Court.

Embry may not have had much of a chance of winning, but he was the perfect lawyer for the case. A cantankerous man, he had a thriving practice representing plaintiffs in personal injury cases, but he and his partners also did a lot of work with labor unions and poor black clients. A native of the state, he knew everyone, and he was not surprised when the local community turned on him after he took on the *Times* as a client. People "stopped speaking to me in the courthouse, in the streets, and some of them got nasty and cussed me out. And Jones [Judge Walter Burgwyn Jones, who presided at the trial] put the word out, old Jones did. Anybody seen associating with me would incur his wrath." And all this just made Embry mad and determined to go ahead.

He may have been the only person who believed he had a chance to win. In his research he had found some old cases from the 1830s that established a qualified privilege for newspapers. "And I knew how to cross-examine damn witnesses." He also had an almost idealistic view of a jury trial, "I believe in people. I was optimistic that the people would do the right thing."

He also had a realistic grasp of local conditions, and expected that his phones would be tapped by the Montgomery police, a situation confirmed by lawyers for the black ministers. Embry took to making important calls about the case from a variety of phones so that police would not be able to listen in. There was no suggestion by any of the defense lawyers that information overheard on the wiretaps was provided to Nachman; rather, the police wanted the information for their own purposes.

Both Loeb and Embry agreed that the best chance to defeat Sullivan was to prevent the case from ever coming to trial. Roland Nachman had filed suit in state court because he knew Alabama law gave him a strong case, and also because he expected a local jury to be sympathetic. But the *Times* was a New York entity, and under the Constitution federal courts had so-called diversity jurisdiction in cases involving citizens of two or more states. The Supreme Court had ruled, however, that if the out-of-state party had a sufficient presence within the state, then state courts could exercise in personam jurisdiction. What constituted a "sufficient presence," though, had never been clearly defined, and the high court pretty much left it to state judges to make that determination. The *Times* did not have much of a circulation in Alabama, but it kept a few stringers on call, and had sent reporters such as Harrison Salisbury into the state to report on what Nachman and others considered local news.

The trial thus began with Embry filing a motion that the *Times* did not do enough business in Alabama to come within the jurisdiction of its state courts. The paper had a daily press run of 650,000, of which only 394 copies (.0006 percent) were sold in Alabama, a number, Embry argued, that did not add up to a meaningful connection to the state. Although the paper kept stringers and sent an occasional reporter, the *Times* did not cover Alabama with any regularity. Moreover, Alabama companies had placed only $18,000 worth of advertisements in the paper in the first five months of 1960, out of total advertising revenue of $37.5 million. All this, Embry argued, did not constitute the substantive connection required for an Alabama court to exercise jurisdiction over the New York newspaper. Embry also emphasized that he was making a "special appearance," one for the sole purpose of arguing that the court had no jurisdiction over his client. Had he made a "general appearance," one in which he represented the client for any other purpose, that by itself could give the court sufficient reason to claim jurisdiction.

It did not work, of course, even though Embry followed the rules in the leading text on the subject, *Alabama Pleading and Practice at Law* by Walter Burgwyn Jones. Among other things, circuit court judge Jones had been connected with Commissioner Sullivan and Governor Patterson a few years earlier in the cleanup of Phenix City, and he was determined to hear the case in his court. A devotee of the Confederacy, in which his father had fought, Jones published "The Confederate Creed," in which he said "I see in the Stars and Bars, the glorious banner of the Confederacy as it waves in the Southern breeze, a symbol of freedom and devotion to constitutional rights, an emblem of honor and character." When in 1961 the city of Birmingham mounted a reenactment to mark the centennial of Jefferson Davis becoming president of the Confederacy, Judge Jones administered the oath of office. Some of the players in the pageant became jurors in a trial in Judge Jones's court, and he allowed them to wear their Confederate uniforms in the jury box. A colorful figure and well known around town, Jones also wrote a weekly column, "Off the Bench," in which he commented on everything from the folly of the administration in Washington to the glory of the Confederacy.

Over the years Walter Jones, as one could expect, had been an implacable foe of the civil rights movement, barring Freedom Riders from demonstrating against segregated buses, forbidding the NAACP from doing business in Alabama, and blocking the U.S. Department of Justice from examining voter registration records in any county in Alabama. He kept seating in his courtroom segregated, and in a libel trial brought after Sullivan's, black spectators wound up sitting in the white section. The next day Jones harangued against "recognized rabble-rousers and racial agitators" for causing an incident and ordered his bailiffs to maintain segregated seating. The case would be tried "under the laws of the State of Alabama and not under the Fourteenth Amendment." He went on to praise "white man's justice, a justice born long ago in England, and brought over to this country by the Anglo-Saxon race."

Despite these personal biases, Jones had a reputation for running a strict courtroom. He also had experience in libel cases, and in fact had presided in *Davis v. Johnson Publishing Co*, the case where Edward Davis had been defamed by *Jet* magazine. In interviews with some of the lawyers afterward, one scholar found that while they spoke about Jones's idiosyncrasies off the bench, they all stated that he knew the law and had run the trial in a straightforward manner. Nachman, who tried a number of cases before Jones, called him a "workman-like judge" who ran a tight ship.

The *Times* lawyers knew they could not expect Judge Jones to dismiss the case summarily, but they still hoped to be able to prove that the *Times* lacked sufficient presence in the state to evade Alabama jurisdiction. On July 25, 26, and 27, 1960, Embry called witnesses to support his contention that the *Times* did little business in the state.

Harold Faber, the national news editor, related that most of the news they picked up regarding Alabama came off the wire services, and from string correspondents who could be dispatched to cover a particular story. The *Times* did not maintain a news bureau in the state nor did it keep regular correspondents stationed there. Joseph B. Wagner, the national advertising manager, who had worked for the *Times* for nineteen years, told the court that the paper had never solicited advertisements in Alabama, and that any Alabama companies that wanted to advertise in the paper would on their own volition contact the Atlanta office. The national circulation manager, Roger J. Waters, testified as to the way the *Times* handled requests for subscriptions from outside the New York metropolitan area, the fact that his office did not solicit business outside that area, and the number of subscribers the *Times* had in Alabama. Finally, John McCabe, the assistant to the comptroller, confirmed that the *Times* did not print in Alabama, did not maintain any offices there, did not have any state residents on its regular payroll, and if fact, had no office of any sort in the state.

Nachman and his associates cross-examined the witnesses carefully, trying to elicit admission that even though the *Times* did not run a regular operation in Alabama as it did in New York, it nonetheless collected news from the state, had stringers who in effect reported on affairs there, and sold newspapers to any resident of the state who wanted to read the paper. By the time they had finished, they had made their point — the *Times* had a connection to Alabama, and Nachman and his associates believed it adequate to maintain in personam jurisdiction.

On August 5, Judge Jones agreed, and ruled that the *Times* did sufficient business in the state to give the court jurisdiction. In the event that appellate courts later said that he was wrong, he gave a second reason why his court could hear the case. Embry had made a mistake in drafting his motion to quash and had therefore, even if inadvertently, made a "general appearance" and thus brought his client within reach of state courts. Embry had, of course, been very careful to avoid that snare and had followed *Alabama Pleadings* to the letter; in effect, Jones just ignored his own rules.

It was a devastating blow for the *Times*, and both Loeb and Embry knew it. Their best chance had been to avoid a trial they both knew would be difficult if not impossible to win. So they now began preparation for the trial, but first the lawyers for the defendants filed various motions, stipulations, and demurrers aimed at limiting the type of evidence and testimony to be admitted, the issues to be examined, and the other minutiae of a trial. Counsel for the four black ministers also asked to have their clients removed from the trial altogether, or at the least, to separate their trial from that of the *Times*. On November 1, 1960, Judge Jones summarily rejected nearly all of the pleadings and demurrers, although the *Times* had a few of its minor points accepted. Jones would in the course of the trial overrule practically all of the objections Embry made, but he understood that Embry was trying to build a record for an appeal, and Jones carefully avoided any act or statement by which the *Times* could claim judicial bias. At one point, when Embry apologized for taking so long on a statement, Jones told him not to worry about it. "I am here as long as is necessary." One of the black lawyers, Fred Gray, afterward said that Jones had treated them well, without condescension, even though he ruled against nearly all of the defense objections.

Trial began on November 1, with Roland Nachman, Robert F. Steiner III, and Calvin Whitesell of Montgomery representing Sullivan. Eric Embry and four other lawyers represented the *Times*, while the black ministers named in the suit — Ralph D. Abernathy, Fred L. Shuttlesworth, S. S. Seay Sr., and J. E. Lowery — were represented by Vernon Z. Crawford of Mobile, S. S. Seay Jr., and Fred Gray. The latter had barely graduated from law school in 1954 when he was swept up in the civil rights movements, and found a good bit of his work — if not his income — came from representing blacks arrested for protesting segregation. He had handled much of the local legal work for the Montgomery bus boycotters (the NAACP and Thurgood Marshall argued the constitutional case in federal court), and had also represented several of the students expelled from Alabama State University in the wake of the sit-in protests

The jury selection went quickly. The pool of thirty-six men included two blacks, and Sullivan's lawyers immediately struck them from the list. The twelve finally chosen posed in the jury box for a picture that the *Alabama Journal* published with their names. Embry protested that this would create pressure on the jurors to vote in favor of Sullivan; Judge Jones overruled the complaint.

Finally the trial on the merits began, and Nachman asked his associate, Calvin Whitesell, to read the advertisement, "Heed Their Rising Voices," to the jury. He had barely started, "As the whole world knows by now, thousands of Southern Negro students — ," when he was interrupted:

> LAWYER CRAWFORD: Your Honor, we would like to object to the reading of that ad unless the counsel who reads it will read what is said and as I recall from reading that ad there is nothing on there that is spelled N-i-g-g-e-r-s. It is spelled N-e-g-r-o and I am sure he is well aware of it and is deliberately —
>
> THE COURT: Read it just like it is.
>
> MR. WHITESELL: Your Honor, I am.
>
> THE COURT: You are not interpolating anything?
>
> MR. WHITESELL: No, sir, Your Honor. . . . He is objecting to the way I pronounce N-e-g-r-o. I have been pronouncing it that way all my life.

Judith Rushin, a reporter for the *Alabama Journal*, wrote: "To newsmen, he did not seem to be saying 'nigger,' but something closer to 'nigra' or 'nigro.'"

(In the stenographic transcript of the trial, which became part of the record reviewed by the appellate courts, the white lawyers are always referred to as "Mr. Nachman" or "Mr. Embry," while the black lawyers are called "Lawyer Gray," "Lawyer Crawford," or "Lawyer Seay," but never "Mr.")

Nachman called Grover Hall as the first witness for the prosecution, and had barely begun his questions when Embry objected. The following colloquy is typical of what happened over the next few days. Embry was like a bulldog, jumping on every statement that could possibly serve as a basis for appeal, a tactic that Nachman understood and, because he was so sure that he had the law on his side, did not try to fight. Judge Jones also understood, and while keeping control of the trial, allowed Embry to build his case, confident that there would be nothing in the record that would lead an appellate court to remand because of judicial error.

Nachman asked Hall if he would read the critical third paragraph in the advertisement, which claimed that after students had sung "My Country, 'Tis of Thee" on the state capitol steps, their leaders were expelled from school and "truckloads of police armed with shotguns and tear-gas ringed the Alabama State College campus."

MR. NACHMAN: I will ask you, Mr. Hall, whether you associate the statements contained in that paragraph with any person or persons?

MR. EMBRY: Go ahead and finish your question but don't answer it, Mr. Hall. Let me object to it before you answer.

MR. NACHMAN: I am through.

MR. EMBRY: Your Honor, we object to that question on the grounds that it invades the province of the jury and it calls for an ultimate inquiry into fact that the jury is to inquire into in this case and it is incompetent, irrelevant and immaterial and it calls for an undisclosed mental operation of this witness and it calls for an unauthorized mental conclusion on the part of the witness. The fact that he is asking about is a fact that is addressed entirely to the jury in this case. It is a fact for the jury to decide, Your Honor. We object to it on these grounds.

LAWYER CRAWFORD: We make the same objection.

THE COURT: You join in the objection?

LAWYER CRAWFORD: Yes, Your Honor. We join in the same objection with the same grounds as these other defendants.

MR. EMBRY: Your Honor, this is an attempt to substitute this witness's opinion for that of the jury . . . and I have an Alabama authority on that point, Your Honor, if you would like to see it.

THE COURT: Well, the way I read these cases here, they hold in some of these cases that it is permissible to ask the witness when you get him on the witness stand after he has read that article whether he understood it to refer to the plaintiff, that is, Sullivan here, and I think that would be admissible —

MR. EMBRY: Your Honor, that's the Iowa case but we have an Alabama case.

THE COURT: Well, let me rule against you — it is a question of identification — let me rule against you and give you an exception.

MR. EMBRY: We except, Your Honor.

LAWYER CRAWFORD: We also would like to except to the Court's ruling in behalf of the other defendants, Your Honor.

Nachman asked Hall two more questions to elicit that he believed the ad referred to the commissioners of the city, and Embry objected to each one, only to be overruled and to add another exception to what would be a very long list by the end of the trial.

Arnold Blackwell, an insurance agent and a member of the Water Works Board, was the next witness, and Nachman asked him a series of questions about whether having seen the ad, he associated it with Commissioner Sullivan. Before he could finally answer that he did, Embry and Crawford objected on the same grounds as they had the questions to Hall, and Judge Jones again denied the objection and allowed them to take an exception.

Embry's game plan, if he had one, appears to have been to object to everything in the hope that when an appellate court worked its way through all of his exceptions to Judge Jones's rulings, it might find at least one ground on which to reverse. Nachman's questions, though, were legitimate. The jury needed to determine whether the advertisement caused readers to associate the charges of police brutality with E. B. Sullivan, and not solely whether it caused them — the jurors — to make that assumption. A libel brings the object of the defamation into public obloquy; if it does not there is no libel. Nachman was therefore on solid ground in questioning Hall and Blackwell about their reactions, as was Jones in permitting those questions.

Also, because the advertisement never mentioned Sullivan's name, Nachman had to prove that the reader of the piece would know to whom the ad referred. It may not have meant much to a reader in New York or New Jersey, who had no idea about the government of a southern city or the names of its officials, but it did make a difference in Montgomery. Of the three elements in a libel case — who published, was it defamatory, and whom did it defame — there was no question but that the *Times* had published the ad. *Any* factual errors in the ad, under Alabama law, made it defamatory. Nachman had to prove two things to the jury, that there were factual errors and that even without mentioning E. B. Sullivan by name, he was the person who had been defamed.

All told, Nachman called six witnesses to make the point that when they read the ad, they associated the charges in it with Sullivan. In addition to Hall and Blackwell, he called Harry W. Kaminsky, the manager of a clothing store and a close friend of Sullivan; William M. Parker Jr., another friend who owned a service station; Horace W. White, the owner of the P. C. White Truck Line, for whom Sullivan had once worked as director of safety; and H. M. Price Sr., the owner of a food equipment business. Only Hall had read the ad on his own; the others had first seen it when Nachman had shown it to them and asked them to testify. All said they believed the ad spoke about Sullivan and his conduct as head of the police. All said that if they had believed the statements, they would have thought the worse of Sullivan. White, for example, said that if he thought the statements true, he would be reluctant to rehire Sullivan. On cross-examination, however, all said that even though they believed the ad referred to Sullivan and his behavior, they did not think the worse of Sullivan because they did not believe the accusations to be true.

Detective Lieutenant E. Y. Lacy, a thirty-two-year veteran of the force, then took the witness stand to answer questions from Nachman regarding police behavior. Nachman asked Lacy whether he had investigated the bombing at the home of Martin Luther King Jr. Embry exploded out of his seat, objecting that the question was "incompetent, irrelevant and immaterial and not relevant to any of the issues in this case." Judge Jones said that he believed the ad mentioned something about a bombing, and Embry had to admit that it did. Once again Jones ruled against him, and once again Embry took an exception.

Lacy then detailed that, in addition to the bomb that had exploded, there had been two attempted bombings, but that in both instances the devices had failed to explode. He also told how he and two other officers, one of them the state director of public safety, had on one occasion dismantled the bomb.

NACHMAN: Did the Police Department have anything to do with the actual bombing? Did the Police Department arrange for the bombing or have anything to do with the bombing?
GRAY: You mean of throwing the bomb?
NACHMAN: Yes, sir.

GRAY: No, sir.

NACHMAN: Did the Police Department do everything they could to apprehend the persons who might be responsible for the bombings?

GRAY: Yes, sir. . . . The Police Department did extensive research work with overtime and extra personnel and we did everything that we knew including inviting and working with other departments throughout the country.

Although Embry and the other defense lawyers took exception, Nachman had made his point. Rather than being responsible for the attacks against King and other civil rights leaders, the police had not only placed themselves at risk in defusing a bomb on King's doorstop but had taken extraordinary, even if ultimately futile, efforts to apprehend the perpetrators.

Nachman then called O. M. Strickland, another police officer, who had been involved in the strange episode of Edward Davis assaulting Ralph Abernathy. This time the court wanted to know how this related to the ad, and Nachman quickly dropped this line of questioning and asked Strickland if he had ever arrested Martin Luther King. The policeman — after a flurry of defense objections — recalled that he had arrested King for trying to enter a courtroom that the judge had sealed off because of overcrowding, and the police had been stationed with orders to let no one else in. King had insisted that he had a right to enter, had been arrested and taken to police headquarters, and had been released almost immediately after posting his own bond. Nachman then asked Strickland whether he had ever assaulted King, triggering a flurry of defense objections, and when Nachman started asking questions about how big Strickland was as compared to King, even Judge Jones thought he had gone far enough and cut off the questioning.

Nachman had up to this point justified his reputation as a good lawyer. Even though Embry had almost continuously objected to his questions and had by the second day accumulated a long string of exceptions, Nachman had at all times remained calm, and after Jones had ruled — nearly always in his favor — had laid down a strong basis for the suit. The *Times* had published an advertisement that had led people to believe that if it was true, then L. B. Sullivan was a bad person unfit to hold public office. They knew better, however, and so did not believe the ad. Then police officers had testified that rather than foment violence, they had done their best to prevent it, even risking their own lives in the process.

Reading the transcript, and noting the great number of exceptions that Embry took to Judge Jones's rulings, one might be forgiven in thinking that Jones was biased against the *Times* and the civil rights leaders. There is little doubt that he opposed civil rights, but in terms of the law he conducted the trial carefully. An expert on Alabama practice, well versed in the state's libel law, he made few if any mistakes, none of which, despite Embry's exceptions, would be a basis for reversal.

On the second day of the trial Nachman called L. B. Sullivan himself to the stand. In a rare few minutes of silence from the defense table, Nachman led Sullivan through his past history, who he had worked for and in what position. Not until the lawyer handed Sullivan a copy of the ad and asked him if the third paragraph, the one involving students at Alabama State College, was true, did Embry jump up to object. Sullivan declared one statement after another in the ad as false, each time eliciting objections from Embry that it was not his place to declare the statements true or false.

NACHMAN: Now, I ask you, Mr. Sullivan, whether to your knowledge it is accurate that "They have arrested him seven times" — for "speeding," "loitering" and similar "offenses."
[*objection, overruled by court, exception taken*]
SULLIVAN: That is false.
NACHMAN: Mr. Sullivan, did you have anything at all to do with procuring the indictment of Martin Luther King on a charge of violating the Income Tax Laws of the State of Alabama?
[*objection, overruled by court, exception taken*]
Sullivan: Nothing whatsoever.
NACHMAN: Did you testify in that case either before the Grand Jury which indicted him or before the petty [*sic*] jury which tried him?
[*objection, overruled by court, exception taken*]

SULLIVAN: I testified at the trial.

NACHMAN: Did you testify with regard to the guilt or innocence of the defendant?

[*objection, overruled by court, exception taken*]

SULLIVAN: I testified as to conditions that existed here in Montgomery.

NACHMAN: Namely as to whether he could get a fair trial —

[*objection, overruled by court, exception taken*]

Nachman then asked Sullivan if he believed that the ad referred to him, and Sullivan emphatically said that it did. The statements in the ad concerned the arrest of people and "truckloads of police," and as commissioner "it is part of my duty to supervise the Police Department and I certainly feel like it is associated with me when it describes police activities." Had he felt "damaged" by these statements? He certainly did. "The statements contained in this ad that reflect upon my ability and integrity and certainly it has been established here that they are not true."

Embry led Sullivan through a grueling cross-examination — when had he first seen the ad, had he ever demanded a retraction, how could a circulation of only thirty-five copies of the *Times* in Montgomery County possible make him feel damaged. At times Nachman objected that Embry was not letting Sullivan answer, jumping in to ask the next question. Sullivan, however, as a police officer had plenty of experience on the stand, and not once did he appear rattled by the defense questions. Embry declared that the ad had not affected Sullivan's standing in the community at all.

EMBRY: Have you ever been ridiculed? Do you feel ill at ease walking about the streets of Montgomery?

SULLIVAN: I haven't had anyone come up to me personally and say they held me in ridicule because of the ad.

EMBRY: Have you been shunned by anyone in a public place or at the house of a friend or in any restaurant?

SULLIVAN: I don't recall.

After Embry had finished with Sullivan, Vernon Crawford stood, one of the few times that a black attorney had asked a question so far.

LAWYER CRAWFORD: Mr. Sullivan, do you consider your police force to be Southern law violators?

SULLIVAN: I certainly do not.

CRAWFORD: Then, Mr. Sullivan, do you consider yourself as Police Commissioner a Southern law violator?

SULLIVAN: I don't consider myself a violator period. Southern or otherwise.

CRAWFORD: Mr. Sullivan, as a result of your not being harmed, as you testified to, you are not held up in public contempt, you are not being ridiculed and you are not ashamed. The purpose of this law suit is the basis for state-wide publicity for running for another office. Is that not correct?

MR. NACHMAN: We object to that, your Honor.

THE COURT: That's not a proper statement.

LAWYER CRAWFORD: That's all. No further questions.

After this strange colloquy, L. P. Patterson, the managing editor of the *Montgomery Advertiser*, took the stand, and Robert Steiner, one of Nachman's colleagues, tried to get Patterson to testify that he had checked the veracity of some of the charges in the ad. Embry objected, and for once the judge agreed, since Patterson had no direct knowledge of any of the events mentioned in the ad. And with that the plaintiff's side rested.

In truth, there was very little the defense could do at this point. It could not deny that the *Times* had published the advertisement. Several witnesses had testified that they believed the ad referred to L. B. Sullivan, even if he had not been mentioned by name, and that if the charges had been true, they would have thought much the worse of him. Sullivan himself had said that he felt the ad had targeted him and that he felt "damaged" by the accusations. Finally, Nachman had shown that several statements in the critical third paragraph of the ad were not true: the students had sung "The Star-Spangled Banner" and not "My Country, 'Tis of Thee" on the capitol steps; students had been expelled not for the demonstration at the capitol but because they sought service at a lunch counter in the county court house; there had been a large number of police at Alabama State College, but they had not "ringed" the campus; the dining hall had never been padlocked to starve the students into submission. A statement in another paragraph mistakenly claimed that Martin Luther King had been arrested seven times, when the correct number was four. All of these might be dismissed as trivial, minor errors that did not in any way alter the main argument of the ad, that southern officials were opposed to civil rights and used all of their resources to harass those struggling for the rights the Constitution promised to them. In a libel suit, however, even one factual mistake could hand victory to a plaintiff, and the *Times* advertisement had more than one.

After the judge rejected their motions to either dismiss the case or direct a verdict for the defendant (a normal ploy at the end of the plaintiff's case and the usual judicial response), the defense called seven witnesses, three members of the *Times* staff and the four ministers named as codefendants.

Gershon T. Aronson, a twenty-five-year veteran of the *Times* who sold advertising for the paper, testified how the ad had come to the *Times*. John Murray had brought it to him late in the afternoon, and he had put it into the production process. Embry tried to show that there had been nothing in the ad to have alerted the paper to any trouble, since it had come from the Union Advertising Agency, a highly reputable firm that placed many ads in the *Times*. On cross-examination, however, Nachman elicited that it was the paper's policy to review all ads of this type, known as editorial ads, to see if they met the *Times's* written acceptability standards, and that policy had not been followed here because some names had been added in handwriting to the bottom of the printed text. On what basis, Nachman wanted to know, did the *Times* assume that these people had actually authorized the use of their names? Aronson responded that they had a letter from A. Philip Randolph, and that a letter by a person well known to them would be taken as authorization. Nachman then led the witness through one example after another of how the *Times* had not followed its own standards in accepting and publishing the ad. At the end of his testimony, observers must have believed that he had done far more for the plaintiffs than for the defense.

The next defense witness also did not help the cause. D. Vincent Redding, manager of the Advertising Acceptability Department, testified that he had looked at the ad and that nothing in it had struck him as false, misleading, or defamatory, and he accepted it "because the ad was endorsed by a number of people who are well known and whose reputation I had no reason to question." Who were some of these people, Embry asked, and Redding named Mrs. Ralph Bunche, the wife of a United Nations official, the Reverend Harry Emerson Fosdick, pastor of the Riverside Church in New York, Mrs. Eleanor Roosevelt, and the socialist leader Norman Thomas—all names that certainly carried weight in New York, all liberals, all known to be strong supporters of civil rights, and therefore, all detested in the South.

On cross-examination Redding conceded that he did not know whether any of these people were knowledgeable about events or conditions in Montgomery and that he had not contacted any of them to ask that question.

NACHMAN: Now, Mr. Redding, wouldn't it be a fair statement to say that you really didn't check this ad at all for accuracy?
REDDING: That's a fair statement, yes.
NACHMAN: That's a fair statement.
REDDING: Yes.
NACHMAN: All right. That's all. No further questions.

Redding was not finished, however, as Fred Gray began questioning him about the names of the four codefendants that had been added by hand, and got him to admit that his office had not checked to see whether they had really agreed to have their names used. Gray, of course, was trying to get the case against the four black defendants dismissed on the grounds that they had never consented to have their names used, and this raised the curious situation in which Embry and Beddow objected to Gray's questioning. If Gray could show that the *Times* had not even bothered to check if people had consented to have their names used, it would only emphasize how negligent the paper had been.

Embry then called Harding Bancroft, secretary of the New York Times Company, and the only official of the paper to testify at the trial. Bancroft testified that they had not published a retraction at Sullivan's request because "we didn't see how the ad reflected on him in any way or how he could be identified by the ad." In fact, the people at the *Times* were "puzzled" by his attitude, and after they had looked into the matter further, they had suggested to Sullivan "that he might want to reply to us indicating how in fact he was involved in the text of the ad."

> EMBRY: What was the occasion of your sending the letter to Governor [Patterson] and not to Commissioner Sullivan?
>
> BANCROFT: Well, the Governor wrote us a letter asking us for a retraction and we replied in what was, in effect, a retraction and apology and the reason we did that because we didn't want anything that was published by The Times to be a reflection on the State of Alabama and the Governor was, as far as we could see, the embodiment of the State of Alabama and the proper representative of the State.

After Bancroft, the attorneys for the four black ministers called each of their clients to the stand and asked them essentially the same question. The testimony of Solomon S. Seay Sr. set the pattern:

> LAWYER GRAY: Tell the Court and the jury whether or not you published that ad in The New York Times.
>
> SEAY: I did not.
>
> GRAY: Did you pay the New York Times or anybody else to publish that ad?
>
> SEAY: I did not.
>
> GRAY: Did you authorize anyone to use your name and affix your name to that ad which appeared in The New York Times?
>
> SEAY: I did not.
>
> GRAY: Did you authorize anyone to use your name in the furtherance of the work of the "Committee To Defend Martin Luther King and The Struggle For Freedom in the South"?
>
> SEAY: I did not.
>
> GRAY: Did you have any knowledge prior to the time that ad was published that the ad was going to come out?
>
> SEAY: I did not

On cross-examination, Nachman asked him about the testimony that A. Philip Randolph had authorized the use of Seay's name, and was that information incorrect. "Emphatically so. Emphatically so, sir."

Ralph Abernathy, Fred Shuttlesworth, and J. E. Lowery all testi-fied that they, too, had had no knowledge of the ad and that they had never been asked nor had they given permission to use their names as sponsors. John Murray, who wrote the ad, was the last witness, and he confirmed that the names of Seay, Abernathy, Shuttlesworth, and Lowery had not been on the original list of signers. When Bayard Rustin had told Murray to add several names, Murray had asked him whether they would be contacted for permission. "He said we don't have to because by virtue of the fact that they all belong to the [South-ern Christian Leadership Conference] and since the S.C.L.C. sup-ports the work of the committee that he felt there would be no problem at all and that you didn't even have to consult them."

Upon the basis of this testimony, the lawyers for the four ministers filed a motion to exclude all testimony as regarding the ad since their clients had not been parties to the creation or publication of the ad, in essence, dismissing all the charges against them. Judge Jones took this under advisement, and then rejected their claim. The jury would decide the guilt or innocence of the *Times* together with the black ministers.

After the defense rested, and before the case went to the jury, several things took place. First of all, each side summed up its case. Robert Steiner spoke for Sullivan and declared that the only way to impress on the *Times* or any other newspaper or magazine (and by this he clearly meant the northern media) to tell the truth was to "hit them in the pocketbook." Sullivan asked $500,000 for the assault on his rep-utation, and Steiner urged the jury to award him the full amount. He then rehearsed all the factual mistakes in the ad, and sneered that "they couldn't even get the song right," referring to the students singing on the capitol steps. As for the statement about police "ringing" the Ala-bama State College campus, "it would take thousands of police prob-ably to ring the campus—approximately twelve square blocks."

Steiner also noted the statement about King's house being bombed, and although Sullivan was not in office when the attempted bombings occurred, "the ad doesn't say so—it was designed to attack the pres-ent city commission. Let The Times explain to you who in the world they were talking about if it wasn't the city commissioners of Montgomery." The fact that the ad included the names of two Negroes from the city (Ralph Abernathy and Solomon Seay), was "proof positive that the ad was talking about Mr. Sullivan."

Fred Gray spoke for the four black defendants, and claimed that Sullivan's attorneys had "failed miserably" to prove that the ministers actually endorsed the ad or knew anything about it. Gray drew laughter from the spectators and from the other attorneys when he asked the jury, "How could these individual defendants retract something — if you pardon the expression — they didn't tract?" The four ministers, he argued, are "the forgotten defendants in this case," and they had no business being charged in the first place. The evidence showed clearly that they had no knowledge of the ad and had never agreed to have their names used. In fact, the only witness for Sullivan who even mentioned his clients had been Sullivan himself, who had sent letters to them asking for a retraction.

Gray's contention that his clients played only a minor role in the proceedings was true, but it was nonetheless a critical one for two reasons — one legal and the other political. It did not matter to Nachman whether the four ministers had the resources to pay even a fraction of what Sullivan demanded as damages, although it later turned out that they were far from being poor church mice. They were Alabama residents, and the primary reason for joining them, Nachman conceded, was to keep the case in state courts and preventing the *Times* from removing Sullivan's suit against the paper to federal court.

Politically, Abernathy, Shuttlesworth, Seay, and Lowery were hardly strangers to the white power structure of the city. They all belonged to the Southern Christian Leadership Conference and had been active in the Montgomery bus boycott and the continuing civil rights protests. Just as the suit intended to send a message to the northern media, it also served as a warning to civil rights activists. Say anything negative about public officials or police behavior, and you will wind up in court facing damages that will keep you in the poorhouse the rest of your lives. The NAACP, according to Fred Gray, kept a close eye on the proceedings, because for Sullivan and the white leaders of Montgomery, "it was a matter of teaching these black ministers who were agitators a lesson and let them know that if you get involved in these type of things, we're gonna come at you on all fronts."

T. Eric Embry remained in character—feisty and challenging the plaintiff's contentions to the end. He accused Steiner of "appealing to every base motive in man by snide references to people living in other parts of the country," and in doing so acknowledged that beleaguered white Alabamians distrusted northerners, who they believed instigated and financed the civil rights revolt. The *Times*, he claimed, had taken every precaution "a normal human being" would take before accepting the ad, a statement that the evidence of his own witnesses contradicted. The only statement that was not substantially correct was that authorities had padlocked the college dining room, and "that statement could not possibly have referred to Sullivan." By the end, however, he knew the verdict would be against the *Times*. "I was trying to appeal to these people's conscience," he later said, and "some of them wouldn't look me in the eye."

Before a jury goes to deliberate, it is charged by the judge with what the law is, and what the jury must determine. Both sides in a case give the judge requests, and they may also ask him to make changes in the charge he or she has drawn. Altogether Embry and the other defense attorneys suggested 140 changes, of which Jones agreed to 46. Many of these suggestions were identical, and merely referred to different defendants. For example, one of the suggestions was "I charge you, gentlemen of the jury, that if you do not find that Rev. Ralph D. Abernathy was responsible for the publication of the advertisement which appeared in the New York Times, dated, Tuesday, March 29, 1960, you must find a verdict in favor of him." Jones agreed to this, as he did to the same request from each of the other black defendants. Copies of the requests that he approved were given to the jury after his oral charge to take with them to their deliberations. Requests that Jones turned down went to the clerk of the court to file with the record. Nachman, sure that the law favored his client, made no suggestions.

Jones denied all requests from defense counsel that the whole or parts of the testimony be struck, that the jury be directed to find the defendants not guilty, or that the case not be sent to the jury. Again, Jones stood on solid legal ground, since Alabama courts followed the "scintilla of evidence" doctrine. The rule applied to civil cases, such as a libel suit, and held that a case had to go to a jury if the plaintiff's evidence, "viewed in its most favorable light, furnishes a mere glimmer, spark, or smallest trace in support of an issue." Jones did not make that rule up, but as a judge in Alabama he had to follow it. (In fact, the rule was and is still followed by a number of states.) Like many of their exceptions and suggestions for jury instructions, counsel for the defense went through accepted motions, knowing they would be ruled against — and rightly so.

Judge Jones gave what was in many ways a model jury charge. He began by joining the attorneys in thanking the jurymen for their interest and patience. Then, before getting to the points of law that needed to be covered, he declared that although he thought it "hardly necessary" to mention it,

> one of the defendants in this case is a corporate defendant and some of the others belong to various races and in your deliberation in arriving at your verdict, all of these defendants whether they be corporate or individuals or whether they belong to this race or that doesn't have a thing on earth to do with this case but let the evidence and the law be the two pole stars that will guide you and try to do justice in fairness to all of these parties here. . . . Please remember, gentlemen of the jury, that all of the parties that stand here stand before you on equal footing and are all equal at the Bar of Justice.

Of course race was a factor, not just at the trial but throughout southern life, and every person involved in the case — judge, plaintiff, defendants, lawyers, witnesses, and the twelve members of the jury — knew that. It would be many years before southern blacks would consider themselves equal at the bar of justice. But whether Jones or anyone else believed it, it was the right thing to say.

Jones then rehearsed the gravamen of Sullivan's complaint, that the advertisement in the *New York Times* of March 29, 1960, "Heed Their Rising Voices," contained false and defamatory matter directed at him, subjecting him to "public contempt, to ridicule, to shame and prejudice, and prejudiced Mr. Sullivan in his public office as Police Commissioner, in his profession, in his trade and in his business and all was done, he claims, with the intent to defame him." Jones also recited the various allegations of error in the advertisement, such as the number of arrests of Dr. King and which song the protestors had sung on the capitol steps.

Regarding the punitive damages, under Alabama law the plaintiff must ask the defendant to make a retraction, and then if he does not, the plaintiff may seek punitive damages. (Nachman had made sure that Sullivan and the other commissioners had asked for a retraction, but the *Times*, probably unaware that Sullivan and the others planned a libel suit, had failed to respond, thus opening the door under Alabama law for Sullivan to ask for $500,000.) The *Times* had entered a plea that the ad had not referred to Sullivan, and the four other defendants had pled that they had nothing to do with the matter and had not given their consent to the use of their names. The plaintiff carried the burden of providing "reasonable satisfaction" to the jury that his allegations of defamation were true. Jones noted that this was not a criminal case, and therefore Sullivan did not have to prove his claim beyond all reasonable doubt. If the jury were reasonably satisfied of his claim, namely, that the average person in Montgomery would find the material in the ad defamatory of Sullivan, then they should find in his behalf.

In terms of the other defendants, under Alabama law every person who has any part in the publication of a libelous statement is held to be strictly liable. Sullivan claimed that even if they had not known about it ahead of time, by their inaction afterward in failing to retract or apologize, they ratified the message of the ad, and should therefore be held liable. "Ratification," Jones explained, "is really the same as a previous authorization and is a confirmation or approval of what has been said by another on his account." If the jurors found from the evidence that the four individual defendants ratified the ad, then they should be found guilty as well; if the jury found otherwise, they should be found not guilty.

In terms of the law, Jones instructed the jury that the ad "belongs to that class of defamation called libel *per se*." Materials under this classification are presumed to be false, malicious, and damaging to the reputation of the person involved. If the jurors found as a matter of fact that the material in the ad was defamatory, they did not need to determine whether the material was false or malicious, and they could vote to award damages.

The law allowed punitive damages in cases of libel per se for two reasons — one to punish the current malefactor, and the other to prevent similar wrongs in the future. Whether the defendants were guilty or not would be a matter for the jury to decide; if the jury found them guilty, they would also determine what damages, if any, should be imposed.

It took the jury only two hours to return with their verdict. Seven months after the *New York Times* had published "Heed Their Rising Voices," twelve citizens of Montgomery, Alabama, found the newspaper, along with Ralph Abernathy, Fred Shuttlesworth, Solomon Seay, and J. E. Lowery, guilty of libel per se. For the defamation he suffered at their hands, the jury awarded L. B. Sullivan punitive damages in the full amount that he asked, $500,000.

# CHAPTER 4

# "Let 'em See the Dogs Work"

There is no question that the *Times* had violated Alabama's libel law. Given the culture of Birmingham in the late 1950s, Sullivan also had little trouble meeting his burden of proof—that a person reading "Heed Their Rising Voices" with its criticism of the local police—could reasonably assume that even if he was not mentioned by name, the sponsors of the ad were attacking him. Once that hurdle had been passed, the rest was easy. The *Times* had been sloppy, had not followed its own rules, and had taken the ad and its contents as written on the assurances of Bayard Rustin and A. Philip Randolph that the material was accurate and the signers had all agreed to the use of their names. While the factual mistakes were minor, the strict libel laws not only of Alabama but of most of the states in the Union did not distinguish between major and minor errors—a factual mistake made the piece libelous per se.

The same could not be said of the guilty verdicts directed at the four black ministers. Uncontested evidence had been introduced during the trial that they had never been consulted about the ad, had had no part in its production, and had never given permission for their names to be used. Even though Alabama law permitted postpublication confirmation to serve as the equivalent of prepublication authorization, the only basis for such an assumption was their membership in the Southern Christian Leadership Conference. Given the hostility in Montgomery to blacks in general and to civil rights activists in particular, the jury apparently found the four men guilty because of their civil rights work and not because they had defamed L. B. Sullivan.

One can also question the $500,000 in punitive damages, the largest award in Alabama history, which would be more than $3.6 million in current dollars. The attorneys for Sullivan made clear that a large damage award would serve to stop the *Times* and other newspapers from printing untrue stories. (Nachman later claimed that he never expected the jury to award the full amount; he thought it a mistake, and a major reason the Supreme Court overturned the verdict.) The judge also instructed the jury that a damage award would serve to stop others from similar behavior in the future. People in Montgomery, Alabama, in 1960 found nearly all northern coverage of the civil rights movement to be distorted, untrue, and derogatory of their way of life. As the *Alabama Journal* editorialized the following day, the jury award to Commissioner Sullivan "could have the effect of causing reckless publishers of the North . . . to make a re-survey of their habit of permitting anything detrimental to the South and its people to appear in their pages."

In the weeks and months after the trial, the strategy seemed to be working, at least as far as the *Times* was concerned. It would take more than three years before the case reached the Supreme Court, years that were difficult not only for the press but especially for the civil rights movement.


The decision in the *Sullivan* case seemed just one more brick white southerners were using to build a wall against desegregation. After the Supreme Court announced *Cooper v. Aaron* in 1958, with its forceful demand that the South stop dragging its feet in implementing *Brown*, opposition increased. Rather than obey the Court, Governor Orval Faubus of Arkansas closed Little Rock schools altogether in 1958 and 1959, and reopened them only following another court order. In Virginia, three cities and two counties also closed their schools to prevent integration, and private "Christian" academies sprang up all over the South, with varying degrees of academic quality but all sharing a "whites only" admissions policy. The pace of desegregation slowed to a crawl; only thirteen additional school districts abandoned segregation in 1958, nineteen the following year, and seventeen in 1960. In Congress, both the House and the Senate passed separate bills to restrict the Supreme Court's jurisdiction over school segregation or to nullify *Brown*, but no measure passed both houses. Six years after *Brown*, thousands of school districts in the South remained segregated, moderate voices had been muted, and politicians from Virginia to

Florida, from the Carolinas to Arkansas, boldly claimed that the Supreme Court decision need not be obeyed.

The federal judiciary, after the hiatus between *Brown II* and *Cooper*, began to grow impatient, and as observers had noted in 1954, if segregation in public schools violated the Fourteenth Amendment's Equal Protection Clause, then state-sponsored segregation in any part of public life could not be sustained. The series of cases that the NAACP Legal Defense Fund brought in the 1950s and 1960s not only kept up pressure on schools districts, but began to impact other areas as well. In *Gomillion v. Lightfoot*, handed down in November 1960 just a few weeks after the Sullivan trial, the Supreme Court struck down an Alabama gerrymandering law designed to negate black voting in Tuskegee. The following month the Court ruled that the Interstate Commerce Act forbade discrimination in bus terminals serving interstate carriers.

Lower federal court judges in the South, despite the fact that they were overwhelmingly southern, held fast to the rule of law despite denunciations and often threats from diehard segregationists. Typically, in a suit challenging a segregated facility, the judge would rule that the old *Plessy* doctrine of separate but equal no longer applied and that continued segregation of public facilities violated the Fourteenth Amendment. An appeal to the Supreme Court invariably resulted in per curiam affirmations of the lower court rulings. In those few cases in which lower courts sustained segregated facilities, the Court remanded with directions to proceed in a manner "not inconsistent with *Brown*." Thus the high court affirmed the end of segregation on public beaches, buses, golf courses, and parks. In *Johnson v. Virginia* (1963), the justices unanimously reversed a black man's conviction for refusing to comply with a state judge's order to move to a section of the courtroom reserved for negroes. "Such a conviction cannot stand," the Court declared, "for it is no longer open to question that a State may not constitutionally require segregation of public facilities."

Somewhat more complex issues arose over segregation in private facilities. Ever since the *Civil Rights Cases* in 1883, the Court had considered private discrimination beyond the reach of the Fourteenth Amendment. In *Shelley v. Kraemer* (1948), however, the Vinson Court had held that state enforcement of restrictive covenants — provisions in deeds barring the sale or rental of property to non-whites — by state courts constituted state action, and was thus prohibited. The Warren Court used this distinction to void the exclusion of blacks from a private theater located in a public park (*Muir v. Louisiana Park Theatrical Assn.* [1958]), and from a private restaurant in a court house (*Derrington v. Plummer* [1957]). In 1961, Justice Tom Clark emphasized that totally private discrimination remained immune from the reach of federal courts under the Fourteenth Amendment, but that a connection to governmental authority brought such discrimination within the definition of "state action." As a result, in *Burton v. Wilmington Parking Authority* (1961), a private restaurant located in a municipally owned and operated parking garage had the necessary connection, and could not discriminate on the basis of race.

One might note that at the time a number of commentators, many of them northern, charged that the Court had reached too far. In *Burton* they could find only a very tenuous connection between the state and the restaurant, which had a separate entrance and was patronized by people who did not use the garage as well as those who did. The connection was probably no more and no less than the connection Judge Jones found between the *New York Times* and the State of Alabama. In modern days there is, however, very little private business that does not have some nexus to public authority, and until 1964 the Court heard several cases trying to determine what limits might apply. The Court was inching its way toward constitutionalizing the old common law rule against discrimination in public accommodations — private facilities such as restaurants, inns, and ferry crossings — that served the public. Eventually Congress took that step when it passed the Civil Rights Act of 1964.

Black leaders took a guarded measure of hope from the election of John F. Kennedy to the presidency in November 1960. During the presidential campaign Martin Luther King Jr. had been arrested in Georgia and sentenced to four months in jail on a minor traffic violation. Richard Nixon, the Republican nominee, tried quietly to intervene but publicly said nothing. An aide convinced Kennedy to telephone King's wife, Coretta, to express his sympathy. At the same time, and unbeknownst to Jack, his brother Bobby telegraphed the judge and requested King's release. The judge for whatever reason agreed; King got out of prison on bail, and gave Jack Kennedy full credit. King's father, the influential Atlanta minister Martin Luther "Daddy" King Sr., had so far been leery of Kennedy because of his Catholicism, but he came around and endorsed the Democrat. In the closely contested election 70 percent of the black vote went for Kennedy, and may have given him victory in some tight northern races such as New Jersey, Michigan, and Illinois—all of which Eisenhower had taken in 1956. Soon after the inauguration, Roy Wilkins of the NAACP called for immediate action to promote voting, education, and jobs for blacks, and the Reverend King handed the president a 100-page memorandum outlining the civil rights agenda.

Because of southern strength in Congress, Kennedy recognized that at least initially he would not be able to get significant civil rights legislation passed and that he would have to act by executive order. Less than two months after taking office he created a presidential Commission on Equal Employment Opportunity, whose energy won the praise of civil rights leaders. Administration officials set an example in testing color barriers, especially in Washington. They refused to speak to segregated audiences, boycotted private clubs that discriminated, and pressured federal employee groups to abandon discriminatory practices. The Justice Department, headed by Robert F. Kennedy, informed all federal judges that the administration intended to follow the Constitution and would enforce their decisions on civil rights. In late 1962 Kennedy signed an executive order prohibiting racial and religious discrimination in housing built or purchased with federal assistance.

But Kennedy had other things on his agenda besides civil rights, and he could not afford to alienate the powerful southern bloc that controlled Congress. The administration did not endorse the "freedom rides" (see below), but intervened only after violence broke out. When Governor Ross Barnett of Mississippi stood "in the schoolhouse door" and refused to allow James Meredith to enroll at Ole Miss, despite a court order, the Justice Department sent 320 federal marshals to the university campus in Oxford, where they were attacked by armed mobs while the state police stood by watching. This was more than an attack on civil rights activists, but constituted an insurrection against the lawful authority of the U.S. government. Just as Eisenhower could not stand by and let Orval Faubus defy a federal court, Kennedy could not allow Barnett — who had promised that the marshals would be protected — to get away with such flagrant disregard of federal authority. The president nationalized the Mississippi National Guard and brought in regular army troops to restore and maintain order. Only after two people had been killed and 375 wounded (about half of them federal marshals) did James Meredith enroll.

The following spring a similar situation took place in Alabama. Governor George C. Wallace had promised in his inaugural earlier in the year to maintain "segregation now, segregation tomorrow, segregation forever." A federal judge ordered the admission of two black students to the University of Alabama, and Wallace vowed to block their registration. Kennedy warned Wallace that if he did so, Kennedy would act immediately. Wallace stood in the schoolhouse door, made his speech before television cameras, and then immediately gave in when Kennedy nationalized the guard. That fall Wallace tried again, and Kennedy again nationalized the guard and ordered them back to their barracks so that school could open peacefully. For five days nothing happened, and then a horrible wave of rioting and bloodshed erupted.

The fact that Kennedy would stand up to Barnett and Wallace reinforced the image in the black community that it had finally had a friend in the White House and an administration that cared. Kennedy also appointed several blacks to high-ranking positions in the government, including Thurgood Marshall to the U.S. Circuit Court of Appeals in New York. Although the president moved more slowly than some black leaders wanted, he understood the reality of the political situation. The country needed far more than executive orders; it needed a comprehensive civil rights law, and in the summer of 1963 he proposed such an act to Congress. But it would not be until after Kennedy's death that his successor, Lyndon B. Johnson, shepherded such a bill through Congress.


While the Legal Defense Fund chipped away at segregation in the courts, the Kennedy administration took a few steps using executive power to promote racial equality. But the civil rights movement, which at one point had been completely a legal attack against separate-but-equal, acquired a new, more dramatic front as young blacks, often joined by their white peers, challenged segregation head-on by refusing to sit in the back of the bus, as Rosa Parks had done, or insisting on being served at segregated lunch counters, or riding on interstate buses sitting next to white people. As Martin Luther King Jr. explained, "We are tired — tired of being segregated and humiliated, tired of being kicked around by the brutal feet of oppression." Although King preached nonviolence, he knew that his confrontational tactics as well as those of other civil rights groups such as the Congress of Racial Equality (CORE) and the Student Nonviolent Coordinating Committee (SNCC), would trigger violence, and he cleverly used those outbursts to enlist the support of white liberals and moderates.

The first sit-in took place on February 1, 1960, in Greensboro, North Carolina. The protests spread quickly across the South, and within a week fifty-four sit-ins were underway in fifteen cities in nine states. Students from Alabama State College in Montgomery joined in on the 25th, in time for an erroneous version of what happened to get into "Heed Their Rising Voices." There had been other attempts at sit-ins in the previous years; CORE claimed to have done the first one during World War II. This time the spark caught, and as it raced across the South it was clear that the level of black resentment against segregation had reached a level that could no longer be contained.

Where the NAACP's legal fight was led from the top, with Thurgood Marshall and his LDF lawyers scouring the country for the right test cases, the sit-ins arose from the bottom, and brought with them a new generation of civil rights activists. A Nashville group included such well-known later activists as John Lewis, Marion Barry, James Lawson, and Diane Nash. Julian Bond got caught up in Atlanta, while Stokely Carmichael, then a student at Howard University in Washington, headed South to become involved. In New York, Robert Moses looked at a picture of the four Greensboro students, was inspired by their "angry, determined" looks, and soon joined the student movement.

In April 1960, Ella Baker, the executive director of the Southern Christian Leadership Conference (SCLC), thought it was time to bring the student activists together, and more than 300 showed up at a conference at Shaw College in Raleigh, North Carolina. While most came from southern black colleges, nineteen students from white colleges in the North also came. Shaw challenged them to fight racial injustice in every walk of life. "The current sit-ins," she told them, "are concerned with something much bigger than a hamburger or even a giant-sized Coke." Before the conference adjourned, the students organized the Student Nonviolent Coordinating Committee (SNCC), with Marion Barry as its chair. Although there were some students from the North, SNCC (which everyone pronounced as "snick"), like the SCLC, focused primarily on Jim Crow in the South, not on the problems of northern blacks. Although they claimed to be more militant than King and his allies, their goals were not very different.

SNCC and the students it organized soon ran into resistance, something they expected since the vast majority of southern whites stood implacably opposed to desegregation. When students had a "wade-in" at a segregated beach in Biloxi, Mississippi, a white man shot and wounded ten black people. Even in the supposedly more moderate upper South resistance remained high. The Woolworth's in Greensboro did not desegregate until July, after it had lost an estimated $200,000 in business, one-fifth of its estimated annual sales. Everywhere lunch-counter owners and the managers of other SNCC targets would call the police, who would arrest the students for trespassing. In 1960 three thousand protesters went to jail, and thousands more were arrested, paid a fine, or were held overnight before release.

The movement spread rapidly, and even reached into Illinois, Ohio, and Nevada. Some accounts place the number of demonstrators involved at 70,000. They challenged segregation not only at lunch counters, but at parks, churches ("kneel-ins"), libraries ("read-ins"), museums, and other facilities. If nothing else, the tenacity of the protesters showed that younger blacks had grown impatient, both with segregation and with what they considered the timid response of black establishment leaders.

The NAACP, the largest and oldest of the civil rights organizations, with 380,000 members, never endorsed the sit-ins. Thurgood Marshall, for example, derided what he called the Gandhian "jail-in" tactics as expensive and impractical, and angered young activists when he told them, "If someone offers to get you out [of jail], man, get out." The president of the all-black Southern University in Baton Rouge, Louisiana, suspended eighteen sit-in leaders and forced the entire student body to resign and reapply so that he could screen the applications and weed out the troublemakers.

A good example of how friction within the black community played into the hands of white officials and often led to violence can be seen in McComb, a town in southwestern Mississippi where segregationists controlled all public offices and the police. SNCC, led by Marion Barry, wanted to challenge the segregationist hold by "direct action" campaigns, including sit-ins. Another leader of the young activists, Robert Moses, agreed on direct action, but also wanted to try to coordinate with local NAACP officials, whom Moses considered vital to any long-term success. The NAACP wanted to concentrate on voter registration, since if they could get blacks the right to vote they would eventually be able to elect black officials. Moses agreed, noting that while sit-ins brought publicity, they were often "a one-event thing," and not something that would sustain the movement.

Barry got his sit-in, and white officials in McComb responded by arresting and jailing the demonstrators for thirty-four days before the SCLC and the NAACP provided bond money. Two of the protesters, high school students in McComb, tried to return to their all-black school after their release, only to be barred by their black principal. This enraged their classmates, more than one hundred of whom dared to march through the town carrying banners and singing "We Shall Overcome." An astounded group of whites surrounded the marchers and savagely beat a newly arrived SNCC worker, the only white person in the march. Police then arrested the SNCC organizers and 116 students, some of whom wound up spending more than a month in jail. The principal expelled all the marchers from the school, and made their readmission conditional on their signing a pledge not to participate in any future demonstrations. Most of the students refused.

None of this pressure from within or without the community succeeded in stopping them. If anything, their inner anger, both at whites and at some of the older black leaders, increased. As James Baldwin wrote in 1961, "To be a Negro in this country and to be relatively conscious, is to be in a rage all the time." The sit-ins had caused some violence, but it was nothing compared to the reaction to the Freedom Riders.

————

The Supreme Court had upheld a black plaintiff's suit against segregated transportation as early as 1941. Arthur Mitchell, a congressman from Illinois, had been ejected from a Pullman car when the train crossed into Arkansas. He filed a complaint, not in federal court, but with the Interstate Commerce Commission, claiming he had been discriminated against in violation of the Interstate Commerce Act. In *Mitchell v. United States*, the high court upheld his claim. Five years later Irene Morgan, a black woman, boarded a bus in Richmond to go to Baltimore, and as Virginia law required, was ordered to the back of the bus. Morgan refused, claiming that as she was an interstate passenger, that law did not apply to her. She was arrested, and the NAACP took on her case. In *Morgan v. Virginia*, a 7–1 Court ruled that in interstate travel, rail and bus lines could not discriminate on the basis of race. But Justice Reed made it clear that the results did not affect state laws governing intrastate travel. Then in 1960, the Court overturned the conviction of a black student for trespassing in a restaurant in a bus terminal that was for "whites only." The ruling in *Boynton v. Virginia* did not break any new constitutional ground, nor did it expand federal powers over interstate commerce, but it did reinforce earlier decisions striking down racial segregation on interstate transportation. (Between *Morgan* and *Boynton*, the Court also ruled against segregation on intrastate transportation in *Browder v. Gayle* [1956], the Montgomery bus boycott case.)

Despite the Court decisions, for the most part blacks understood the dangers of pressing their claim, and the majority of them, especially in the Deep South, acquiesced, albeit reluctantly, in continued segregation. James Farmer, the head of CORE, decided that in the wake of the *Boynton* ruling, the time had come to challenge segregation on the trains and buses. Blacks would embark on "freedom rides" into and through the Deep South, and use facilities, such as restaurants and restrooms, in the terminals where the buses stopped.

Even though the law was on the black riders' side, Farmer expected that whites would respond with violence. They informed the White House, the Justice Department, and the Federal Bureau of Investigation of their plans. On May 5, 1961, seven blacks and six whites got on two buses—one Greyhound and one Trailways—in Washington, D.C., heading toward Alabama, Mississippi, and New Orleans. The plan was to have at least one interracial pair sitting in adjoining seats and at least one black rider sitting in the front seats usually reserved for white passengers. The rest would be scattered through the bus.

Minor trouble occurred in Virginia and North Carolina, with a few riders arrested in Charlotte, North Carolina, but the first violence came in Rock Hill, South Carolina, where whites clubbed John Lewis and knocked him down when he tried to enter the white restroom. The real trouble came when the buses reached Alabama. Birmingham police sergeant Tom Cook, an avid supporter of the Ku Klux Klan, and Police Commissioner Bull Connor decided the rides would end in Alabama. They assured Gary Rowe, a member of a violent Klan gang—and unbeknownst to them an FBI informer—that when the bus came into town the Klan would have fifteen minutes to attack the riders before the police showed up. Rowe reported this to J. Edgar Hoover, who did nothing about it and did not inform Attorney General Kennedy, to whom he supposedly reported.

When the riders in the Greyhound bus came to Anniston, Alabama, a mob attacked the vehicle, slit its tires, and smashed the windows. The crippled bus pulled out of the terminal but broke down several miles out of town, and was then firebombed by the mob that had been chasing it in cars. As the bus burned, the whites held the doors shut, intending to burn the passengers to death. Reports vary on exactly what happened, but either an exploding fuel tank or a rider brandishing a revolver caused the mob to retreat, allowing the men to get off the bus. Seeing their quarry still alive, the mob returned to beat the riders, and only warning shots fired into the air by a highway patrolman who came on the scene stopped what would have become a massacre. The victims, most of them burned and beaten, were taken to a hospital, but at 2:00 AM they had to leave because the staff feared that a mob outside would attack. The Reverend Fred Shuttlesworth, one of the codefendants in the *Sullivan* case, organized several cars of blacks who drove through the mob, picked up the Freedom Riders, and spirited them away.

When the Trailways bus pulled into the Anniston depot an hour after the Greyhound bus had burned, eight Klansman boarded it and proceeded to beat the Freedom Riders, leaving them semiconscious at the back of the bus. The bus nonetheless continued on to Birmingham, where thirty Klan members wielding baseball bats, pipes, and tire chains attacked the riders. One rider, a 61-year-old man, was left permanently brain-damaged. As Bull Connor had promised, the police were nowhere in sight. The beaten riders broke off their trip and flew to safety in New Orleans.

If the Klan and their accomplices thought that violence would break the resolve of the young activists, it had just the opposite effect. Diane Nash and John Lewis coordinated a new group of SNCC volunteers, joined by CORE veterans from Nashville, that went back into Alabama and Mississippi. Once again they were met by violence, and Lewis was savagely beaten in Montgomery. (This was fully reported not only in the *Times*, but in other organs of the northern press, and without fear of reprisal, since television crews caught all the brutality on film and broadcast it to a sickened nation.)

The buses went to Mississippi after Attorney General Robert Kennedy worked out a deal with Senator James Eastland for Mississippi to provide police protection on the highway, but allowed Jackson police to arrest the riders when they entered the bus terminal in Jackson. Police arrested James Farmer and a group of riders, and a local judge convicted them of breach of the peace and fined them $200 apiece. When they refused to pay the fines or post bail, he sentenced them to thirty-nine days in jail before they finally posted bond. Many of them wound up in the maximum-security wing of the state penitentiary at Parchman, where the guards tried to break their unity by knocking them down with water from fire hoses, closing the cell windows during the daytime to increase the already unbearable temperature, and blasting them with cold air from exhaust fans at night. All the efforts proved unsuccessful.

Governor Ross Barnett of Mississippi thought that if southern officials adopted strong enough measures, the freedom rides would stop, but more volunteers kept coming. Jackson police arrested 328 riders before the end of the summer, two-thirds of them college students, three-fourths male, and more than half black. The rides stopped only in December after the Interstate Commerce Commission banned bus and railway companies from using segregated facilities. Southern cities, dependant on those carriers, had little choice but to finally desegregate.

But the violence continued. In 1963 Martin Luther King determined to confront racism in what was generally considered the most thoroughly segregated city in America — Birmingham, Alabama. Since the end of World War II there had been more than fifty racially motivated bombings of black homes and businesses. In the city's businesses, even the then booming steel mills, blacks held only the lowest-paying jobs. Everything in the city was segregated, even the drinking fountains. When federal courts ordered the desegregation of municipal parks and playgrounds, city officials closed them rather than integrate. The commissioner of public safety, Bull Connor, and his men regularly terrorized black inhabitants, and in large measure Connor's vicious response to King's campaign focused attention on the city and brought new support to the civil rights movement, a goal that King anticipated.

King launched a series of boycotts, sit-ins, and demonstrations in April; aware that he hoped to arouse sympathy, city officials ordered initial restraint. King was arrested for violating a state court order barring demonstrations, and in the week he spent incarcerated he wrote "Letter from a Birmingham Jail." Its commitment to racial justice and nonviolence made it one of the most widely read documents of the movement. Even while King was in jail, the demonstrations continued, and the police arrested hundreds of protestors. With the ranks of volunteers depleted by the arrests, King decided to send out some 1,000 children, of whom more than 900 were arrested. The next day more children gathered at King's church, and Connor ordered them to stay inside. When some of them came out, Connor lost whatever shreds of restraint he may have had. Either unaware of the new power of television or not caring about it, Connor ordered firemen to turn high-pressure hoses on the children, knocking them down and leaving many on the sidewalk unconscious and bleeding. Policemen then turned on the marchers and began beating them with nightsticks, while others allowed police dogs to get close enough to the demonstrators to be able to bite them. All this in front of television cameras that broadcast the sight to a sickened nation.

Connor reveled in it, and newsmen reported that when his police officers held back a group of white people from attacking, he told the police, "Let those people come to the corner, sergeant. I want 'em to see the dogs work. Look at those niggers run." The demonstrations continued, and water from a high-pressure hose knocked the Reverend Fred Shuttlesworth against a church wall, where he collapsed into unconsciousness. When an ambulance came to take him to a hospital, Connor told one and all, "I wish they'd carried him away in a hearse."

Although King and his lieutenants in the SCLC preached nonviolence, Connor's arrest of more than 2,000 children, along with the vicious use of fire hoses and police dogs, proved more than the protestors could tolerate. Some of them began throwing rocks and bottles at the police, the first time that a large number of African Americans had broken from the nonviolence King preached. As one might have expected, this led whites to escalate their violence, and in turn more blacks took to the streets with rocks and bottles. Police reacted furiously, beating blacks at random. Over the next several months more than 100,000 people took part in demonstrations in Birmingham, and police arrested more than 15,000 of them. The violence reached a horrible climax in September when a bomb blew up a Birmingham church, killing four little black girls.

The violence continued in Birmingham and elsewhere in the South, but finally, as northern businesses canceled plans to open facilities in the Deep South, southern moderates awakened to the fact that segregation could destroy the economic growth the region had enjoyed after the war. In Birmingham, the white elite promised to desegregate public eating facilities and to hire black salespeople, but the most galling segregationist practices remained.

The violence finally led John Kennedy to move off center, and he told his aides to prepare a civil rights bill; on June 11, 1963, he went on national television to announce his support in an eloquent and passionate talk. After detailing the injustices visited upon black people, he asked "who among us would be content to have the color of his skin changed and stand in [their] place." That night an assassin shot Medgar Evers, an NAACP field secretary in Mississippi, in the back, and he collapsed in a pool of blood at his kitchen door, where his wife and three children awaited him.

Against this background the appeal of the Birmingham jury's decision against the *New York Times* and the four black ministers slowly worked its way to the United States Supreme Court.

CHAPTER 5

# The Road to the Alabama Supreme Court

While violence raged in the streets of Birmingham and elsewhere, authorities used the decision in *Sullivan v. New York Times* to harass the press, hoping to force northern media to stop, or at least to cut back on, their coverage of events in the South. The violence, however, as well as television broadcasts of white policemen battering black protesters, made it impossible to ignore events.

Everyone, of course, expected the *Times* to appeal, but most lawyers thought that, given the standards of the Alabama libel statute and the fact that the Supreme Court had rarely decided any cases dealing with state libel laws, the newspaper would have a difficult time escaping not only the judgment in Sullivan's suit, but the damages pending in the other suits as well. Before the *Times* could get to the U.S. Supreme Court, it had to go through the posttrial motions as well as review by Alabama's high court.

About this time Claude Sitton, the *Times* reporter based in Atlanta who covered the South, flew into Montgomery to bring the paper's readers up to date on other developments in Alabama. He checked into his hotel, left his bag there, and strolled over to the *Advertiser* to chat with reporters and editors, a pattern he had followed on several occasions. Rex Thomas, the Associated Press bureau chief in Montgomery, spotted Sitton in the newsroom, and warned him that local officials knew he was in town and had assigned a deputy sheriff to serve him with some sort of subpoena.

Sitton immediately called the hotel bell captain, whom he knew from his earlier visits, and asked him to get his bag from his room and take it to the Hertz car rental agency across the street. Sitton practically ran through the *Advertiser* newsroom to a window that opened on a back fire escape, climbed down to the ground, and, following back alleys, walked to the Hertz office as fast as he could without calling attention to himself. He rented a car, drove immediately out of town, and then followed back roads rather than the main highway to the Georgia state line.

The Sitton story was not unusual. Harrison Salisbury, whose reporting had generated so much hostility in Alabama, recalled that the tactic of silencing the press seemed to be working. Lawyers advised reporters for the *Times* not to enter Alabama, since subpoenas in new suits might be served on any employee of the paper, and it made the *Times* rely on wire service accounts for more than a year. Other media, including magazines and even television networks, according to Salisbury, questioned "the usefulness of sending a reporter into a southern state to cover a Rights controversy and to make them think twice about reporting the facts, harsh and raw as they often were."

There can be no question that many white southerners hoped the suit would chill press coverage. The day after the jury returned its verdict in the *Sullivan* case, the *Alabama Journal* predicted that the $500,000 award "could have the effect of causing reckless publishers of the North . . . to make a re-survey of their habit of permitting anything detrimental to the South and its people to appear in their columns." The South, the paper went on, suffered libels every day, and was subject to more calumnies than it had been "in the days of the New England fanatical abolitionists, Uncle Tom's Cabin and Simon Legree." Northern papers had felt themselves safe from reprisal for their mistruths because they were far away, but they no longer had such protection. The *Times* had been summoned more than a thousand miles to face justice. "Other newspapers and magazines face the same prospect. The only way to prevent such long distance summons is to print the truth."

The *Montgomery Advertiser* ran a headline about the various libel cases still pending in the courts: "State Finds Formidable Legal Club to Swing at Out-of-State Press." And a formidable club it was. According to one source, libel actions from Florida to Texas rang up a total of more than $300 million in awards or requested damages against the media. The *Times* itself faced judgments in the Alabama suits alone of more than $3 million, and new suits based on the Salisbury articles threatened to add millions more. James Goodale, who became general counsel for the paper, later wrote that the few people realized at the time how financially vulnerable the *Times* was in 1960, wracked by labor strife and as a result earning relatively small profits. Television stations came under attack as well, and the Columbia Broadcasting System, which had aired a news program on the difficulties of blacks trying to register to vote in Montgomery, found itself facing a $1.5 million libel suit.

The sheriff of Etowah County, Alabama, Dewey Colvard, sued the Curtis Publishing Company for $3 million, following an article in the *Ladies Home Journal* by Lillian Hellman that accused Colvard and his deputies of police brutality during racial demonstrations in the summer of 1963.

Tom King, a candidate for mayor of Birmingham, threatened suit against the *Saturday Evening Post* for an article he claimed constituted "a gross defamation of the city of Birmingham and its citizens." The article, by Birmingham-born novelist Joe David Brown, charged his hometown with being the only big city in the United States that had not even tried to get its black and white citizens to meet and work out some solution to the race problem, a failure that made "Birmingham a backward big city by any standards." King's opponent, former police commissioner Eugene "Bull" Connor, also blasted the article.

The *Saturday Evening Post* also faced two lawsuits by University of Alabama football coach Paul "Bear" Bryant. The *Post* carried an article on what the writer, Furman Bisher, called the growing brutality of college football, and mentioned, among other teams, Alabama's Crimson Tide. Bryant claimed he had been defamed and sued the *Post* and Bisher for $500,000. Far more damaging, however, was an article that claimed that former Georgia coach and athletic director Wallace Butts revealed secrets of the Georgia defense to Bryant just a week before Alabama trounced the Bulldogs, 35–0. That case would eventually wind up in the Supreme Court, and it helped to define libel law after *Sullivan*.

Local newspapers that had applauded the use of libel laws to keep northern media from spreading lies found that the sword of libel could be swung widely. William A. McDaniel, a Gadsden, Alabama, fireman, sued the *Birmingham* (Ala.) *News* for libel and invasion of privacy after it erroneously identified him as Robert Shelton, grand dragon of the Ku Klux Klan. At the trial, where he won $15,000 in damages, a lawyer for the paper asked him if he had suffered any financial losses. His reply: "I couldn't say."

Anthony Lewis, the long-time Supreme Court reporter for the *Times*, gave an account of how officials in Birmingham, Alabama, planned to use the *Sullivan* verdict not only against the media but against civil rights groups as well. In 1963 a group called the Inter-Citizens Committee, formed by black ministers, published a six-page pamphlet about what had happened to Theotis Crymes, a 26-year-old black man. On the night of March 19, 1960, as Crymes drove home, a police car stopped him. The officer stood him up against the police car, and then shot him in the back, paralyzing him from the waist down. When Crymes asked why, the office told him, "Shut up, nigger." The FBI investigated and determined the assailant to be Roy Damron, the police chief of Helena, Alabama. A federal grand jury indicted Damron, but an all-white jury acquitted him.

When Birmingham police received a copy of the pamphlet, they sent it to the city's Law Department. William A. Thompson, the assistant city attorney, read it and suggested that the distributors of the pamphlet could be prosecuted for criminal libel for the statements it made about Chief Damron.

The pamphlet reported what had happened, and according to the *Alabama Journal*, the only way the press — or anyone for that matter — could escape libel suits was to tell the truth. But the *Sullivan* verdict brought the whole matter of "truth" itself into question. The rules of libel as Judge Jones had interpreted them made it practically impossible to write about the realities of life in the Deep South in the early 1960s — the riots, the violence inflicted by white police officers on protesting blacks, the lynchings, or indeed, anything about racism or segregation. Any publication that circulated a few copies in Alabama, or sent a reporter into the state, could be hauled into court by any official, named or unnamed, who claimed that stories about voter registration or school segregation or lunch counter sit-ins reflected badly on his job performance and reputation.

Claude Sitton filed a story from Sasser, Georgia, in July 1962, that clearly caught the mood and the intention of many white officials: " 'We want our colored people to go on living like they have for the last hundred years,' said Sheriff Z. T. Mathews of Terrell County. Then he turned and glanced disapprovingly at the thirty-eight

Negroes and two whites gathered at the Mount Olive Baptist Church for a voter registration rally. 'I tell you, cap'n, we're a little fed up with this registration business.'" Police officers went through the parking lot calling out the license numbers of the vehicles, and then Mathews strode into the church and told the gathering that they were not behaving properly, that they had good lives, and that they should stop causing trouble. It is little wonder that civil rights workers called Terrell County "Terrible Terrell" for its racial oppression.

Mathews and many white southerners had good reason to fear voter registration. Terrell County had 8,209 black residents, and 4,553 whites. But while 2,894 whites were registered to vote, only 51 Negroes were on the rolls. In Terrell County and elsewhere, if the majority blacks got to vote, it would be the end of white control of the local government, its services, and especially the police forces. This eventually did happen, after the 1965 Voting Rights Act, backed by federal enforcement, gave southern blacks power at the polls.

Sitton and other reporters continued to gather news from the South, and the *Times* continued to print it despite the libel suits. Gradually public opinion in the North began to change, due in part to press coverage of the civil rights struggle but also because every evening television news brought live coverage of violence in southern streets into northern living rooms. Yale law professor Alexander Bickel gave television a good deal of credit for focusing northern attention on civil rights. Segregation, he noted, was an abstraction, and northerners could not fathom just what it meant to have a segregated school system, nor did many of them really care. The televised riots, however, "brought instantly, dramatically and literally home to the American people, and showed what it meant concretely. Here were grown men and women furiously confronting their enemy: two, three, a half dozen scrubbed, starched, scared and incredibly brave colored children. The moral bankruptcy, the shame of the thing, was evident."

The sense of outrage would build until Congress finally passed the Civil Rights Act of 1964. This was, in fact, the truth about conditions in the South in the early 1960s, the truth that southerners did not want publicized and that they tried to suppress through application of the libel laws.

---

Following the trial, lawyers for the *Times* and the four ministers moved for a new trial, a usual tactic following a loss, and Judge Jones scheduled a hearing in early February 1961. The *Times* moved for a continuance, that is, a delay so they could prepare more material, and Jones put off the hearings for a month. However, because the lawyers for the ministers had not separately asked for a continuance, Jones ruled that they had not acted within the allowable time frame and thus forfeited the right to ask for a new trial. Jones declared their property should be seized and sold to pay the $500,000 judgment against them, or, if they wished to delay seizure, to post a million dollar bond. (Sullivan clearly expected that all or most of the award would come from the *Times*, and not from the ministers. When there are joint defendants in a civil suit, however, all are responsible for the damages. If one of the parties has no assets, then the others have to pay the full amount.)

Normally such seizure would not take place until a judgment became final after all appeals had been exhausted. Clearly the verdict would be appealed to the Alabama Supreme Court, and probably to the U.S. Supreme Court. Only if the highest court affirmed the judgment would it then become final. Following Judge Jones's ruling, however, the sheriff's office immediately took Ralph Abernathy's five-year-old Buick Century, and seized the bank accounts of all four men. Abernathy also owned a small plot of land in the western part of the state, and a sheriff sold that at auction. Solomon Seay told newsmen that he had little property that could be impounded. His house was in his wife's name, and he believed his auto was registered with one of his sons as owners. In the meantime, a jury had awarded $500,000 against the *Times* and the four men in a suit brought by Mayor Earl James, and other suits by City Commissioner Frank Parks and Governor John Patterson would soon be tried. Because the *Times* had filed its motion in time, no move was made to seize any of its assets.

News of the seizure, reported in the pages of the *Times*, outraged its publisher, Arthur Hays Sulzberger, and he asked Louis Loeb if there was any way he could legitimately help them. Loeb felt personal sympathy for the men, but as the lawyer for the *Times* he had to advise Sulzberger to stay out of it. If their cases and that of the *Times* were identical the paper might be able to do something to help, "but unfortunately they are not because they do not have the question of jurisdiction which is the main string to our bow for eventually obtaining a reversal." Loeb also recommended that the *Times* keep its correspondents out of Alabama for a year, lest one of the parties suing it serve notice on a reporter, and thus destroy any hope of winning the argument that Alabama had no jurisdiction. The *Times* would continue to work with the ministers' attorneys in the appeals, and if victorious, the paper could then help the four men recover their assets.

Abernathy, Seay, Lowery, and Shuttlesworth also went into federal district court to seek an order stopping execution of the judgment. The ministers charged that Governor Patterson and the city commissioners "conspired and planned — utilizing their official positions as well as the judicial machinery of the state, to deter and prohibit the plaintiffs and their supporters — from utilizing their constitutional rights — by instituting fraudulent actions against the plaintiffs, without any basis in law or fact." The presiding judge, Frank M. Johnson Jr., was one of the heroes of the civil rights movement, and on several occasions had ordered desegregation of public facilities. But he denied the request to stop seizure of their property because they had failed to exhaust all of their remedies in state court. A few days later Judge Jones ruled against the *Times* in its request for a new trial. The next step would be an appeal to the Alabama Supreme Court, which had proven itself a defender of white supremacy and a foe of civil rights organizations.

One needs to keep in mind that while the *Sullivan* case wound its way through the court system, the *Times* defended itself in other lawsuits as well. *Sullivan* would be key because it was the first. Just as his victory in Judge Jones's courtroom encouraged other angry white officials to go after the *Times*, a victory in the Alabama Supreme Court and in the U.S. Supreme Court would mean that the considerable assets of the New York Times Company could be seized to pay those judgments as well.

The first ray of hope came in June 1961, when the U.S. Court of Appeals for the Fifth Circuit ruled that the *Times* and one of its reporters could not be sued for libel in Alabama over an article on segregation that had appeared in the newspaper. Judge Harlan H.

Grooms of the federal district court for the northern district of Alabama had denied the paper's motion to quash service in seven lawsuits that had been consolidated for hearings. The suits grew out of Harrison Salisbury's articles describing racial tensions in Birmingham. Seven plaintiffs, including Eugene "Bull" Connor and the other city commissioners, all charged that the articles caused them to suffer "public contempt, ridicule, shame and disgrace," and sought damages totaling $3.1 million. Grooms had ruled that notice to the paper of suit, even though not delivered in person, had been achieved by so-called substitute service through the Alabama secretary of state.

A unanimous Court of Appeals panel reversed Grooms. Speaking through Chief Judge Elbert R. Tuttle, it ordered the case remanded to the district court, with directions to enter a judgment for the *Times* and for Salisbury, quashing the service. Interestingly, the court cited a ruling by the Alabama Supreme Court holding that in an action for libel against a newspaper, the injury occurs at the place where the newspaper is primarily published (*Age-Herald Publishing Co. v. Huddleston* [1921]). "It is thus clear that whatever else may be in dispute, none of the activities of Salisbury, and therefore of The Times, performed or done in Alabama, ripened into a cause of action in that state" (*New York Times v. Connor* [5th Cir., 1961]).

Judge Grooms, hardly chastened by the Court of Appeals, ordered that the suit go forward. He obeyed the appeals court order regarding the quashing of service, but said there were sufficient other grounds on which to proceed with the case. Connor and the others won, as expected, and not until 1966, following the Supreme Court's ruling in *Sullivan*, did the Fifth Circuit finally dismiss the suit.

The *Times* also managed to quash a few other suits by removal to federal courts, which found either service illegitimate or the suits fraudulent. But until the *Sullivan* suit could be settled, the newspaper did not know whether it would go free of judgment or owe millions.

If the *Times* had received little sympathy from Judge Jones, it could expect none from Alabama's highest court. Following *Brown*, only a handful of school boards in the South voluntarily desegregated, and none in the Deep South. That meant there had to be lawsuits, and the NAACP's Legal Defense Fund mounted nearly all of them. It followed, then, that if a state wanted to stop desegregation, it had to neutralize the NAACP, and southern states adopted a strategy modeled on congressional action against the Communist Party — demand membership lists and make the organization as well as membership in it illegal. Although ultimately unsuccessful, the strategy hamstrung the organization for years, and Alabama managed to keep the NAACP out of business in that state from 1956 until the summer of 1964. The Alabama Supreme Court at the time consisted of seven justices, all white males, elected to six-year terms. Because they stood for election, they tended to be just as anti–civil rights as a George Wallace or any other statewide politician in Alabama at the time, and they led the attack against the NAACP.

On June 1, 1956, Attorney General (and later governor) John Patterson went into Judge Jones's court and claimed that the NAACP was violating state law by doing business without registering. Jones had no interest in hearing from the NAACP, and in a clear abuse of his judicial authority issued a restraining order without waiting for the organization to respond. "I intend to deal the NAACP a mortal blow," he declared, "from which they shall never recover."

The NAACP stood ready to register if state law required it to do so, but Jones would not allow it. Instead, he ordered the organization to produce its records, including its membership list. This the NAACP could not do without putting its members at the mercy of the Klan, White Citizens Councils, and the police. When it refused to do so, Jones imposed a penalty of $10,000, increased to $100,000 after five days, and continued the injunction.

The NAACP appealed to the Alabama Supreme Court, asking it to suspend the injunction so it could register. The court said the NAACP had to follow the "established rule" and file for a writ of certiorari. The NAACP did, and the court dismissed it, declaring the allegations in the filing were insufficient. The NAACP refiled with more detailed allegations. The court then said that the way to challenge the injunction was by mandamus, not certiorari, and it was too late to file for that. Thus Judge Jones's injunction stayed in place even though the NAACP had never had a hearing, not in his court and not in the Alabama Supreme Court.

The Supreme Court easily recognized the blatant lawlessness of the Alabama Supreme Court, and in June 1958 handed down *NAACP v.*

*Alabama*. Justice John Marshall Harlan spoke for a unanimous Court and stated, for the first time, that it was "beyond debate that the freedom to engage in association for the advancement of beliefs and ideas is an inseparable aspect of the 'liberty' assured by the Due Process Clause." Compelled disclosure of membership may constitute an effective restraint on the freedom to associate, and at times "inviolability of private association is indispensable."

As usual, the Court remanded back to Alabama with instructions to amend its ruling in light of the decision, but the Alabama Supreme Court refused to do so, simply reaffirming its decision. The U.S. Supreme Court again reversed, and the Alabama court refused to lift the injunction or to send the case back to the trial judge to give the NAACP a hearing. Again the NAACP went to Washington, and finally, after more delays, the Alabama court allowed the case to go to trial.

Naturally the NAACP lost, it appealed, and the Alabama court refused to hear the case for a year. When it did, it created a new and convoluted procedural rule that it said the NAACP had not followed. Therefore the trial court's judgment was affirmed without reaching the NAACP's constitutional claim. The NAACP went to the U.S. Supreme Court for the fourth time, and for the fourth time it won. The normally patient and gentlemanly Justice Harlan ended his opinion: "Should we unhappily be mistaken in our belief that the Supreme Court of Alabama will promptly implement this disposition, leave is given the Association to apply to this Court for further appropriate relief." This time the Alabama Supreme Court finally gave up. Congress was about to pass the 1964 Civil Rights Act, and the mood of the country as well as of the more moderate elements of southern society had changed. The people of Alabama no longer found L. B. Sullivan or Bull Connor or a lawless state court so attractive.


During the trial Eric Embry had raised a number of "exceptions" to Judge Jones's rulings. Both men understood the game; Embry was not trying to insult Jones, but was laying the basis for an appeal. Jones did not take offense, aware of Embry's strategy but confident in the correctness of his rulings. In fact, to avoid any suspicion of bias, Jones went out of his way to make it easy for Embry to note his exceptions.

In appealing the decision to the Alabama Supreme Court, Embry grouped his exceptions into eighteen specific claims, each alleging a defect in either the plaintiff's suit or one of Judge Jones's rulings. The court essentially had three options to respond. First, the justices could find merit in a claim of sufficient weight to undermine the integrity of the trial procedures, and order a new trial on that basis. Second, they could recognize some merit in the claim, but also decide that it did not in and of itself seriously affect either the outcome or the procedure. Third, they could find it without merit, and dismiss it.

Roland Nachman and his colleagues had already won their case, but they had to respond to Embry's exceptions, and in doing so defend both the legitimacy of Sullivan's suit and the correctness of Judge Jones's ruling. Both Embry and Nachman cited prior cases to justify their positions, and following are three of the challenges by Embry, and the corresponding responses from Nachman.

JURISDICTION:

EMBRY: If a newspaper published in New York libels a resident of Alabama, the cause of action for libel arises in New York, even though a small portion of the issue containing the libelous matter is mailed or shipped to subscribers and newsdealers in Alabama. *Age Herald Pub. Co. v. Huddleston*, 207 Ala. 40, 92 So. 193; *Weir v. Brotherhood of Railroad Trainmen*, 221 Ala. 494, 129 So. 267; *Bridwell v. Brotherhood of Railroad Trainmen*, 227 Ala. 443, 150 So. 338; *Ogden v. Association of U.S. Army*, D.C., 177 F. Supp 498.

NACHMAN: Under Alabama law, when a newspaper publishes a libel in New York and distributes it in Alabama, the cause of action arises in New York and in Alabama. *Johnson Publishing Co. v. Davis*, 271 Ala. 474, 124 So. 2d 441; *Scripto, Inc. v. Carson*, 362 U.S. 207, 80 S.Ct. 619; *WSAZ v. Lyons*, 6 Cir., 254 F.2d 242.

EXCESSIVE AND UNJUSTIFIED DAMAGES:

EMBRY: A verdict in the amount of $500,000 in a libel action where the plaintiff shows no actual damage and there is no evidence of wrongful intent on the part of the defendant, is so plainly excessive as to demonstrate conclusively that the verdict is the result of bias, passion, prejudice or other improper motive upon the part of the jury and should be set aside and a new trial ordered.

*Crowell-Collier Publishing Co. v. Caldwell,* 5 Cir., 170 F.2d 941; *Johnson Pub. Co. v. Davis,* 271 Ala. 439, 124 So.2d 441.

NACHMAN: Damages must be left to the jury, whose judgment ordinarily will not be interfered with unless the amount is so excessive as to show passion or prejudice or other improper motive. *Johnson Pub. Co. v. Davis,* 271 Ala. 439, 124 So.2d 441.

FIRST AMENDMENT:

EMBRY: The characterization of a publication as a libel under state law does not of itself establish that it is not entitled to federal constitutional protection, and a reviewing court must determine whether the attacked expression is suppressible within constitutional standards. U.S. Constitution, Amendments I and XIV; *Beauharnais v. People of Illinois,* 343 U.S. 250, 72 S.Ct. 725; *Roth v. United States,* 354 U.S. 476, 77 S.Ct. 1304.

NACHMAN: The Fourteenth Amendment is directed against state action and not private action. *Collins v. Hardyman,* 341 U.S. 651, 71 S.Ct. 937; *U.S. v. Cruikshank,* 92 U.S. 542, 23 L.Ed. 588. Libelous utterances are not within the area of constitutionally protected speech and press. *Roth v. United States,* 354 U.S. 476, 77 S.Ct. 1304. The First Amendment of the Constitution of the United States does not protect commercial advertising. *Valentine v. Chrestensen,* 316 U.S. 52, 62 S.Ct. 920; *Breard v. City of Alexandria,* 341 U.S. 622, 71 S.Ct. 920.

Both sides looked for support primarily in prior Alabama decisions, since the case had been tried in a state court and under state law. In the third exception listed above, despite its awkward phrasing, Embry tried to get some sort of First Amendment protection for his client, but at that time he really had no support for such an assertion. The Supreme Court had handed down very few decisions regarding libel, and none of them even suggested that a newspaper enjoyed some sort of constitutional immunity against libel charges.

Less than two decades earlier, a unanimous Court, in *Chaplinsky v. New Hampshire* (1942), had confidently listed "fighting words," obscenity, and libel as forms of expression outside First Amendment protection. With few exceptions, the Court had left libel a matter for state law. In 1952 the justices split 5–4 in *Beauharnais v. Illinois.* Justice

Frankfurter spoke for the majority in upholding a state law prohibiting group libel and denying that libel came within the constitutional protection of free speech. The state legislature had as good a reason to try to prevent defamatory attacks on groups as on individuals, and he saw no reason for the high court to interfere. Justice Black, already arguing an absolutist view of the First Amendment, saw criminal libel as unconstitutional, while Justice Jackson believed the law overbroad. Nothing in any of the opinions suggested that laws regarding defamation of individuals violated the Constitution.

*Valentine v. Chrestensen* (1942) added commercial speech to the three categories listed in *Chaplinsky*, and one wonders why either side cited *Roth v. United States* (1957), a case in which the Court upheld the conviction of Stanley Roth under a federal obscenity statute. Although Justice Brennan's opinion tried to carve out areas of protection — where works had serious literary value, for example — he still maintained that obscenity stood outside the umbrella of First Amendment protection.

The two sides also cited Supreme Court precedent in trying to establish whether the local state court had in personam jurisdiction over the *Times*. Precedent was important because congressional acts conferring jurisdiction on federal courts, dating back to the Judiciary Act of 1789, were not clear, and thus blurred the lines between federal and state court jurisdiction. From the time the issue first arose in the late nineteenth century, the high court had consistently held that for a state court to take jurisdiction of a cause, the due process clauses of the Fifth and Fourteenth Amendment required that it have jurisdiction over the person of the defendant as well as subject-matter jurisdiction over the cause itself. Originally, in *Pennoyer v. Neff* (1878), Justice Stephen Field had held that under the Tenth Amendment a state had exclusive jurisdiction and sovereignty over persons and property within its territory, but could not exercise such authority over persons or property outside its borders.

Revolutions in communications and transportation, and the nationalization of commerce, soon made the second part of Field's position insufficient. In *International Shoe Co. v. Washington* (1945), the Court modernized the concept of in personam jurisdiction by requiring that a person or a corporation have "minimum contacts" with the state so as not to offend "traditional notions of fair play and substantial justice." States quickly exploited this ruling by enacting so-called long-arm statutes extending state court jurisdiction to out-of-state entities that had minimal contact sufficient to maintain contractual or tortious suits. The Supreme Court as recently as 1957 had supported these statutes, and in *McGee v. International Life Insurance Co.* wrote:

> Looking back over this long history of litigation a trend is clearly discernible toward expanding the permissible scope of state jurisdiction over foreign corporations and other nonresidents. In part this is attributable to the fundamental transformation of our national economy over the years. Today many commercial transactions touch two or more States and may involve parties separated by the full continent. With this increasing nationalization of commerce has come a great increase in the amount of business conducted by mail across state lines. At the same time modern transportation and communication have made it much less burdensome for a party sued to defend himself in a State where he engages in economic activity.

The Alabama statute that allowed Judge Jones to exercise jurisdiction not only met Supreme Court standards but reflected the criteria of similar laws in other states. Eric Embry was reaching mightily to try to get Supreme Court decisions supporting his arguments about libel, the First Amendment, or limits on in personam jurisdiction.

Associate Justice Robert B. Harwood delivered the opinion of the court on August 30, 1962. The 60-year-old Harwood had been a member of the state legislature and attorney general of Alabama, and had sat on the Court of Appeals for seventeen years until Governor Patterson named him to fill a vacancy on the Supreme Court. He had won a full six-year term earlier in the year, and so was the junior member of the court. A descendant of an old Alabama family, Harwood, unlike some of the other members of the court, had a career that took him outside the bounds of Alabama law and politics. A graduate of the University of Alabama and its law school — where he later taught — he had gone to Harvard for graduate study and earned a masters of law degree. He had been an assistant U.S. attorney during the 1930s, and during the war had served as an officer in the Judge Advocate General's Department.

(Although the opinion was unanimous, only Chief Justice J. Ed. Livingston and associate justices Robert Tennent Simpson and Pelham J. Merrill were noted as joining the opinion. There were no dissenting or concurring opinions, so one surmises that the other three justices — Thomas S. Lawson, John L. Goodwyn, and James S. Coleman — silently concurred in the opinion.)

It was clear from almost the opening paragraph that the *Times* would lose. In going over the facts of the case, the court noted that the paper maintained a staff correspondent in Atlanta, Claude Sitton, who covered eleven southern states, including Alabama; that Sitton sometimes spent a week to ten days on his visits to Alabama; that between 1956 and April 1960, regular staff correspondents spent 153 days in Alabama to gather news articles; that the paper published forty-nine of these articles based on their correspondents' reporting; that after Sitton was advised by a lawyer to leave the state the *Times* relied on a regular stringer in Montgomery and had three stringers in the state; that in terms of business, two solicitors for "Sales" as well as two employees of the *Times* had at various times come to Alabama seeking business; and that between 1956 and April 1960, businesses in Alabama paid for $26,801.64 in advertisements in the paper. All of this provided the sufficient contact for in personam jurisdiction by Alabama courts over the *New York Times*. Justice Harwood traced the evolution of the Supreme Court's views from *Pennoyer v. Neff* down through *International Shoe* and *McGee.* "We are clear to the conclusion that the activities of The New York Times," he declared, "are amply sufficient to more than meet the minimal standards required."

Harwood's correct depiction of the Supreme Court cases supported his conclusion, but he could have reached the opposite finding, that Alabama courts lacked jurisdiction. In *Age Herald Publishing Co. v. Huddleston* (1921), the Alabama court had found that jurisdiction for libel lies in the state where the publication is produced, a case that the U.S. Court of Appeals had cited in one of the various *Times* suits. But that decision had come four decades earlier, and while it certainly served his purpose to ignore the case, it also made good legal sense to follow the more recent decisions of the Supreme Court.

Embry had argued that Judge Jones had erred in characterizing what Embry had believed to be a "special appearance" for the sole purpose of denying jurisdiction, and labeling it a "general appearance." The court said Jones had not erred, and since it was a general appearance, the *Times* had in effect waived all objections to any possible defects in the manner that process had been served, that is, how it had been notified to appear in the Alabama court. "The conclusions of the trial court in this aspect are in accord with the doctrines of a majority of our sister states, and the doctrines of our own decisions."

This last sentence typifies how the Alabama court handled this case. The justices clearly understood that the suit grew out of the civil rights disturbances in Montgomery, and given their ongoing conflict with the U.S. Supreme Court over the NAACP case, they wanted the opinion so thoroughly grounded in established law that there would be no grounds for the Supreme Court to reverse. This was actually not hard to do, since the law was emphatically on Sullivan's side. Harwood also wanted to emphasize that this was not some idiosyncratic Alabama law, but that the main precepts grew directly out of Supreme Court precedent regarding the law of libel and in personam jurisdiction, and that the state's law tracked that of most other states as well. Had this case come up in another state, Harwood implied time and again, the results would have been the same, and he cited not just Alabama precedents but opinions from other states as well. At one point he wrote, "we will not excerpt further from the decisions from other jurisdictions in accord with the doctrine of the above cases, but point out that innumerable authorities from a large number of states may be found set forth in 25 A.L.R2d, pages 838 through 842." *American Law Reports*, a compendium of holdings from all U.S. jurisdictions arranged by topics, was a standard reference work for lawyers and judges.

In the key objections raised by Embry, he claimed that the advertisement was not directed at Sullivan, that it was not libelous per se, and that the plaintiff had failed to show that he had been in any way damaged. Here the court followed Alabama precedent: words that tended to injure a person in his reputation, profession, trade, or business, or "bring the individual into public contempt," were libelous per se. Moreover, whether the publication had such an effect was not to be determined by "the critical analysis of a trained legal mind, but must be construed and determined by its natural and probable effect upon the mind of the average lay reader." Under that doctrine, the determination would be left to a jury. In this case, the jury had found it libelous, and the appeals court had no grounds to overturn that judgment. Once the publication had been found libelous per se, Sullivan did not have to show particular damages; he could ask for punitive damages, and that amount would be set by the jury.

As for Embry's efforts to invoke the First Amendment as protection for the *Times*, the court had no trouble dismissing it, since "the First Amendment of the U.S. Constitution does not protect libelous publications." Nor could the Fourteenth Amendment be invoked, since it applied only to state action and not to private action. Harwood then methodically but briefly went down each of Embry's exceptions and found no merit to any of them. Embry had also asked that the damages be reduced, but the court noted that in all cases where the judgment had been reduced, the defendant could claim that there was some substantial truth in what it had said. In this case the *Times* could not make that claim.

"It is our conclusion that the judgment below is due to be affirmed, and it is so ordered. Affirmed."

The decision came as no surprise. Embry had done as well as anyone given the facts of the case, the law of libel as it then existed in Alabama and most of the country, and a hostile court dead set against civil rights. The *Times* would, of course, appeal the decision to the United States Supreme Court, but if it hoped to win there it would need a new and far different strategy.

# CHAPTER 6

# A New Game Plan

Although Eric Embry argued the case before the Alabama Supreme Court, several names appeared as counsel for the *Times*, including Herbert Brownell Jr. and Herbert Wechsler. Brownell had been attorney general in the Eisenhower administration, and was now a senior partner at Lord, Day, and Lord, the firm that handled legal matters for the paper. Wechsler taught at the Columbia Law School, and Louis Loeb, who knew him well, invited Wechsler to join the legal team defending the *Times*. Wechsler played a small role in the Alabama Supreme Court appeal, advising Embry on federal jurisdiction for some of his points, but after the paper's loss in that tribunal he took over the task of seeking review in the U.S. Supreme Court. Wechsler faced formidable obstacles in that the Court had tended to leave libel decisions alone, matters to be decided by state courts under state law. More importantly, even if he could get the Court to grant certiorari — a writ that goes to the lower court and brings the case up for review — he had to come up with an innovative means by which the justices could justify overturning Sullivan's victory.

Herbert Wechsler was no stranger to the Supreme Court. After graduating Columbia Law School he had clerked for Justice Harlan Fiske Stone, and then returned to Columbia to teach. In 1940 he went to Washington to work for the Justice Department, and argued five cases before the Supreme Court. After the war he remained with the department, in charge of the War Division during the Nuremberg war crimes trials. He then returned to Columbia, where he taught until his retirement in 1978, also serving as director of the American Law Institute.

A man of great intellect and presence, he could — and did — strike some people as arrogant. Eric Embry thought the New Yorker looked down on the southern lawyers handling the case, and perhaps he did. Both friends and foes described him as having a razor-sharp intellect and an unwillingness to abide either fools or what he considered false doctrine. An expert in constitutional law and in federalism, he and Henry M. Hart Jr. had cowritten one of the most influential casebooks in American law, *The Federal Courts and the Federal System*, first published in 1953.

Wechsler was one of the leading lights of the so-called process school of jurisprudence, who believed that the results in any particular case mattered less than that the decision had been reached through the correct process, with rules that applied consistently across the board. In 1959 he gave the Holmes Lecture at Harvard, entitled "Toward Neutral Principles of Constitutional Law," which became one of the most cited law review articles in the second half of the twentieth century and is considered a key document of process jurisprudence. Although he personally despised racism and segregation, he criticized the Court for its opinion in *Brown v. Board of Education* for failing to justify its ruling with principled arguments that went beyond the case.

Wechsler and counsel for the ministers had three months from the time of the Alabama Supreme Court decisions to file petitions for certiorari. Louis Loeb told him he could call on the resources of Lord, Day, and Lord, but Wechsler also wanted to bring in his former student and now colleague at Columbia, Marvin Frankel. Between his graduation and his return to the law school Frankel had served in the office of the solicitor general, representing the government before the Supreme Court, and also had six years in private practice. The two men knew and respected each other, and Wechsler would feel secure with the quality of Frankel's work.

As the men began their research, they realized two things. First, the law of libel in Alabama did not differ that much from the laws in other states or the common law of England. Once the plaintiff had made a plausible claim that a publication harmed his or her reputation, the burden of proof rested on the defendant to show the truth of the publication, since in a libel suit falsity was presumed. Second, a conviction in a libel suit presumed damages, and the plaintiff did not have to show any quantifiable measurement for these damages, such as one did in other tort actions, such as physical injury or property damage, that is, the car was destroyed, and a new car will cost × dollars.

Years later Wechsler recalled that at the time he knew very little about libel law. "I remember it came as a shock to me in doing the background reading to realize the nature of the burden put on the defendant. . . . And it had to lead you to believe that libel law as it stood on the books was not really enforced in those terms in this country, probably because juries moderated it in practice." In Montgomery, however, the jury had not moderated the severity of the law, nor was there any legal issue raised by their refusal to do so.

Although Wechsler, as an expert in jurisdictional matters, would raise questions before the high court that the Alabama courts lacked jurisdiction, he recognized that by itself that would not be a winning argument. Gradually he came to believe that he should base his case on the First Amendment's guarantees of freedom of speech and of the press. Before he could proceed, however, he had to convince the people at the *Times* that they should try to take the case to the Supreme Court.

Wechsler attended a meeting with executives from the New York Times Company, and found them to be dispirited and totally unfamiliar with the strategy he proposed, namely, that the libel laws of Alabama and elsewhere constituted an abridgement of freedom of the press and therefore violated the First Amendment. "To my amazement," he recalled, "the Madisonian and Jeffersonian doctrines [of a free press] had not penetrated to the upper reaches of *The New York Times*." They wanted to stick to their tried and true policy — never settle a libel case, publish the truth, and pay for the occasional loss — at a time when the judgments in Alabama were mounting into the millions and the paper was on shaky economic ground.

So Professor Wechsler lectured them on what the meaning of the First Amendment is, why it was important that the *Times* raise questions of what constituted a free press, and that even if all the Court did was decide that factual shortcomings in a libel case could invoke constitutional issues, that would be a victory. He could see that he had not won them over, but in fact he had convinced the only man who counted, Orvil Dryfoos, who had just taken over as publisher of the *Times* on the retirement of his father-in-law, Arthur Hays Sulzberger.

Dryfoos met with Louis Loeb afterward, and then Loeb called Wechsler and told him to go ahead.

A strategy of invoking the First Amendment may seem perfectly logical a half-century after the fact, but at the time Wechsler made a big gamble. Just as the Supreme Court had left libel law to the states, it had said very little about the reach of the Press Clause. Law professor Lucas Powe, an authority on media law in America, declares that "for all practical purposes the modern constitutional law of freedom of the press began with . . . *New York Times v. Sullivan.*" Little came before, and what did provided hardly any support for Wechsler's strategy.

According to Sir William Blackstone, the great eighteenth-century commentator on English law, freedom of the press meant that while there could be no *prior* restraint on publication, a person could be punished for what had been said *after* publication. The rule that government could not prevent publication but could punish the words determined *Patterson v. Colorado*, decided in 1907. Thomas Patterson, a Democratic senator from Colorado and a newspaper publisher, ran a series of editorials, stories, and cartoons in his papers ridiculing the Republican-dominated Colorado Supreme Court. He was particularly incensed that the court had invalidated a referendum granting home rule to Denver. At the request of the court, the state's attorney general brought contempt proceedings against Patterson, and under state law, Patterson could not even offer the truth of his charges as a defense. His statements, involving cases then pending before the court, were declared to be an obstruction to justice. In his appeal to the U.S. Supreme Court, Patterson claimed that the court had violated his state and federal constitutional rights by precluding him from demonstrating the truth of his accusations. He based this claim primarily on the Colorado constitution, which guaranteed free speech to all its citizens, and he did not try to invoke the First Amendment.

Justice Oliver Wendell Holmes Jr., speaking for a 7–2 majority, upheld the conviction, and relied on Blackstone's view that truth or falsity had nothing to do with criminal libel: "the provocation, and not the falsity, is the thing to be punished criminally." Holmes broke no new ground in this case, but merely reaffirmed that states had the power to punish so-called bad tendencies in speech. Because exercising this power did not violate any federal rules, he dismissed the case.

In 1907 the process of incorporation — the application of the protections of the first eight amendments to the states through the Due Process Clause of the Fourteenth — had not yet begun. The first right to be incorporated, that of freedom of speech, did not occur until the middle of the 1920s, and the Court incorporated the Press Clause in 1931 in *Near v. Minnesota.*

An explosion of "yellow" journalism had led the Minnesota legislature in 1925 to pass a Public Nuisance Abatement Act, authorizing suppression of any "malicious, scandalous and defamatory newspaper, or other periodical." The law aimed particularly at silencing the *Saturday Press*, a tabloid that had exposed corruption in the state government, albeit in a lurid and at times irresponsible manner. The publisher, an unsavory character named Jay Near, often ran articles attacking Jews, Catholics, blacks, and labor unions. Civil libertarians opposed the law because they claimed that it enforced prior restraint on publishers, a type of censorship that Blackstone had held could not be imposed on the press. Robert McCormick, the very conservative Chicago publisher, recognized that the type of law applied against the *Saturday Press* could also be used against papers like his own and assigned his legal staff to handle Near's appeal to the Supreme Court.

Had the case come up even a few months earlier it might well have been decided against Near. At the time Chief Justice William Howard Taft would have joined the conservatives to uphold the state law, but Taft had died and Charles Evans Hughes now occupied the center chair. The new chief justice sided with the liberals and moderates to void the law as a form of prior restraint, condemning the act as "the essence of censorship." The case marks the first of many cases in which the Court would strike down efforts at prior restraint. More important, Hughes declared that "it is no longer open to doubt that the liberty of the press and of speech is within the liberties safeguarded by the due process clause of the Fourteenth Amendment from invasion by state action."

*Near* marked an important milestone in freedom of the press, in that it applied the Press Clause to the states, and one legal expert at the time called it "the most important decision rendered since the adoption of the First Amendment." It also reinforced the principle that government cannot impose prior restraint on the press absent an overwhelming and clearly demonstrated necessity, a standard so high it has never been met in the Court. As Alexander Bickel wrote, "prior restraints fall on speech with a brutality and a finality all their own. . . . Indeed it is the hypothesis of the First Amendment that injury is inflicted on our society when we stifle the immediacy of speech."

But prior restraint was not the issue in the *Times* case. Alabama had not stopped the paper from publishing the advertisement, but wanted to punish the paper for violating its libel law, an action that conformed perfectly to Blackstonian doctrine. Wechsler thus had little material to build on, and no precedents to support a claim that Alabama's libel laws violated the First Amendment.

Press Clause jurisprudence had remained unchanged since *Near*, but Wechsler took some hope from the fact that the high court had gradually expanded the protection of the Speech Clause. In 1919, Holmes had essentially applied the theory that government could punish speech for a "bad tendency," and then enunciated the rule that "the question in every case is whether the words used are used in such circumstances and are of such a nature to create a clear and present danger that they will bring about the substantive evils that Congress has a right to prevent" (*Schenck v. United States* [1919]). The problem with this test is that in the hands of conservative justices, all seemingly radical statements appeared clearly and presently dangerous.

Later that year Holmes changed his mind, and in a brilliant dissent in *Abrams v. United States* he began the modern speech-protective jurisprudence of the First Amendment. He set forth the idea of a marketplace of ideas, in which all ideas must be allowed free expression, and the best ideas will win out. Brandeis expanded on that notion in *Whitney v. California* (1927), tying the notion of free speech to the democratic process. From then on the Court, with one noteworthy exception, kept broadening the constitutional protection for free speech. That exception came in 1951 in *Dennis v. United States*, at the height of the McCarthy-era excesses, when the Court upheld federal laws making it a crime to teach communism. Then the Court moved back on track, and in 1969 would bury the whole notion of seditious libel as a crime in *Brandenburg v. Ohio*. But would the justices be willing to apply their increasingly liberal notion of what free speech means to an area that had traditionally been outside their jurisdiction?

Although the entire First Amendment protects freedom of expression in one form or another, there are significant differences between interpretations of free speech, free press, and freedom of religion. In speech and in religion error had never been a determining factor. Street corner advocates could orate at length on the problems of this or that political system, and few people paid any attention to whether they got their facts right. The Supreme Court itself had held that government could not inquire into the truth or falsity of a religious belief, since by its nature such belief could not be proved or disproved (*United States v. Ballard* [1944]). But libel and slander required attention to facts and to truth, and somehow or other Wechsler had to convince the Court that the very nature of libel laws violated the Constitution.

A possible solution came in a proposal from his colleague. Marvin Frankel suggested that the law of libel, as it had been used by Alabama, was as oppressive of free speech as the doctrine of seditious libel had been in the eighteenth century, especially as it had been expressed in the Sedition Act of 1798, a law that had evoked classic defenses of free speech and press by James Madison and Thomas Jefferson.

The Alien and Sedition Acts of 1798 resulted from growing tensions between the United States and France. The Federalist Congress provided a new standing army and a small navy, and authorized the arming of American merchant ships. It also passed four measures aimed at aliens and critics of the government. Whatever their wisdom (tripling time for naturalization and giving authority in peacetime to deport aliens deemed dangerous and in wartime to jail them), the three alien acts clearly fell within the powers over immigration and naturalization under Article I. The Sedition Act, however, provided punishments of up to two years in prison and a fine of $2,000 for combining or conspiring to oppose any measures of the government, or to "write, print, utter or publish . . . any false, scandalous and malicious writing . . . against the government of the United States, or either house of Congress . . . or the President . . . with intent to defame . . . or to bring any of them into contempt or disrepute." The vice president, against whose followers the law was aimed, was conspicuously omitted from the proscriptions; one could say whatever they wanted to about Thomas Jefferson. Given the high level of political incivility at the time, the historian George Brown Tindall wryly noted that "considering what Federalists and Republicans said about each other, the act, applied rigorously, could have caused the imprisonment of nearly the whole government."

The Adams administration did not apply the law rigorously or even-handedly. It secured fifteen indictments, all against Republicans, and Federalist judges charged the juries in so biased a manner that guilty verdicts resulted in ten cases, despite the absurd triviality of the allegedly seditious comments. In a series of articles Congressman Matthew Lyon of Vermont ridiculed John Adams's "continual grasp for power" and "unbounded thirst for ridiculous pomp, foolish adulation, and selfish avarice," for which he spent four months in jail and paid a fine of $1,000. Thomas Callender, in *The Prospect before Us*, said that the American people in the election of 1800 had a choice between Thomas Jefferson ("that man whose life is unspotted by crime") and John Adams ("that hoary headed incendiary . . . whose hands are reeking with blood"). For this a Federalist judge fined him $200 and sent him to jail for four months, but since he could not raise money for a bond guaranteeing his good behavior, he languished behind bars until Jefferson became president in March 1801 and pardoned him and all the others sentenced under the act.

Wechsler and Frankel knew that the cases had never been tried in the Supreme Court, and given Blackstone's views, it is possible that the high court would have sustained the law. They took great interest in the resolutions written by Thomas Jefferson and James Madison, and passed respectively by the Kentucky and Virginia legislatures in November and December of 1798. The two documents, in arguments that greatly interested the two lawyers, condemned the Sedition Act as an unconstitutional infringement of freedom of the press.

The Kentucky and Virginia Resolutions, however, also denounced the law as an infringement upon states' rights, and set forth a theory of the Union as a compact of states. Whenever Congress passed a law that exceeded its delegated powers, the states had the right and the power to interpose themselves between their citizens and the national government and to refuse to enforce such laws within their borders. This latter theory, of course, would be resurrected by John C. Calhoun in the years prior to the Civil War, and by defenders of segregation in the 1950s and 1960s. States' rights played a central role in the South's opposition to *Brown*, and Wechsler (a recognized scholar in the field of federalism) and Frankel surely understood that southerners would raise this cry at the idea of a federal court overturning what had clearly and always been a matter of state jurisdiction. They, however, ignored the matter, and Nachman, well aware of the Supreme Court's previous record on civil rights, referred to it only obliquely.

In enacting the legislation the Federalist sponsors followed what was considered good law at the time. The Sedition Act did not impose any prior restraint, but provided punishment for bad speech. Many people at the time, both in England and the United States, held that an attack on government was an attack on the people themselves. Supreme Court Justice Samuel Chase summarized the Blackstone/Federalist position: "Since ours is a government founded on the opinions and confidence of the people, if a man attempts to destroy the confidence of the people in their officers, their supreme magistrate, and their legislators, he effectively saps the foundation of their government. A republican government can only be destroyed in two ways; the introduction of luxury, or the licentiousness of the press." Opposition to Federalist policies was the same as opposition to the government and therefore opposition to the people. To the Republicans a seditious libel law served the governing majority as a tool to beat down opposition, and the clearly partisan manner in which the law had been enforced proved their argument.

There is, despite the claims of the Originalists, very little in the debates in Congress or the states' ratification of the First Amendment to tell us exactly what the Framers meant by the phrase "Congress shall make no law . . . abridging the freedom of speech, or of the press." We know that during the debate over the ratification of the Constitution, Federalists such as Alexander Hamilton thought a listing of rights unnecessary, but because of anti-federalist sentiment Madison and others agreed to add a bill of rights at the first Congress, which they did. But what did it mean?

Jefferson, Madison, and their allies had been thinking about that matter even before the Sedition Act, and they, of course, had a completely different view of the nature of public criticism of government. In Great Britain, sovereignty lodged in the Parliament, which stood as the protector of the people against executive usurpation. In the United States, Madison explained, "the people, not the government, possess the absolute sovereignty." Because of this, the American theory of the press had to be different from that of Great Britain. The abolition of prior restraint might be a sufficient check on the royal prerogative, but under the American Constitution the press must be free "not only from the previous inspection of licensers, but from the subsequent penalty of laws." It would be a "mockery to say that no laws should be passed preventing publications from being made, but that laws might be passed for punishing them in case they should be made."

This, of course, was the argument that the lawyers for the *Times* had been seeking, a rejection of the Blackstonian view and its replacement by a theory of press freedom that did away with penalties for criticizing government. Historically, American law had been moving away from Blackstone as the source of legal authority ever since the Revolution, and in northern states especially, there had been some sensitivity to criticism of public officials. In an 1890 Massachusetts case, for example, the defendant Collier had hinted that Malcolm Sillars, a member of the Massachusetts House of Representatives, had taken a bribe. Sillars sued but unsuccessfully. "It is one of the infelicities of public life," declared the Massachusetts court, "that a public officer is thus exposed to critical and often to unjust comments." But these had to be tolerated (*Sillars v. Collier* [1890]). But while this tolerance for some criticism of public officials existed in a few jurisdictions, parts of Blackstone's *Commentaries* continued to exist in American law long after lawyers and students stopped consulting the four volumes. Wechsler believed it was time to bury the whole notion of punishment for disparaging comments on public officials. In a democracy the press needed freedom to comment. More than a decade before the Sedition Act, Jefferson had written: "Were it left to me to decide whether we should have a government without newspapers or newspapers without a government, I should not hesitate for a moment to prefer the latter."

Before Wechsler could make the argument that the Court should strike down the Alabama law as well as the judgment against the *Times* on First Amendment grounds, he had to convince the Court to take the case. He did this through a "Petition for a Writ of Certiorari to the Supreme Court of Alabama," filed on November 21, 1962, which listed Herbert Brownell and Thomas F. Daly of Lord, Day, and Lord as attorneys for the plaintiff. But the petition, as everyone knew, had been written by Wechsler with Frankel's help.

A petition for certiorari is not an argument on the merits, or to be more precise, implicates the merits only partially. In appealing from a lower court decision, the petitioner has to show that there are important constitutional issues involved and that the lower court either failed to take these questions into account or got them wrong. The petitioner also has to confirm that the high court has jurisdiction under one or more federal statutes to hear this case.

Key to the granting of certiorari is the "rule of four" — four justices have to agree to take the case. They do not have to agree with the petitioner that the lower court erred, but only that there is an important issue that needs resolving. It may be that cases with similar factual situations resulted in diametrically opposite conclusions in different circuit courts, and then the Supreme Court needs to resolve the differences so that the law is uniform in the federal judiciary. In this case four justices would have to agree that the *Times* had raised a significant constitutional issue that brought into question what had been established law.

The rules of the Court impose a format on petitions for certiorari, because the justices want the key question or questions laid out succinctly — they want to know exactly what is involved should they take the case. Wechsler, a veteran litigator in the high court, knew precisely what to do. The first eleven pages essentially summed up the case from the time the advertisement had been printed, through the trial in the local circuit court, to the decision of the Alabama Supreme Court. It also laid out the four questions that Wechsler believed merited the attention of the Court:

Whether, consistently with the guarantee of freedom of press in the First Amendment as embodied in the Fourteenth, a state may hold libelous *per se* and actionable by an elected City Commissioner, without proof of special damage, statements critical of the conduct of a department of the City Government under his jurisdiction which are inaccurate in some particulars.

Whether there was sufficient evidence to justify, consistently with the guarantee of freedom of the press, the determination that statements, naming no individual but critical of the Police

Department under the jurisdiction of the respondent as an elected City Commissioner, were defamatory as to him and punishable as libelous *per se*.

Whether an award of $500,000 as "presumed" and punitive damages for libel constituted, in the circumstances of this case, an abridgement of freedom of the press.

Whether the assumption of jurisdiction [in this case] transcended the territorial limitations of due process, imposed a forbidden burden on interstate commerce or abridged freedom of the press.

Fortunately for Wechsler, Embry — perhaps at Wechsler's suggestion — had raised the First Amendment issue in the Alabama Supreme Court, because normally the high court will not allow the introduction of new arguments that have not been argued in the lower court. Where Embry's exceptions had dealt almost entirely with matters of jurisdiction and interpretation of state law, Wechsler ignored them. Even his fourth question, dealing with jurisdiction, had been raised only to bolster his claim that all aspects of this case, in one way or another, involved the freedom of the press guaranteed by the First Amendment.

On page 12 Wechsler got to the heart of his argument, "Reasons for Granting the Writ." His first sentence summed up his whole argument — "The decision of the Supreme Court of Alabama gives a scope and application to the law of libel so restrictive of the right to protest and to criticize official conduct that it abridges the freedom of the press."

Libel law, resting on assumed falsity and presumed damages, not only sounded like seditious libel, but its effects were in some ways worse. Even the 1798 Sedition Act required that the defendant's purpose was to bring the "official into contempt or disrepute," while a statement adjudged libelous per se is, as the trial court instructed, *presumed* to be false and malicious. The offended official need not prove that any harm actually took place; all a jury needed to believe was that it might have tended to diminish his reputation. Such rules, Wechsler argued, cannot be reconciled with "this Court's rulings on the scope of freedom of the press safeguarded by the Constitution."

Of course the Court had never really made any such rulings, and so Wechsler had to rely on decisions flowing from other parts of the

First Amendment, such as the Speech and Religion Clauses. The Court, he claimed, started with the assumption that "one of the prime objectives of the First Amendment is to protect the right to criticize 'all public institutions' " (*Bridges v. California* [1941]). He then cited *Cantwell v. Connecticut* (1940), to the effect that in both religion and politics sharp differences arise, and often vituperous discussion may follow. But the people of this nation, aware of history, have ordained "that in spite of the probability of excesses and abuses," freedom of religion and of speech are essential in a democracy. Even if there are errors, "half-truths," or "misinformation," there can be no denial of speech in the absence of a clear and present danger of the perversion of justice (*Pennekamp v. Florida* [1946]).

Wechsler knew that the Court had on several occasions placed libel outside the protection of the First Amendment, and understood he had to address that issue. Libel, he claimed, "like obscenity, contempt, advocacy of violence, disorderly conduct or any other possibly defensible basis for suppressing speech of publication, must be defined and judged by standards which are not repugnant to the Constitution." The application of libel law in Alabama failed this test because, like the Sedition Act, it stifled criticism of official conduct.

Whether he knew it or not, in this section, and in the arguments he would later make in the brief and in oral argument, Wechsler gave the justices the solution to the problem. They would not be able – nor would they want – to do away with libel law completely. It existed to preserve reputation, and men and women needed a way to clear their names and to punish those who slandered them. By focusing on criticism of public officials, Wechsler drew a line between private citizens, who should be protected in their reputation, and people who held public office and should not be shielded from criticism of how they fulfilled their obligations.

Wechsler also had to deal with the problem of errors in the advertisement, because libel laws in most states automatically made factual error libelous per se. Again he focused on the First Amendment, arguing that the factual errors were not substantial enough to alter the general message of the advertisement, which, as criticism of public officials, needed to be protected. From a constitutional point of view, minor factual errors should not serve as a pretext to deprive the press of its freedom.

There were many reasons to challenge the decisions in Judge Jones's court, and Embry had hit most of those in his exceptions. Wechsler brilliantly took many of those objections and clothed them in the language of a precious right protected by the Constitution. Embry, for example, said that the $500,000 award of damages was excessive considering that Sullivan had not even been mentioned by name. Jones, Embry, and the Alabama officials all understood that a large award would serve as a club against the press, but Wechsler said that the ability to use such a club went too far in terms of the First Amendment. He cited Justice Brandeis that a "police measure may be unconstitutional merely because the remedy, although effective as a means of protection, is unduly harsh or oppressive." Surely a half-million-dollar award based on a piece that had a few minor and irrelevant errors should be seen as "unduly harsh and oppressive." He again quoted *Cantwell* that "the power to regulate must be so exercised as not, in attaining a permissible end, to infringe the protected freedom."

As expected, Wechsler spent several pages denying that the Alabama courts had jurisdiction, in part because this was his specialty, and also, perhaps, as another avenue for the Court to go if it would not embrace his expansive view of the First Amendment. But the Press Clause remained the heart of his argument. The Court had over the years expanded the meaning of free speech; it had for all intents and purposes done away with the crime of seditious libel; to allow the judgment to stand would be to violate a tradition that went back to the Founding Era, and would impose harsher consequences than the 1798 Sedition Act that history had discredited. "For the foregoing reasons, it is respectfully submitted that this petition for a writ of certiorari should be granted."

The black ministers filed their own petition, since the circumstances of their case differed markedly from that of the *Times*, and they also had a new law team. I. H. Wachtel, a high-powered Washington business lawyer, had had his conscience pricked by Martin Luther King. He volunteered to help King, and his first task was to defend Ralph Abernathy, Solomon Seay, Joseph Lowery, and Fred Shuttlesworth. Where Wechsler focused on the First Amendment, Wachtel emphasized race and civil rights. The trial had been held in a segregated courtroom, where the black lawyers were referred to as "Lawyer," never as "Mr." After a review of the facts, Wachtel began his section on why certiorari should be granted: "This case cries for review. The grave constitutional issues involved here and the impact of this decision on civil rights and the desegregation movement—burning issues of national and international importance—are clear and indisputable. What has happened here is further evidence of Alabama's pattern of massive racial segregation and discrimination and its attempt to prevent its Negro citizens from achieving full civil rights under our Constitution." Wachtel pounded home the message of the civil rights struggle and its importance to this case. Eight years after *Brown* no public schools in Alabama had been desegregated. The only reason to have included the four ministers in the suit was "to silence people from criticizing and speaking out against wrongful segregation activities." The trial pitted white against Negro, "before an all-white jury, and an all-white judiciary." If the Court did not take the case, Wachtel warned, "not only will the struggles of Southern Negroes toward civil rights be impeded, but Alabama will have been given permission to place a curtain of silence over its wrongful activities. This curtain of silence will soon spread to other Southern States in their similar attempts to resist civil rights and desegregation."

M. Roland Nachman, who had argued the case for Sullivan at trial and before the Alabama Supreme Court, filed the brief for the respondent in opposition, and he used the same argument he had before—the lower courts had got it right; the procedures and results in Judge Jones's court followed accepted law. The Supreme Court, therefore, had no reason to accept the case, and he tried to show this in the eight questions he asked.

1. Does a newspaper corporation have a constitutionally guaranteed absolute privilege to defame an elected city official in a paid newspaper advertisement so that the corporation is immune from a private common law libel judgment in a state court where, because of the admitted falsity of the publication, the newspaper is unable to plead or provide state afforded defenses of truth . . . ?

2. When the only claimed invasion of a corporation's constitutional rights is that a city official successfully sued it for damages . . . and when the corporation does not contend that the state trial proceedings have been unfair, does the corporation bring to this Court a federal question subject to review within this Court's certiorari jurisdiction?

3. Are libelous utterances in a paid newspaper advertisement within the area of constitutionally protected speech and press?

4. When an admittedly false newspaper advertisement . . . charges that city police massively engaged in rampant, vicious, terroristic and criminal actions . . . is it an infringement of the newspaper's constitutional rights [when a jury finds it guilty in a private common law libel suit] so as to present any federal question for review in this Court?

5. . . . May this Court consistently with its decisions and the 7th Amendment review on certiorari a state jury finding, in a trial concededly fair, and . . . when this state jury verdict embodied in a final state judgment has been approved by the state's highest appellate court?

6. May this Court consistently with its decisions and the 7th Amendment re-examine facts tried by a state jury . . . when review is sought on assertions that the verdict is wrong and general and punitive libel damages merely excessive?

The last two questions dealt with jurisdiction, whether there had been a special or general appearance, and whether the *New York Times* had sufficient presence in Alabama to warrant jurisdiction; in both instances Nachman suggested that this was not the sort of matter the high court normally reviewed.

Where Wechsler had spoken about a free press and Wachtel about civil rights, Nachman tried to give the Court a quite different interpretation. "This lawsuit arose because of a willful, deliberate and reckless attempt to portray in a full-page newspaper advertisement for which The Times charged and was paid almost $5,000, rampant, vicious, terroristic and criminal police action in Montgomery, Alabama, to a nationwide public of 650,000. The goal was money-raising. Truth, accuracy, and long-accepted standards of journalism were not criteria." The *Times* had not even followed its own standards of checking on the accuracy of the advertisement; not a single person in any department had bothered to look into the allegations made in the ad. The "nation's most influential newspaper" ran a paid advertisement that libeled his client with "violent, inflammatory and devastating language."

Nachman realized, however, that merely denouncing the *Times* for its failure to check facts would not be enough; the *Times* itself had conceded that errors existed, but claimed that they made no difference. Nachman had to convince to Court not only that the grounds the petitioners had put forward lacked merit, but that history demanded that the judgment be left alone. Libel did not enjoy the protection of the Constitution. "Throughout its history, this Court has never held that private damage suits for common law libel in state courts involved constitutional questions." If Wechsler could quote Jefferson, so could he, and cited a letter from Jefferson to Abigail Adams in 1804 explaining his opposition to the 1798 Sedition Act. That law had been unconstitutional because it had been a federal statute. Libel should be a matter of state law, he told her, and he believed in the necessity of such laws as restraints on "the overwhelming torrent of slander which is confounding all vice and virtue, all truth and falsehood in the U.S. The power to do that is fully possessed by the several state legislatures."

Nachman also, and quite effectively, countered the argument of the *Times* as a victim in the lawsuit by pointing out that the press can be the villain in a libel dispute. John Henry Faulk, a radio personality, had lost his job and had been unable to find work for years after he had been tarred as pro-Communist by *Red Channels* magazine. He had sued the publisher for libel, and a jury in New York awarded him $3.5 million, which an appellate court reduced to $500,000. The *New York Times* in an editorial had praised the jury verdict, predicting it would have a "healthy effect" on warding off future irresponsible slanders. The "enormity" of the wrong done to L. B. Sullivan required a similar response, and Nachman hoped that "the decision below will impel adherence by this immensely powerful newspaper to high standards of responsible journalism commensurate with its size."

One of the questions that Nachman put in his response essentially said, albeit tactfully, that not only did the Court not have to take this case because there were no new issues, but given its precedents, it should not: "May this Court consistently with its decisions and the 7th Amendment re-examine facts tried by a state jury in a trial concededly fair?" especially after those findings had been reviewed and confirmed by the highest state appellate court. Nachman cited nearly a dozen prior cases showing "the uniform course of decision by this Court for over a hundred years in recognizing the legal autonomy of state and federal governments" (quoting *Knapp v. Schweitzer* [1958]).

The *Times* had no basis, either in the Constitution or in prior Supreme Court decisions, to challenge the jury verdict, and the Court itself was bound to follow long-established precedent, especially when dealing with a matter of federalism. This was a state suit, decided by a state judge and local jury, and confirmed by the state's highest court. The Court had no need to take this case.

If this had been simply a Press Clause case, the odds against getting certiorari would have been high. Press Clause jurisprudence up to that point had essentially been the rule of no prior restraint. Libel had remained outside the umbrella of First Amendment protection, and the Court had steadfastly held libel to be a matter of state law. As Roland Nachman later noted, the only way he could lose was if the Court changed one hundred years of libel law. Nor would Wechsler have stood much of a chance on challenging the jurisdiction of the Alabama courts, since the high court had consistently upheld state long-arm statutes. The key lay in the fact, as Wachtel claimed and as the justices well understood, that *New York Times v. Sullivan* at heart was a civil rights case, albeit one that clearly implicated the First Amendment. The members of the Court would also have been aware of how the Alabama high court had defied it in the NAACP case. Wechsler surely was right in focusing on the First Amendment, giving the justices the jurisprudential handle they needed to enter the case.

Nachman filed his response to the *Times* brief on December 15, 1962, and a few days later answered Wachtel's petition for the black ministers. The clerk of the Court organized the various briefs and responses and circulated them to the nine chambers. Sometime in the next few weeks the justices took the matter up in conference, and according to a note in Justice William O. Douglas's file, all of the justices agreed to take up the case.

On January 7, 1963, John F. Davis, the clerk of the Supreme Court, notified counsel for the *Times*, the ministers, and Sullivan, as well as the clerk of the Supreme Court of Alabama, that the Court had granted certiorari in No. 606, *The New York Times v. Sullivan*, and No. 609, *Abernathy, et al. v. Sullivan*.

# Briefing the Court

Normally, cases accepted for review at the beginning of January would be argued that spring and decided before the Court adjourned for the summer, but the Court already had a full calendar for the rest of the term. Lawyers on both sides would therefore have until September to write and file their briefs, and then condense those arguments down into talking points for their oral arguments.

There is some debate among scholars, practitioners, and even judges over the value of oral argument, but there is no debate over the importance of the briefs that each side files with the court. The brief is the story of the case, and includes the full record from the proceedings of the trial court up to the decision of the highest appellate court to have reviewed the case, and gives counsel their chief opportunity to persuade the Court. Oliver Wendell Holmes Jr. said that he was only rarely influenced by oral argument, but always relied on the record and briefs. Briefs and records are delivered to chambers well before oral argument, so that justices and their clerks have time to read and analyze them, and to see what issues they want to pursue. A good brief not only may convince a justice to favor that side, but in difficult cases may provide the jurisprudential roadmap on how best to frame that opinion.

In the early days of the Court there were no briefs, and not until 1821 did the Supreme Court rules require all parties to submit written briefs. Since then the rules on briefs have changed several times in regard to format and length, but the crucial parts are the same. There should be a succinct statement of the case and of the questions involved, and the argument should specifically point out the authorities relied upon, cases as well as non-case material such as statutes, monographs, and articles.

The modern court rules emphasize that a "brief must be compact, . . . concise, and free from burdensome, irrelevant, immaterial, and scandalous matter." Experience led to this rule, since early in the twentieth century there were no page limits imposed, and Justice John H. Clarke complained of briefs with more than a thousand pages. Should such a brief be submitted today, it would be "disregarded and stricken by the Court." Experienced lawyers can put what they need into fifty pages or less, and in 1980 the Court adopted Chief Justice Warren Burger's suggestion that fifty pages be established as the maximum size.

Because many of the cases brought to the Court are argued by lawyers inexperienced in appellate work, the justices have to contend with what Charles Evans Hughes described as "diffuseness": a lack of clarity, focus, and analysis. Too many lawyers see a brief as little more than a setting down of facts and the relevant law, and fail both in imagination — what might these facts mean if we look at them anew — and in analytical rigor, that is, what are the implications for the development of law if we accept one argument over another. Poorly written and inadequate briefs hurt the client's chance of success.

In a 1942 article in the *ABA Journal* on appellate briefing, Justice Wiley Rutledge advised lawyers to "make your briefs clear, concise, honest, balanced, buttressed, convincing, and interesting. The last is not the least. A dull brief may be good law. An interesting one will make the judge aware of this." An unfocused brief, even if it has good law, may lose a case because it fails to hold the justice's attention. An effective brief brings home why the case, and its proper solution, should occupy the justice's attention.

Herbert Wechsler's experience as a teacher (he was considered one of the best at Columbia) as well as the dozen arguments he had made in the high court gave him a clear understanding of what he had to do in the brief for the *New York Times*. Wechsler's wife, Doris, his colleague from Columbia Marvin Frankel, and Ronald Diana, a young associate at Lord, Day, and Lord, did research, prepared memoranda on questions Wechsler wanted answered, and went over his drafts with a critical eye. But this was 1963, and the practice of law was much different than it is a half-century later. There were no gigantic law firms with dozens or hundreds of associates who could be assigned to research and other chores; there was no Internet where cases, authorities, and other materials could be accessed by a few keystrokes. The most modern piece of technology in law offices was an IBM electric typewriter, and most lawyers, including Wechsler, wrote out drafts and then revisions in pen or pencil on long yellow legal pads.

Everyone at the *Times* and at Lord, Day, and Lord understood that in this last stage Herbert Wechsler would be in charge. (On the petition for certiorari the lawyers for the *Times* had been listed as Herbert Brownell and Thomas F. Daly of Lord, Day, with Wechsler's name, along with that of Embry, as "of counsel," a clearly subsidiary ranking, even though he had written the petition. In the argument brief, Wechsler's name accompanied that of Brownell and Daly, while Louis Loeb, Eric Embry, Marvin Frankel, Ronald Diana, and Doris Wechsler made up the list "of counsel.") As it turned out, Wechsler was on sabbatical from Columbia that spring, so he could devote most of his time to the brief. When the prestigious American Law Institute offered him the post of executive director, Wechsler got them to agree to hold the offer until after he had finished the *Times* case.

Wechsler worked hard himself and expected no less of his colleagues. Frankel later said that he believed between them they read everything ever published on the issues — not just libel law, but history, press matters, and even ten years worth of the *Alabama Lawyer*. Doris Wechsler worked on some of the jurisdictional questions, and tried to draft a section. As she related, Herb "had some very clear ideas about how it should be handled and did it his way, which was much better than anything I had attempted. Mine was more pedestrian."

There is nothing pedestrian in the brief for the petitioner, but neither is it flashy. The tone is measured, hyperbole is avoided, and Wechsler carefully followed a strategy that he believed few other lawyers at the time shared, namely "a sense that a Supreme Court brief should be a document that a Supreme Court justice can use in writing an opinion favorable to the briefer." Wechsler understood that because he was asking the justices to make a dramatic break from precedent, he needed to present a plan by which they could do that, a rationale why they should abandon long-standing rules regarding state law and libel.

Throughout the summer of 1963 the four of them — Herbert and Doris Wechsler, Frankel, and Diana — worked away. The Wechslers normally spent part of the summer on Cape Cod, but not that year. Extremely methodical, Wechsler read everything he could before committing anything to paper. "It was a hot summer," Frankel later said, and "Herb was a very severe senior partner, but it was marvelous. Finally there came a night when Herb and Doris and I were working, I believe in their apartment, and Herb said, 'That's it. All we need now is the cite checking.'" The job of checking to make sure that cases are correctly cited and that quotations are accurate is a tedious one, usually assigned to an associate or even a student assistant, and Frankel suggested that one of the younger lawyers at Lord, Day could do it. No, said Wechsler, "I'm not going to trust that to anyone else," and he did it himself. After showing it to people at the law firm and the *Times*, he filed it with the clerk of the Supreme Court on September 6, 1963.

The brief ran 102 pages, about twice what would be allowed under the current rule of the Court, with 12 pages listing cases and authorities cited and about 25 pages recounting the history of the case, from the trial court through the Alabama Supreme Court. Wechsler recited the same four questions he had listed in the petition for certiorari — whether consistent with the First Amendment a state could hold statements made in criticism of government officials libelous per se; whether there was sufficient evidence, again consistent with press freedom, to justify the award; whether the size of the award, in the circumstances, abridged press freedom; and whether the state court's assumption of jurisdiction violated both the First Amendment and the Commerce Clause.

This time, however, he answered those questions, and in a particular manner. The *Times* lawyers knew that precedent regarding libel law favored Sullivan; the Court had always taken a hands-off approach to state libel law, and had consistently held libel outside the umbrella of First Amendment protection. In the brief Wechsler would concede that this had been the case, but only because in the prior decisions of the Court the cases had never involved criticism of public officials. The Court could intervene in this case because the state of Alabama had violated the First Amendment by the way it had used its libel laws against a legitimate and *protected* form of speech, one hallowed in

American history — citizen criticism of their government and of its officials.

By taking this approach the Court would not have to give libel full protection under the First Amendment; private persons who had been defamed could still go into state courts to clear their name and seek appropriate damages. The fact that there had been errors in the advertisement made no difference; one did not expect political speech to be completely accurate, and by casting the ad as a form of political speech — which it clearly was — Wechsler could invoke other traditions in the law that the Court could use to decide in his favor.

Other than noting that the ad dealt with one of the great issues facing the country and that stifling press comment could adversely affect the movement, Wechsler did not talk very much about civil rights, leaving that to the lawyers for the four ministers. He had one message, and he pounded it home in almost every paragraph — the Constitution guaranteed free expression; political speech had always been considered the core value protected by the First Amendment; political speech included criticism of the conduct of elected or appointed government officials; freedom of the press meant that newspapers and other media could engage in political speech, and must, for the sake of democracy, be allowed to do so without fear of libel suits; the manner in which Alabama had applied its libel law unconstitutionally violated freedom of the press; for the sake of democratic institutions such abridgement could not be allowed to happen.

Again, Wechsler utilized the 1798 Sedition Act as an analogy to the Alabama libel law (and by implication, similar laws in other states), and he claimed that the law "first crystallized a national awareness of the central meaning of the First Amendment." In the House debate on the bill, John Nicholas of Virginia had warned that a law ostensibly directed against falsehood "must be a very powerful restriction of the press, with respect to the publication of important truths," since men would be deterred from printing "anything which should be in the least offensive to a power which might so greatly harass them." James Madison, in his Virginia Report, warned that if such laws had been in effect the colonies might never have freed themselves from Great Britain, nor the people of the United States thrown off "the infirmities of a sickly Confederation."

In a statement that would find its way into Justice Brennan's opinion, Wechsler noted that although the Court had never passed on the Sedition Act, "the verdict of history surely sustains the view that it was inconsistent with the First Amendment." He then cited a number of opinions as well as historical and legal treatises supporting this view, "which reflect a broad consensus that, we have no doubt, is part of present law." The lesson, of course, that Wechsler wanted the Court to acknowledge is that any effort to prevent criticism of public officials either by the press or by the citizenry could not be sustained under the Constitution. That nothing "justifies repression of the criticism of official conduct was the central lesson of the great assault on the short-lived Sedition Act."

Wechsler, for a variety of reasons, kept his focus on the 1798 law, and not on the World War I statutes that substantially reenacted the earlier proscriptions. The prime tactical reason may have been that the Court had never passed on the constitutionality of the first Sedition Act, historians had generally condemned it, and no less powerful authorities than Thomas Jefferson and James Madison had denounced it. The World War I statutes had precipitated the beginning of modern free speech jurisprudence, but the Holmes and Brandeis views on free speech had not yet won total victory. The Court had never declared the 1917 and 1918 laws, or any of the many state laws modeled on them, to be unconstitutional. The Warren Court would eventually do so, but not until 1969.

Nonetheless, the Court had been moving away from support of seditious libel for more than four decades, and Wechsler made the point over and over that Alabama's law of personal libel, as applied in this case, amounted to little more than a sedition act, punishing the press for criticism of government. Courts had long held that municipal governments could not sue their critics for libel, and "no court of last resort in this country has ever held, or even suggested, that prosecutions for libel on government have any place in the American system of jurisprudence" (quoting *City of Chicago v. Tribune Co.* [Ill. 1923]). That rule also held for any effort to convert libel on government into libel of the officials who compose government.

Wechsler also noted that the Court had on numerous occasions declared that the whole purpose of constitutionally protected expression was "to assure unfettered interchange of ideas for bringing about of political and social changes desired by the people" (quoting *Roth v.*

*United States* [1957]). Such political expression cannot be restricted by any test of truth, whether that test be administered by courts, executives, or juries, and this meant that such speech also could not be limited because it might diminish the reputation of government or its officers.

Nor could the dialogue be restricted because it might be offensive to some. The daily dialogue of politics, according to Justice Robert Jackson, included the "effort to discredit and embarrass the Government of the day by spreading exaggerations and untruths and by inciting prejudice or unreasoning discontent, not even hesitating to injure the Nation's prestige among the family of nations." And still it must be protected (quoting *Communications Assn. v. Douds* [1950]). Going back even further, Wechsler cited the nineteenth-century jurist David Brewer, who, talking about political discourse and criticism of the courts, said, "the moving waters are full of life and health; only in the still water is stagnation and death." The First Amendment, noted Wechsler, "guarantees that motion shall obtain."

Wechsler needed to show that the Court itself shared this view, and he used the analogy of contempt citations from the bench for statements supposedly injurious to judges' reputations or their conduct of trials. "It is settled that concern for the dignity and reputation of the bench does not support the punishment of criticism of the judge or his decision, whether the utterance is true or false." And indeed, the Court had so ruled. In *Bridges v. California* (1941) the Court had reversed state court contempt citations against labor leader Harry Bridges and the *Los Angeles Times*, and extended First Amendment freedom of the press to published comments on pending court decisions. A few years later in *Pennekamp v. Florida* (1946), the Court overturned a contempt citation against the *Miami Herald* and one of its editors, John D. Pennekamp, for criticizing the handling of certain cases in state courts. Such editorials, no matter how critical, wrote Justice Stanley Reed, posed no clear and present danger to the operations of the Florida judicial system.

If the weapon of a contempt citation cannot be used against critics of judges, then comparable criticism of an elected political official cannot be chastised because it allegedly diminishes his reputation. "If political criticism could be punished on the ground that it endangers the esteem with which its object is regarded, none safely could be uttered that was anything but praise." Wechsler noted that public officers are immune from libel suits in their official communications, even if they denigrate a private citizen. "It would invert the scale of values vital to a free society if citizens discharging the 'political duty' of 'public discussion' did not enjoy a fair equivalent of the immunity granted to officials as a necessary incident of the performance of official duties."

Wechsler thus provided the Court the means by which it could depart from a century of abstention from reviewing state libel decisions, and he wanted the new rule to be as broad as possible. The libel laws of Alabama and other states served the functional equivalent of a sedition law when applied to comments in the press about the policies or conduct of government and its officials, and thus violated the First Amendment protection of the press. Criticism of government was at the heart of political speech, and thus had to be fully protected, even if it included factual errors. If a person entered the political arena, he had to expect the criticism — even strong and virulent criticism — that came with the territory.

But what about the claim of the Alabama Supreme Court that the First Amendment did not apply to state libel laws? Nachman had, in his response to the petition for certiorari, quoted Jefferson's approval of the states' controlling libel laws. This gave Wechsler the opportunity to address another issue. "That distinction lost its point with the adoption of the Fourteenth Amendment and the incorporation of the First Amendment freedoms in the 'liberty' protected against state action." The Court could indeed address the issue of the use of libel laws as a weapon against the press because the Court had, in other cases, already applied the First Amendment to the states.

In his final section Wechsler discussed the matter of whether the Alabama courts had legitimate jurisdiction to try a New York newspaper that had minimal contacts with the state. Wechsler had to deal with jurisdiction, if only as a last resort should the Court not agree with his argument about libel. Here again he realized that the Court's decisions had validated so-called long-arm statutes, so his attack took two forms. First, he tried to show that the contact that the *New York Times* had with the State of Alabama did not meet the minimal standards that the Court had spelled out in *International Shoe Co. v. Washington* (1945) and its later applications. These cases all required that the foreign corporation have some sort of "base" in the state, and this could hardly be said of a newspaper whose Alabama readership comprised only 0.06 percent of its daily circulation and 0.2 percent of the Sunday edition, and from which it drew only 0.046 percent of its advertising revenue. "The occasional visits of correspondents to the State to report on events of great interest to the nation places *The Times* in Alabama no more than in Ankara or Athens or New Delhi, where, of course, similar visits occur."

The problem with this approach is that it would have involved the courts in countless case-by-case determinations of what measured up to the rather indefinite standards of "substantial" or "minimal" contact. The Court had realized that it would be impossible to draw some bright line to mark off contacts that made a foreign corporation amenable to state jurisdiction and those that did not, and it most certainly did not want to go down that route. Wechsler hoped that by his showing how little presence the *Times* had in Alabama, the justices would say that it failed the test. In fact, state courts had exercised jurisdiction with as little contact as, or even less contact than, the *Times* had in Alabama.

It was worth the shot, but then Wechsler went back to the central theme of his argument, the First Amendment. It was one thing to exercise long-arm jurisdiction in commercial matters, but quite another to do so for the sole purpose of silencing legitimate—and protected—speech. Freedom of the press included newsgathering and circulation, and thus had to be safeguarded. "Neither can continue unimpaired if they subject the publisher to foreign jurisdiction on the grounds and scope asserted here." There could be no doubt that the exercise of jurisdiction constituted state action, and thus brought it within the reach of the First Amendment as embodied in the Fourteenth, especially when it has "the collateral effect of inhibiting the freedom of expression, by making the individual the more reluctant to exercise it" (quoting *Smith v. California* [1959]). If a court could take jurisdiction of a libel action on the basis of sporadic newsgathering and trivial circulation, "it can and will do so not only when the plaintiff has a valid cause of action but also when the claim is as unfounded and abusive as the claim presented here." The negative impact on freedom of the press far outweighed the desire of a state to provide its residents with a convenient forum, especially when that power could be used to stifle a constitutional freedom.

All told, Wechsler had prepared a brilliant brief, and it did everything that needed to be done. Written in a calm and deliberative manner, it nonetheless reflected the drama of the historic although not always successful fight to ensure free speech and press against efforts to silence criticism. He invited the justices not to abandon the entire law of libel, but only where it could apply to criticism of government and of its officials — a trend, he assured them, that they had been following for more than three decades. He stayed focused, concentrating on one issue and one only, that of a free press, and he hoped that the importance of free expression would win the Court to his side. In only one passage did he allude to the civil rights struggle, and even there he bent it to his main argument: "This is not a time — there never is a time — when it would serve the values enshrined in the Constitution to force the press to curtail its attention to the tensest issues that confront the country or to forego the dissemination of its publications in the areas where tension is extreme."

Roland Nachman had essentially lost the first round when the justices granted certiorari. That meant that at least four members of the Court agreed with Wechsler that important questions in this case needed review by the high court; it did not mean that a majority of the Court agreed with Wechsler's analysis. Unlike the response to the certiorari position, where Nachman had essentially *asserted* that the lower courts had gotten it right and the results should not be disturbed, he now had to *prove* that they had not erred. While he recognized that previously the high court had deferred to state decisions in this area, he also knew that the Supreme Court had become far more concerned with the First Amendment issues that the *Times* brief had raised and that he would have to respond to them. Although he tried to ignore civil rights arguments, Nachman must have realized at some point that the Court that had issued *Brown*, striking down decades of constitutionally accepted segregation, and had repeatedly involved itself and the federal judiciary in areas traditionally reserved to state control, would have no qualms entering another such precinct. Once certiorari had been granted, it had become a whole new ball game. Nachman's wins in front of Judge Jones as well as in the Alabama Supreme Court would not matter unless he could win in Washington as well.

{ *Chapter 7* }

This meant he had to convince the justices that the trial court had been correct in its judgment, that Alabama law as applied in the trial did not violate any First Amendment freedom, that jurisdiction had been properly invoked, and that the *Times* had not been a victim of anything except its own negligence, which did not carry constitutional protection. It was a difficult task, and he summed up his argument in four major categories.

*First*, the Constitution conferred no absolute immunity to defame public officials. The advertisement was libelous per se, and such statements had no constitutional protection. As a result, damage awards by the jury may not be disturbed.

Nachman wanted to make clear that the villain in the case was not Alabama, nor Judge Jones, nor the jury, but the *New York Times*, "perhaps the nation's most influential newspaper, [which] stooped to circulate a paid advertisement to 650,000 readers — an advertisement which libeled respondent with violent, inflammatory, and devastating language. The *Times* knew that the charges were uninvestigated and reckless in the extreme." When confronted with the libel charges, the newspaper had ample defenses under Alabama law. Substantial truth in all material aspects would be a complete defense, while privilege and fair comment would also suffice. But when the allegations are false, there is no privilege, and this was the rule in the vast majority of American states. Moreover, this was not a case in which the paper had pled truth and the jury had not believed it; representatives of the *Times* had admitted that the ad contained several factual errors. Beyond that, the paper and its representatives conceded there had been a fair trial.

Justice Black had written that when a case is tried "in accordance with regular court procedure, submitted to a jury as provided by the constitution and laws of that State, and in harmony with the traditions of the people of this nation . . . no proper interpretation of the words 'due process of law' can justify the conclusion that appellant has been deprived of its property contrary to due process" (*United Gas Public Service Co. v. Texas* [1938]).

Despite the efforts of the *Times* to raise a federal question, none existed, for libelous statements had never been protected by the Constitution. Moreover, throughout its history the Supreme Court had never held that private damage suits for common law libel in state courts involved constitutional questions. Nachman protested that the brief for the *Times* tried to secure meanings in key cases that the Court had never intended, and he argued that the Court had meant exactly what it said in *Roth v. United States*, that "the First Amendment was not intended to protect every utterance. . . . Libelous utterances are not within the area of constitutionally protected speech." That the libel appeared in a commercial advertisement argued even more strongly against clothing it in constitutionally protected garb, and he insisted that the Court should be taken at its word when it said that commercial speech also stood outside the First Amendment.

Even in the Court's most famous Press Clause case, *Near v. Minnesota* (1931), Justices Holmes and Brandeis, icons of free speech jurisprudence, had joined in Chief Justice Hughes's statement that "punishment for the abuse of the liberty accorded to the press is essential to the protection of the public, and that the common law rules that subject the libeler to responsibility . . . are not abolished by the protection extended in our constitutions." In the past twenty years the Court had declined to review forty-four libel cases coming from state and federal courts. It reviewed three, and in those three found that the defendants enjoyed a qualified immunity because of their position.

As for the give and take of political discourses, the type of immunity that the *Times* sought would cover things that should never be protected, false statements to the effect that the secretary of state had given military secrets to the enemy, that the governor of a state poisoned his wife, that the mayor and city council are corrupt, or that the head of public health polluted the water supply. The Court in *Pennekamp*, even while dismissing the contempt citation, nonetheless held that judges and other public servants, when faced by defamation, have remedy in damages for libel.

In its recourse to history, the *Times* could not prove that the Constitution granted it an absolute privilege to defame a public official because that had never been the case. Nachman cited Zechariah Chafee, "an old and close friend of free speech and press," who noted that the men of 1791 who wrote and ratified the First Amendment did not regard damage suits for libel as objectionable. Around 1800 there were several convictions in Massachusetts alone for libels attacking the conduct of the legislature and of public officials.

The question of whether an utterance is libelous per se had always been a question for a jury to decide, and in this case, following state law in a trial admittedly fair, a jury had determined that the advertisement in question constituted a libel against Commissioner Sullivan and had awarded him damages, the amount of which was also traditionally in the jury's discretion. Only recently a New York court had refused to disturb a verdict of $3.5 million in a libel suit, of which $2.5 million was punitive, noting that punitive damages have always been at the discretion of the jury. "The jury, representing the community, assesses such a penalty as, in its view, is adequate to stop the practices of the defendant and others having similar designs" (*Faulk v. Aware, Inc.* [1962]).

Nachman reminded the Court that it had always considered itself barred by the Seventh Amendment from setting aside state and federal jury damage awards as either inadequate or excessive. ("In Suits at common law, where the value in controversy shall exceed twenty dollars, the right of trial by jury shall be preserved, and no fact tried by a jury, shall be otherwise re-examined in any Court of the United States, than according to the rules of common law.") Nachman cited several cases, concluding by quoting from *Knapp v. Schweitzer* that many cases showed "the uniform course of decision by this Court for over a hundred years in recognizing the legal autonomy of state and federal governments." Nothing in the *Times* argument should lead the Court to abandon this practice.

*Second*, the Court had no reason to review a jury determination that the advertisement concerned L. B. Sullivan. Once again, he charged, the *Times* wanted to turn what had always been a factual determination by a jury into a constitutional matter, and he urged the Court to remain true to its longtime practice: "This Court simply does not go behind these factual determinations and review a state court judgment, entered on a jury verdict and affirmed by the highest appellate court." He charged it was "patently frivolous" for the *Times* to say that "no ordinary person of reasonable intelligence could possibly read this advertisement as referring to the Montgomery police commissioner." The jury was not bound by the Constitution to take the *Times*'s construction of these words, but was free to determine for itself what they meant.

This argument, that the Court historically did not enquire into the factual conclusions of a legitimate state jury, may have been one of the strongest that he could have made. Although Sullivan had not been mentioned by name, the advertisement did attack the behavior of the police, and traditionally the claim that the allegations referred to him would have been a question of fact for the jury. Nachman then cited a dissenting opinion by two sitting members of the Court, Hugo Black and William O. Douglas in *Galloway v. United States* (1943): "Either the judge or the jury must decide facts and to the extent that we take this responsibility, we lessen the jury function. Our duty to preserve this one of the Bill of Rights [the Seventh Amendment] may be peculiarly difficult, for here it is our own power which we must restrain."

Wechsler, no matter how much he clothed his argument in First Amendment precedent, was asking the Court to abandon a century of precedent in very important areas — federalism, respect for state law, and deference to jury findings. While freedom of speech and press mattered a great deal to the Court, so did these ideals. In the end the justices would have to determine which they valued more.

*Third*, there was nothing unusual in this case to give the Court reason to depart from a clear-cut record and from its long-established constitutional standards. Wechsler had referred in his brief to other libel suits then pending against the *Times* in Alabama, and labeled them as "companion cases." Nachman objected, and claimed that with the exception of the two suits by the other Montgomery commissioners, this case stood on its own, and the Court needed to limit itself to the record of this case. The other cases had not yet been decided, and no one knew for sure what would happen. The fact that the advertisement involved racial matters did not give it immunity from the law, and the enormity of its wrong was clear. The paper had defamed people, and a jury had found it guilty and assessed damages. This happened all the time. If the paper had been more careful and less arrogant, it would have checked its facts, corrected the errors, and would then have been able to plead truth as a complete defense. Alabama law, as that in all states, provided safeguards to protect constitutional rights.

But, when a newspaper — or an individual — cannot avail itself of these defenses because "it has indeed defamed in a commercial advertisement, no constitutional right, privilege or immunity expounded by this Court during its entire history shields a newspaper from damages in a common law libel suit."

*Finally*, Nachman argued that the *Times* had been properly before the Alabama court, which clearly had jurisdiction. In fact, he claimed, because both the trial court and the Alabama Supreme Court held that the paper had made a general rather than a special appearance, "an adequate independent state ground as to jurisdiction is a bar to review here."

The *Times* claimed that the Alabama Supreme Court "has incorrectly interpreted its own decisions," and therefore it was in error on the jurisdictional question. The Supreme Court should not even be looking at that issue, but even if it were appropriate to do so, the state court had indeed followed its own precedents, which reflected practices in other states. In the end, though, the important question was not whether the paper had made a general or a special appearance, or even if the Alabama courts had got this matter wrong. "The crucial test is simple. Did the *Times* have sufficient business contacts with Alabama so that suit against it there accorded with traditional concepts of fairness and orderly administration of the laws?" The courts below, after "painstaking analysis of the jurisdictional facts of record," held there was indeed sufficient contact, and their conclusion comported not only with the standards of due process but with the Court's own decision. (Nachman cited the unanimous opinion in *McGee v. International Insurance Co.* [1957] that one contract negotiated entirely by mail with a predecessor company gave California sufficient contact with a successor company, and upheld a default judgment against the latter firm.)

"For the foregoing reasons," Nachman concluded, "it is respectfully submitted that the writ of certiorari should be dismissed as improvidently granted; in the alternative, respondent respectfully submits that this case should be affirmed."

In the companion case of *Abernathy v. Sullivan*, Wachtel, as he had in the certiorari petition, hit hard on the patent unfairness of the Alabama proceedings. The four men first learned of the *Times* ad when they received a letter from Sullivan, which did not include the full ad, but quoted from the two paragraphs on which the commissioner based his complaint. He then demanded that each of them "publish in as prominent and public a manner" as the *Times* ad "a full and fair retraction of the entire false and defamatory matter." The petitioners could not possibly comply, and before they even had time to consult lawyers and receive appropriate advice, Sullivan instituted his suit.

Wachtel charged that the proceeding before Judge Jones was "a race trial, in which they were from first to last placed in a patently inferior position because of the color of their skins." The trial took place in a segregated courtroom, "the one room, of all rooms, where men should find equality before the law."

There was relatively little law in the brief, at least compared to the ones submitted by Wechsler and Nachman, but it had more than its share of passion. Wachtel wanted to make sure that the justices understood that at the heart of this case was the great issue of the time, the black struggle for equality. In that courtroom "where Sullivan, a white public official, sued Negro petitioners represented by Negro counsel before an all-white jury, in Montgomery, Alabama, on an advertisement seeking to aid the cause of integration, the impact of courtroom segregation could only denote the inferiority of Negroes and taint and infect all proceedings."

Although the closing remarks of counsel at the trial had not been officially transcribed and included in the record, Wachtel reported a remark supposedly made by Robert Steiner, one of Sullivan's lawyers: "In other words, all of these things that happened did not happen in Russia, where the police run everything, they did not happen in the Congo where they still eat them, they happened in Montgomery, Alabama, a law-abiding community." It would have been difficult for anyone reading the brief not to understand.

In addition to the briefs for the appellants and respondent, the Court may also receive briefs from amici curiae, friends of the court, parties who have an interest in the issues raised in a case. A person or group may file an amicus brief if both of the litigants agree, or failing that, if the Court grants permission. In his brief Nachman had taken a shot at the "*Times* and its powerful corporate newspaper friends," and by this he meant the companies that published the *Washington Post* and the *Chicago Tribune*. Both papers clearly understood the risk that a decision confirming the jury verdict would have on their reporting of civil rights struggles in the South. The *Times*, of course, agreed to their request, but Sullivan's lawyers did not. So they asked permission of the Court, which granted it over Nachman's objections.

Interestingly, Nachman did not object to the American Civil Liberties Union and its New York chapter filing an amicus brief, since he must have known that the ACLU would come down on the side of greater freedom for the press. The ACLU posed two questions, whether Alabama libel law as applied abridged the right to publish discussion and criticism of the government, in contravention to the First Amendment, and second, whether the trial denied petitioners due process and equal protection of the laws as guaranteed in the Fourteenth Amendment.

The ACLU was particularly concerned that the lower courts had refused to recognize the difference between criticism of a private person, which might be defamatory, and that of a public official, which it believed to be fully protected. It also took issue with Sullivan's claim that commercial speech such as a paid advertisement deserved less constitutional protection than did other forms of expression. The first assertion pretty much mirrored Wechsler's arguments (interestingly, his sister-in-law Nancy F. Wechsler worked on the brief), but the ACLU went further in arguing that paid advertisements, especially when dealing with political matters, should be protected.

One could never know how public officials would react to criticism, and if one reacted as Sullivan had, then the newspaper faced punishment for what the brief called a "concealed 'libel,'" one that might not be apparent to the average reader. "If newspapers are to be liable without fault to heavy damages for unwitting libels on public officials in political advertisements, the freedom of dissenting groups to secure publication of their views on public affairs and to seek support for their causes will be greatly diminished." Only recently, the brief reminded the Court, it had ruled in a case involving a radio station that "if a station were held responsible for the broadcast of libelous material, all remarks even faintly objectionable would be excluded out of an excess of caution" (*Farmers Educational & Cooperative Union v. WDAY Inc.* [1959]).

Groups advocating particular issues, such as the NAACP and, by implication, the ACLU itself, did not have the resources to publish a newspaper or operate a radio or television station, but they could raise the money for advertisements such as "Heed Their Rising Voices." To make newspapers liable for the political views of such advertisers would mean that they would no longer carry those views, for fear of lawsuit, and this shut down important voices in the political dialogue.

The briefs from the *Chicago Tribune* and *Washington Post*, as expected, fully endorsed the *Times*'s position. The former compared the Alabama law to a seditious libel act, and recounted how government officials had tried to quash criticism, going back to *De Scandalis Magnatum* in 1274 and continuing in the colonies and afterward. It included horror stories of how politicians tried to cow newspapers by threat of suit, and gave some detail to one of the cases that Wechsler had mentioned, *City of Chicago v. Tribune Co.* (1923). "The mayor of Chicago, William Hale Thompson, whose administration was marked by graft and corruption, sought to silence [the *Tribune*], his bitterest and most vocal critic. Thompson caused a libel suit for ten million dollars to be filed against the *Tribune* on behalf of the City of Chicago." The Supreme Court of Illinois voided the action, and declared it repugnant to the guarantees of free speech and press. The U.S. Supreme Court should do no less.

The *Post* brief expanded upon one of Wechsler's arguments, that in criticism of public officials, utterances that even if possibly defamatory "because of overstatement or exaggeration" should be given protection at least when honestly made in the belief that they are true. Essentially, all criticism should be protected except in cases where the publisher knew the charges to be unfounded. The brief cited another recent case, *Smith v. California* (1959), in which the state had prosecuted a bookstore owner for having an obscene book in the store. The Supreme Court reversed the conviction because there had been no evidence that Smith knew the volume was obscene. Knowledge of an act, or "scienter" in the legal phrase, would have to be shown. Otherwise comments on government and its officials should be totally immune to libel suits.

The main issues had been put out as forcefully as possible — Wechsler arguing that the case should be governed by a new standard of freedom for the press akin to the protection afforded to speech, Nachman urging the Court to stick to its traditions of leaving matters like libel to the states and respecting the decisions of local juries, and Wachtel reminding the justices that the case had come up for one reason only, the horrible treatment suffered by blacks in Alabama and other southern states. With the filing of all the briefs, the litigants and their lawyers now waited for the Court to schedule oral arguments.

# CHAPTER 8

# "May It Please the Court"

On the morning of January 6, 1964, the marshal of the Supreme Court of the United States, formally dressed as always, stood and called out, "All rise!" As the audience clambered to their feet, the nine members of the nation's highest tribunal filed in through the red velvet curtains in back of the bench and stood behind their chairs as the marshal called out the traditional opening.

"Oyez, oyez, oyez. The honorable, the Chief Justice and the Associate Justices of the Supreme Court of the United States. All persons having business before the honorable, the Supreme Court of the United States, are admonished to draw near and give their attention, for the Court is now sitting. God save the United States and this honorable court."

It had been almost four years since "Heed Their Rising Voices" had appeared in the *New York Times*, years during which a jury trial in Montgomery had found the newspaper and four of the advertisement's signers guilty of libel, a verdict confirmed by the Alabama Supreme Court. This was the last chance for the *Times* to escape what would surely be a ruinous series of libel judgments in Alabama and elsewhere, and it all depended on the nine men who now took their seats in back of the raised bench.

In the center chair sat Chief Justice Earl Warren, who had arrived in Washington in the fall of 1953. As part of a political deal the year before, Warren, the popular three-term governor of California, had endorsed Dwight Eisenhower for the Republican nomination for president. In return, Ike offered to give Warren the first seat that opened on the high court. Eisenhower no doubt thought of Warren as an associate justice, a side judge, rather than the nation's highest judicial office, and the president probably subscribed to journalist John Gunther's description of Warren as a genial second-rater, "honest, likeable, and clean . . . with little intellectual background, little genuine depth or coherent philosophy." He will, Gunther predicted, "never set the world on fire or even make it smoke." Fred Vinson's unexpected death, however, left the chief justiceship open, and Eisenhower somewhat reluctantly named Warren.

The man who would one day be called "Super Chief" had risen slowly but steadily in California politics. His record, generally, had one flaw. During the war he had given in to the patriotic hysteria and urged the removal of Japanese Americans from the West Coast. Aside from that incident, he had run an enlightened local district attorney's office, had been a crusading attorney general, and as governor of California had compiled a progressive record that attracted the liberal wing of the Republican Party. Moreover, despite the Japanese American stain, Warren had demonstrated throughout his career sensitivity to civil liberties, and during the Red Scare of the early 1950s had spoken out forcefully against Joseph McCarthy and the imposition of loyalty oaths.

Most people failed to see that Warren's genial exterior covered a steely will that had been tempered in the political furnace. Warren was never a great legal thinker, and some of his opinions have been criticized for naiveté and lack of systematic analysis. But his political skills, his ability to work harmoniously with people of different backgrounds, his talent for putting together majorities while keeping his own vision in mind, made him one of the most effective chief justices ever to occupy the center chair. Even his critics give him credit for fashioning the unanimous Court that handed down *Brown v. Board of Education* in 1954.

If he lacked a coherent jurisprudential philosophy, Warren had definite ideas about what the Constitution meant in protecting individual rights. Government, he believed, had a positive role to play in a rapidly changing society and economy, and courts in particular had a special obligation to articulate civil rights and liberties and to protect them from intrusion by the state. As his biographer and former clerk G. Edward White described it, Warren came to the Court with a "penchant for activism" and a strong "moral passion."

Immediately to the right of the chief justice (the left for those facing the bench) sits the senior associate justice, on his left the next most senior, and then alternating, with the most junior justice seated furthest on the chief's left. During the entire time Earl Warren presided over the Court. Hugo Lafayette Black sat at his right hand. Black had been a populist senator from Alabama and a firm supporter of Roosevelt's New Deal. He had also been leery of courts interposing their will against that of the people's elected representatives, and thus had enthusiastically endorsed Roosevelt's attack on the Court in 1937. As a reward, Black received Roosevelt's first appointment to the Court, and served there from 1938 until his death in 1971. There had been a major news scandal shortly after he took the oath of office when it was discovered that Black had been a member of the Ku Klux Klan, but that blew over and civil rights groups would later praise his decisions on equal protection for minorities.

During his first few terms on the bench Black's deficiencies in legal knowledge embarrassed the brethren. Black understood this, but he had a good head, learned quickly, and worked hard; by the early 1940s a clear constitutional vision had emerged in his opinions, one that he would advocate constantly for the next three decades on the bench. While courts should defer to legislative policy decisions, they had a clear obligation to play an activist role in the defense of civil liberties and individual rights. Black read constitutional wording literally. Where the First Amendment said that Congress shall make no law abridging freedom of speech, it meant just that: Congress shall make *no* law limiting speech. Black also believed that the Fourteenth Amendment "incorporated" the protections of the Bill of Rights and applied them to the states. On the other hand, Black did not believe in so-called natural rights, which could be grafted onto the Constitution by judges, and he dissented from a ruling that a right to privacy existed; he could not find the word "privacy" in the Constitution.

To the left of Warren sat William O. Douglas, Black's friend and ally. Douglas had been Sterling Professor at Yale Law School and one of the leading lights of the Realist movement, which, among other things, acknowledged that judicial prejudices played a major role in decision making. During the New Deal he had gone to Washington to join the Securities and Exchange Commission, and in the late 1930s, as the SEC chairman, he had led the fight to force Wall Street to accept reform and regulation.

Douglas may have been the smartest man on the Court; William

Brennan said he was one of the few real geniuses he had ever met. But he never fully immersed himself in the business of being a judge. In his first few years he wrote some well-reasoned opinions, but as time went on his opinions grew shorter and deliberately avoided the type of analysis (law review opinions, he called them) that could influence lower court judges and help refine doctrine.

Probably more than any other member of the Warren Court, Douglas can be characterized as a results-oriented justice, interested only in the right result and not too concerned with explaining the jurisprudential steps one took to get there. As the years went by he moved closer to Black's absolutist view of constitutionally protected rights, especially speech. But it would be a mistake to see him as Black's shadow. Douglas, more than any other member of the Warren Court, stood willing to constitutionalize rights not found spelled out in the document, so long as he considered them basic to individual liberty. In the best common law tradition, Douglas ignored contemporary reliance on either precedent or textual analysis to discover a right to procreation as well as to privacy.

Sitting next to Black was Tom Campbell Clark. A protégé of Sam Rayburn, the Texas-raised Clark had come to the Justice Department in 1937 and had uncomplainingly helped direct the relocation of more than 100,000 Japanese Americans during the war. He had also prosecuted war contract frauds uncovered by the Truman Committee, and he and Harry Truman soon became friends. When Truman became president in 1945, he wanted some people around him he knew and trusted, and named Clark attorney general.

During the Truman administration Clark served as chief enforcer of the controversial loyalty program, and he brought these attitudes with him to the Court in security cases. But he also developed sensitivity to civil rights, and he entered the government on the side of the NAACP for the first time in the restrictive covenants case, *Shelley v. Kraemer* (1948). Despite his southern origins, he backed Truman in his civil rights program.

After the 1951 steel seizure case, in which Clark and a majority of the Court had ruled against the administration's takeover of the steel mills, Truman called Clark "my biggest mistake. . . . He's about the dumbest man I think I've ever run across." Court historians have disagreed, and some consider Clark one of the most underrated justices in modern history. He wrote his own opinions (unlike other Truman appointees) and while basically conservative was also open-minded. Under Warren's tutelage he grew receptive to viewpoints he might have earlier dismissed. Clark, for example, delivered the Court's opinion in the landmark case of *Mapp v. Ohio* (1961), which applied the Fourth Amendment warrant requirements to the states.

On the other side of the bench sat Eisenhower's second appointment, John Marshall Harlan, whose grandfather had been the sole dissenter in *Plessy v. Ferguson* (1896). Often known as Harlan II, he was basically conservative, but he brought great learning and high legal skills to the Court, and quickly earned a reputation as a "lawyer's judge," one whose opinions spoke not only to theoretical concerns but also to the practical issues that lawyers, judges, and prosecutors needed to understand. A Harlan opinion always received great respect and a careful reading in the other chambers, even if one did not agree with its conclusion. One scholar declared that Harlan's opinions "have not been exceeded in professional competence by any Supreme Court Justice since Brandeis."

Although Harlan came to be looked on as "the conservative conscience of an ever more activist Court," his conservatism was a far cry from either of the Truman appointees and certainly from that of the Four Horsemen, the opponents of the New Deal in the 1930s. He respected precedent, but did not make it his only criterion; while willing to overrule an earlier decision, he demanded a very strong case for doing so. He did not accept Black's blanket application of the Bill of Rights to the states, and in criminal cases tended to see whether the police and prosecutorial behavior passed a "fundamental fairness" test. His was a Burkean conservatist, married to a concern for individual rights, especially those protected under the First Amendment.

Eisenhower's next appointment would in the long run prove perhaps the most influential. Although the president and his attorney general, Herbert Brownell, believed William Joseph Brennan Jr. to be a moderate, he soon emerged as the Court's most important liberal and Chief Justice Warren's right-hand man. During the 1960s the regular conference of all the justices would invariably be preceded by a private meeting between the two to plan strategy — Warren handling the political aspects of coalition building and Brennan providing the jurisprudential arguments.

Brennan's influence, however, derived not from his judicial skills, which, while impressive, were not overwhelming. Instead, much of it came from his personality, his friendliness, his political instincts, and above all, from his uncanny ability to define a liberal consensus that could bring in centrists and even some conservatives. Brennan could massage an opinion to cut away the sharp jurisprudential edges and thus make it palatable to those who would never have accepted the results if Black or Douglas had proposed them. Brennan got on well with his colleagues and understood that a vote against him on one case never precluded a future vote for his position in another.

Brennan's priorities in terms of individual rights emerged fairly early and clearly. The Bill of Rights gives to every person enormous protection against the state. The citizen cannot be stopped from expressing views, petitioning the government, or exercising the whole range of liberties Americans held dear. The government, on the other hand, must always be held in check, and the judiciary has the responsibility to make sure there is no established church, no infringement on the rights of people accused of crimes, no interference with personal autonomy or privacy. Brennan may have been the judicial activist par excellence, because unlike Douglas (who said the only soul he had to save was his own), Brennan concentrated on writing opinions that could serve as guides to lower court judges, and thus make his high court opinions the law of the land.

Eisenhower's last appointment, Potter Stewart, proved to be one of the ablest and most interesting men on the Court. At age 44 he had been one of the youngest men ever appointed to the high court, and gave off an air of vigor and youth that at times seemed almost out of place on the bench. Stewart loved being a judge, and once remarked that it involved "all the fun of practicing law without the bother of clients." Although Douglas characterized Stewart as a conservative, almost all labels seemed meaningless when applied to him. Stewart himself said that he had enough trouble figuring out what liberal, conservative, or activist meant in the political world, and they had no meaning on the Court. Asked to describe himself, he declared simply: "I am a lawyer." One of his law clerks called him the quintessential common law judge, and that may be the best clue to understanding him.

Although common law judges are nominally bound by precedent, they also have the obligation of squaring the legal rules of the past with current needs, fulfilling Holmes's famous aphorism that "the life of the law has not been logic; it has been experience." Stewart could parse cases with the best of his colleagues, but he had a keen sensitivity to how law would actually work in the real world and of the danger of erecting inflexible and irrelevant rules. He felt many people would remember him only for his comment in a 1964 case when he declared he would not attempt to define pornography, "but I know it when I see it." Overall his decisions are perhaps more conservative than liberal, but certainly not hidebound. A common law judge tries to figure out what rules will do the least harm to past decisions and still keep the law flexible for current needs.

At the far end of the bench on Warren's right sat John Kennedy's first appointment, Byron R. White, who brought an impressive lists of first with him—first All-American back, first former pro football player, and first Supreme Court clerk to become a member of the Court. White had impressed Kennedy by his personal courage in handling the Freedom Riders' protests in Alabama in the spring of 1961. Aside from civil rights—for which he remained a strong advocate during his three decades on the bench—White tended to be pragmatic and conservative, a lot like Stewart, but more dispassionate and reserved. During the Warren years it would be difficult to classify him, but he grew more conservative over time, and seemed to have found his home with the conservatives of the succeeding Burger and Rehnquist Courts.

The newest appointee, Arthur Joseph Goldberg, had been Kennedy's secretary of labor. The youngest of eleven children of an immigrant fruit peddler, he had worked his way through Northwestern Law School, graduating first in his class. He then developed a highly successful labor law practice, and became counsel to the AFL-CIO. Goldberg got along with his colleagues, championed an activist role for the Court, and was not afraid to take on new issues. He noted that his predecessor, Felix Frankfurter, "always was fearful that the Court would injure itself [by taking controversial issues]. . . . Well, it's not the function of a Supreme Court Justice to worry about the Court injuring itself. It's the sworn duty of a Supreme Court Justice to do justice under law and apply the Constitution." His good friend Bill Douglas could not have said it better.

Goldberg's appointment changed the whole tenor of the Court. The brilliant Felix Frankfurter, once he realized that Earl Warren would not follow his advice, opposed him on a number of issues, and became the leader of the Court's conservative bloc in the late 1950s and early 1960s. By 1964 many of Frankfurter's allies had left the bench — Robert Jackson, Sherman Minton, Harold Burton, and Charles Whittaker — to be replaced by liberals or moderate conservatives. With the appointment of Goldberg to replace Frankfurter, the liberal bloc now had five solid votes — Warren, Black, Douglas, Brennan, and Goldberg — and the era that historian Scot Powe has called "History's Warren Court" began. (The Court became even more liberal when Abe Fortas replaced Goldberg in 1965, and Thurgood Marshall replaced Clark in 1967.)

*Brown* and its follow-up decisions of the 1950s helped accelerate the civil rights movements, and the Warren Court never abandoned its commitment to equal protection. But look at some of the major cases decided by the Court after Goldberg joined it:

- *Engel v. Vitale* (1962), which struck down mandatory school prayer as a violation of the Establishment Clause;
- *NAACP v. Button* (1963), which voided a Virginia barratry law used to prevent the NAACP and other civil rights organizations from bringing anti-segregation suits;
- *Gideon v. Wainwright* (1963), which held that the Sixth Amendment right to counsel applied to the states and that lawyers had to be provided in all felony cases;
- *Gray v. Sanders* (1963), a lead-up to *Reynolds v. Sims* (1964), which required all state legislatures to reapportion on the basis of one-person, one-vote;
- *Abington Township v. Schempp* (1963), which extended the logic of *Engel* to prohibit Bible reading as well;
- *Sherbert v. Verneri* (1963), which required states to make accommodations for religious beliefs when determining state-sponsored benefits, such as unemployment compensation;
- *Massiah v. United States* (1964), the first in a series of cases that would expand and tie together the Fifth and Sixth Amendment rights of persons accused of crimes, and which would culminate in *Miranda v. Arizona* (1966);

- *Heart of Atlanta Motel v. United States* and *Katzenbach v. McClung* (1964), which upheld in broad terms the 1964 Civil Rights Act;
- *Freedman v. Maryland* (1965), which struck down state censorship of motion pictures;
- *Griswold v. Connecticut* (1965), which established a constitutional right of privacy;
- *South Carolina v. Katzenbach* (1966), which upheld the Voting Rights Act of 1965;
- *Harper v. Virginia State Board of Elections* (1966), which struck down the use of poll taxes in state elections;
- *Loving v. Virginia* (1967), which struck down state laws against interracial marriages;
- *Katz v. United States* (1967), which made all wiretaps subject to Fourth Amendment requirements that police first seek a warrant with probable cause;
- *Duncan v. Louisiana* (1968), which held that the Sixth Amendment right to a jury trial applied to the states in all cases that, if in federal court, would require a jury;
- *Epperson v. Arkansas* (1968), which struck down a state law forbidding the teaching of evolution in public schools;
- *Tinker v. Des Moines Independent Community School District* (1969), which upheld the rights of students to engage in nondisruptive political protest even in schools;
- *Stanley v. Georgia* (1969), which upheld the right of a person to watch allegedly obscene films in the privacy of his home;
- *Brandenburg v. Ohio* (1969), which finally did away with the crime of seditious libel in the United States.

This is, of course, only a partial list, and extends to 1969. But the lawyers arguing *New York Times v. Sullivan* in January 1964 certainly saw the way the Court had been going. Roland Nachman claimed that the only way he could lose was if the Court abandoned more than a century of precedent, but in cases such as *Brown v. Board of Education*, *Engel v. Vitale*, and others, the Court had done just that, and it could not have filled him with optimism. While Herbert Wechsler might have taken some comfort from the fact that the Court had shown itself more receptive to protecting civil liberties, especially First Amendment rights, there was no guarantee that they would agree to his proposal that the Press Clause trumped the libel laws of all fifty states and the District of Columbia.

Up until the Civil War, oral argument could be the determining factor in a case, even after the Court demanded briefs starting in 1821. Moreover, unlike today, when except in rare cases oral argument is limited to one hour, lawyers could speak for days. The story is told that when Daniel Webster, arguing in the Dartmouth College case, ended with the words "It is a small college . . . and yet there are those who love it," many in the room were in tears, including Chief Justice John Marshall. Webster won the case.

In our time, because every case is briefed, the record is provided, and clerks provide bench memoranda of the important legal questions involved, a number of commentators believe that oral argument is no longer important. Some justices practically ignore it, and William O. Douglas supposedly used the time to answer his mail, although he apparently kept one ear open in case anything interesting might be said.

Under the rules of the court, advocates may not read their arguments, and the Court frowns on the type of oratorical flourishes that nineteenth-century lawyers such as Webster used. Justices will pepper the lawyer in front of them with questions, often to the point that he or she may not be able to develop the points essential to the case. A good lawyer can answer the questions and do so in a manner to emphasize his or her argument. A successful oral argument is not a lecture but a conversation, one in which the justices learn something new about the case.

In the brief a lawyer is making the best and strongest argument possible, but in oral argument the justices will raise questions about those arguments. How far are you willing to go in extending the law? Would this apply in all cases or only ones in which certain conditions governed? Why should we reverse a precedent that has served us well? And the lawyer must answer these questions, even if he or she is being bombarded by questions from other justices.

Court watchers say that while few cases have been won in oral argument, many have been lost. Under what can sometimes be relentless questioning from the bench, even the most experienced advocate may slip up. To give a recent example, in a case dealing with the McCain-Feingold campaign finance reform law, an assistant solicitor general was attempting to defend the law's provision that there could be no electioneering communication in a period before primary or general elections. One of the justices asked did that mean that if a book had been written attacking or defending a candidate, the government could ban circulation of that book prior to the election. The flustered attorney said that yes, that would be possible, and even those justices in favor of the law were appalled at this statement.

Wechsler and Nachman both had previously argued before the Supreme Court and knew what to expect. Wechsler had more experience, a dozen or so cases, but Nachman was considered a very good lawyer, one who could think quickly on his feet. In 1964 the Court allowed two hours for oral argument, a long time to defend your position against questions designed to probe the weakness of your case.

It was clear from the start that the justices were paying close attention to the arguments in this case. They had copies of the briefs before them and the record nearby, and when asking questions often referred to a specific page. Shortly after Wechsler began at 12:30, Justice Brennan called out, "I am sorry, I am having difficulty hearing you." Wechsler began again, in a stronger voice: "The writ calls for review of a judgment of the Supreme Court of Alabama which in our submission poses hazards for the freedom of the press not confronted since the early days of the Republic." As in his briefs, Wechsler would emphasize his main theme — the civil law of libel had been unconstitutionally used by state officials to punish statements critical of their official conduct. The second question involved how far a state could reach to impose this type of punishment, the jurisdictional matter, but as it turned out Wechsler never really got to develop this matter. For him and for the justices, the core issue remained freedom of the press.

The justices listened intently and without interrupting Wechsler while he went over the history of the case — the appearance of the advertisement in the newspaper, the demands for retraction, the letter to the governor but no letter to Sullivan because his name had not been mentioned, the resulting lawsuit, and the suits still pending. The subject matter of the ad had been civil rights, and he went through the various paragraphs talking about the students and about the Reverend King. Wechsler also noted that the title of the ad, "Heed Their Rising Voices," had come from a *Times* editorial, "which indicates accurately the sympathy with which this newspaper has viewed the Negro mass demonstrations in the South." The text of the ad "was thus a statement of protest," but once having traversed this territory, he said little more about civil rights.

Wechsler had to deal with the question of accuracy, since under Alabama law truth served as a complete defense in libel law. The *Times* had been unable to avail itself of this defense because of the factual errors in the ad. He admitted that factual errors existed: "the statement was inaccurate in saying, as it did, that the students refused to register. They didn't refuse to register. And more than that, the ad was wrong in stating that their dining hall was padlocked in an attempt to starve them into submission." Martin Luther King Jr. had not been arrested seven times, as the ad claimed, but only four.

Wechsler could not understand how anything in the advertisement referred either directly or indirectly to L. B. Sullivan. "The pleading did not separate out any particular statement. And under the Alabama practice no innuendo need be alleged. So we are at a loss — and it gives, I may say, a very unreal quality to this proceeding — we are at a loss to know precisely in what respect the Respondent claims that he was libeled." The best he could suggest is that because the ad mentioned the police, and Sullivan served as commissioner in charge of the police, then anything said about the police should be interpreted as an attack on him. Wechsler considered this view "fantastic," but the trial court agreed with it, and the Alabama Supreme Court approved as well.

Only the Reverend King had been mentioned by name in the ad, and in all other instances the ad referred to plural subjects: "they," "southern violators," "police." At this point Justice White asked whether the ad referred necessarily to local police. Could it also include state police? "It could be the state police," Wechsler agreed. "It could be."

Justice Harlan seemed puzzled by the fact that the suit had taken place when there had been so little presence by the newspaper in Alabama.

MR. JUSTICE HARLAN: How many days was this advertisement published?

MR. WECHSLER: One day,

MR. JUSTICE HARLAN: Just one day?

MR. WECHSLER: Just March 29th.

MR. JUSTICE HARLAN: 394 copies, you say?

MR. WECHSLER: 394 copies went to Alabama, of which some 350 went to mail subscribers . . . and the balance went . . . to news dealers in Alabama, who simply sold them. So I suppose you would get the New York Times at a few newsstands in Alabama the way you would get the Montgomery Advertiser in Times Square in New York City if you look for it.

Wechsler then jumped back to his First Amendment argument, noting that the courts below had refused to even consider it because the First Amendment did not protect libelous statements. The trial judge had told the jury that the statements were libelous per se, and when a statement is libelous per se, then falsity and malice are presumed, so the plaintiff did not have to prove damages. The amount of punitive damages would be set by the jury. This caught Justice Brennan's ear.

MR. JUSTICE BRENNAN: In any event I gather there is no proof of actual damages, other than as flows from the supposed presumption?

MR. WECHSLER: Exactly. . . . He was asked if he could show he was hurt in any way, and in no way was he hurt. And the record is absolutely clear on that.

Wechsler had now used up more than half the time allotted him. He had described the advertisement in detail in order to bolster his arguments that the material was generally true and that in no way did it refer to Sullivan. He had asserted that this use of libel law violated the First Amendment, but he now needed to expand that theory and convince the justices of the unconstitutionality of what had happened.

MR. WECHSLER: Our first proposition is that this action was judged in Alabama by an unconstitutional rule of law offensive to the First Amendment, and offensive on its face to the First Amendment. Taking that rule, what it amounts to is that a public official is entitled to recover presumed and punitive damages subject to no legal limit in amount for the publication of a statement critical of his official action of an agency under his general supervision, if the court finds that the statement tends to injure reputation – which the court did find here – and the jury finds that the statement makes a reference to him.

The only defense available is if the statement is true in all its factual and material particulars. . . . So in that sense, as applied to this kind of a statement, we are attacking the constitutionality of the majority rule as it appears in the black letter law.

MR. JUSTICE BRENNAN: The basic assumption behind that contention, if I understand you correctly, is that a state fashioning of a common law rule may violate the Constitution.

MR. WECHSLER: Certainly. Certainly we assume that, but I shouldn't suppose that is controversial. That was assumed in the Bridges case, for contempt. It was true in the Cantwell case.

MR. JUSTICE GOLDBERG: . . . The state may obviously fashion libel and slander rules without offending the First Amendment. It is the particular rule which is fashioned under these circumstances that you assail?

MR. WECHSLER: This rule, as applied to officials, the criticism of official conduct, which we submit is what the First Amendment of the Constitution of the United States, I would not say was exclusively about, but was primarily about, we are actually making here, in relation to this rule of law, the same argument that James Madison made and that Thomas Jefferson made with respect to the validity of the Sedition Act of 1798.

MR. JUSTICE BRENNAN: How far does this go, Mr. Wechsler? As long as the criticism is addressed to official conduct?

MR. WECHSLER: Yes.

MR. JUSTICE BRENNAN: To official conduct? Are there any limits whatever which take it outside the protection of the First Amendment?

MR. WECHSLER: If I take my instruction from James Madison, I would have to say that within any references that Madison made, I can see no toying with limits or with exclusions.

MR. JUSTICE BRENNAN: The First Amendment gives it, in effect, an absolute prudence to criticize –

MR. WECHSLER: The First Amendment was precisely designed to

do away with seditious libel, the punishment for criticism of the government and criticism of officials.

MR. JUSTICE GOLDBERG: And this applies not only to newspapers but to everybody?

MR. WECHSLER: Exactly. Of course.

MR. JUSTICE GOLDBERG: In other words, you are not arguing here for the special rule that applies to newspapers?

MR. WECHSLER: Certainly not. We are talking about the full ambit of the First Amendment.

This was the heart of the argument — the First Amendment to the Constitution had meant to protect citizens and newspapers when they criticized public officials for the conduct of their office. Seditious libel had been instituted to protect the reputation of the Crown and the king's deputies, and the truth of the charges mattered not. The Framers, according to Wechsler, intended to do away with seditious libel in any form, and the State of Alabama had attempted to use the common law rules of libel as a bludgeon against criticism of public conduct. This could not be allowed, even if there were minor errors in the allegations.

Wechsler and the justices traded comments on what could be used as a defense in Alabama, and the *Times* attorney showed them how difficult it would be if there was even a single factual error. One could not even avail oneself of the defense of fair comment in an editorial if one statement was untrue. But how far could one take this? If a minor factual error existed, it was one thing; but what if there was major falsehood?

MR. JUSTICE GOLDBERG: So to follow this through, it is a logical conclusion that a citizen would have the right under that broad proposition to state falsely, knowingly, and maliciously that his Mayor, his Governor, had accepted a bribe of one million dollars to commit an official act, and . . . the Mayor could not sue for libel?

MR. WECHSLER: That is right. What he would have to do is to make a speech, using his official privilege as Mayor, to make a speech answering this charge. And that of course is what most

Mayors do, and what the political history of the country has produced.

But what about the jury findings, some of the justices wanted to know. Traditionally the high court had deferred to findings of fact made by the jury. Did Wechsler believe the Court should review those facts? Definitely, he responded, because in this case the jury determination had yielded a constitutional violation.

All told, Wechsler had made a strong case, but he and the justices understood that in order for the *Times* to win, the Court would have to forge an entirely new rule of what the First Amendment protected, and how far that protection extended. To do so, as Roland Nachman reminded them, would mean abandoning decades of precedent and fealty to other constitutional provisions.

Nachman began by addressing what he termed "a sharp difference" between Wechsler's analysis of the facts and his. Where the lawyer for the *Times* had seen a great conspiracy to silence the press, he saw the case as a normal civil suit — there had been a jury trial, a verdict, a motion for a new trial, and review in the state's highest appellate court. Moreover, the very substantial record that had been produced supported the finding that the *New York Times* had libeled L. B. Sullivan. As for the constitutional issue, "we are here after a jury trial, with all that means in terms of the Seventh Amendment."

Justice Goldberg then wanted to know if Nachman believed that the Seventh Amendment applied to the states through the Fourteenth. Nachman said that he did, and because of that, appellate courts had no more right to review state jury verdicts than they did federal jury verdicts. Both subtly, and sometimes more overtly, Nachman essentially told the high court that it had no business, and no precedent, to review what the Alabama jury had determined.

He then reviewed the case, and his view of what the advertisement and subsequent events meant stood diametrically opposed from Wechsler's analysis. The *Times* had refused to retract regarding Sullivan, because it had claimed that the ad did not refer to Sullivan. But a jury had found that it did, and that meant the failure to retract implicated the paper in libel per se and the subsequent damages. The *Times* did not plead truth, which Alabama law made clear was a complete defense against libel, because it could not. "If the *Times* had felt this ad was true or any part of it was true, it could have set that out in its plea, but it did not." This reflected not on Alabama law, but on the mistruths in the advertisement.

Wechsler had emphasized that Sullivan had not been mentioned in the ad, and therefore the jury had no basis to conclude that he had been libeled. But the jury had clearly determined that the ad referred to Sullivan, and he read from the transcript of the trial to prove that witnesses testified they did not believe the allegations against the commissioner were true. At this point one of the justices broke in.

MR. JUSTICE GOLDBERG: I don't know what references you are making, but if the witness were asked, "Would you believe it true that Mr. Sullivan bombed Mr. King's home?" I assume the answer would be "No, I would not believe it is true." Is that the type of questioning you have reference to?

MR. NACHMAN: No, sir. The type of question I have reference to is whether the ad — the words in the ad — I am addressing myself to Mr. Wechsler's contention, as I understand it, sir, that this was only incorrect in some particulars. I am saying that what went to the jury was an admission really by counsel for the *New York Times* from the very outset of this case, from the pleadings, from what happened during the trial, and from the evidence . . . that this was false not just in some particular but completely false, and there was no attempt made at the trial by the *Times* to say that any of this was true.

MR. JUSTICE GOLDBERG: I looked over the record, and I thought there was evidence at the trial which showed the truth in part of the allegations of the ad. There were some inaccuracies, as I read the record, in the ad, and it is correct there was no attempt to show that Mr. Sullivan bombed the house, et cetera, but I didn't read the record to do what you are now saying, in saying that the ad at large and every sentence of it was totally and completely false. Are you arguing to us the case went to the jury on the posture that this ad was from beginning to end totally false?

MR. NACHMAN: Yes, sir.

MR. JUSTICE GOLDBERG: You are?

MR. NACHMAN: What I am saying, sir, is that there was evidence from the *Times* itself, from the pleadings, from statement of its counsel, from evidence in the case, in addition to this, which could justify a jury verdict that the entire ad was false. . . .

MR. JUSTICE BRENNAN: May we reexamine that?

MR. NACHMAN: We say no, sir, unless there is no basis whatever. It is devoid of reason. In the Thompson case—

MR. JUSTICE WHITE: You mean reexamine the facts?

MR. NACHMAN: That's right. We say that the Seventh Amendment protects this verdict unless this Court finds there is no reasonable basis whatever for it, no evidence at all to support it. Thompson versus Louisville—

MR. JUSTICE BRENNAN: The Seventh Amendment?

MR. NACHMAN: Yes, sir.

MR. JUSTICE BRENNAN: A state trial?

MR. NACHMAN: A state trial—the jury verdict reexamined otherwise in accordance with the rules of common law, which we understand the rules of common law protect State verdicts as well as federal verdicts.

Nachman actually stood on fairly solid ground here, and just as Wechsler had asked the Court to forge a new rule on the First Amendment, so Nachman wanted the Court to adhere to the rules it had followed, namely that it would review only matters of law and would not second-guess juries on findings of fact. Moreover, he tried to place a constitutional mantle over this practice, claiming that the Seventh Amendment protected jury findings from appellate reversal. The wording of the amendment would seem to support his argument—"no fact tried by a jury shall be otherwise re-examined in any Court of the United States." He stood on far less firm ground when he claimed that the Court had incorporated the Seventh Amendment and applied it to the states. In cases to that time the Court had read the amendment as applying only to cases tried in federal courts, and under common law judges could overturn jury findings in particular circumstances. The Court might well have used this case to do what he urged, incorporate the amendment.

He also wanted the Court to adhere to its precedents in holding libel outside First Amendment protection. When Justice Brennan asked him whether the high court could reexamine whether the statements in the advertisement had been libelous as a constitutional matter, Nachman urged the justices to do as they had in the past, leave "the characterization of publications as libelous or not libelous to the States." Of course, if the finding had been ridiculous, for example a person had stated that so-and-so had blond hair and a court had found that libelous, it could certainly be reviewed. The conduct charged in this case, however, "is within the normal, usual, rubric framework of libel. . . . We think we are well within the classic definition of libel."

Nachman steadfastly stuck to his guns: jury verdicts should not be overturned, and there was no First Amendment issue here. The great *New York Times*, one of the most influential newspapers in the country, had not even followed its own rules. It had been unable to plead truth because there were falsehoods in the ad; it did not matter if some parts of it were correct, because it was within the traditional purview of a jury to find that the ad referred to Sullivan and that it was false in its entirety, and they could award appropriate damages. When Justice Harlan wanted to know if there had been any actual damages, Nachman replied, "In the sense of showing any actual out-of-pocket loss of money at that time, no, sir, there was no showing of that. But we submit that the jury could fairly take into account future loss of earnings. . . . That is allowed in Alabama."

Justice White wanted to follow a thread that Wechsler had made, on the extent that newspapers would be immune from libel for criticism of public officials.

> MR. JUSTICE WHITE: So you are saying this case unavoidably represents the question of whether or not a person may tell a deliberate lie about a public official. Is that the issue?
>
> MR. NACHMAN: No, sir, that is not the issue.
>
> MR. JUSTICE WHITE: Doesn't it present that issue? Whether you may publish a deliberate lie?
>
> MR. NACHMAN: Yes, your Honor, we think that the defendant in order to succeed must convince this Court that a newspaper corporation has an absolute immunity from anything it publishes. . . . As I understand their contention and as I understand what they said it to be, if a newspaper charges, say, a mayor or police

commissioner with taking a bribe, that there is absolute immunity against a libel suit in that regard. We think that is something brand new in our jurisprudence. We think that it would have a devastating effect on this nation.

MR. JUSTICE WHITE: But if it were held here that a newspaper can publish a falsehood which it thought to be true, that would still not save the *Times* here?

MR. NACHMAN: You mean a reasonable belief in truth?

MR. JUSTICE WHITE: Yes.

MR. NACHMAN: No, sir, not under Alabama law. It would have to be true.

It is impossible to say that any given statement swayed the justices one way or the other, but clearly Justice White and some of the others found this statement disturbing. It is one thing to publish allegations that are known to be false; it is quite another to publish something that a reporter or editor has every reason to believe true and later discovers it is in error. Under Nachman's theory the latter would put a newspaper at as much risk as the former, and clearly have a chilling effect on the First Amendment. Wechsler had claimed that if one had to worry that any critical statement might be open to suit, papers would never print anything but praise.

There was one final issue that Nachman wanted to address, and that was Wechsler's argument that a significant difference existed between libelous statements about public officials and those made against private citizens. "We submit this Court and no other court has ever made a distinction between libel of public officials and libel of private persons."

Before he could finish, however, Justice Brennan had some more questions about the size of the jury award. Had the jury come in with a verdict for $5 million instead of $500,000, would Sullivan still be entitled to it? Of course, Nachman responded, the size of the award is entirely in the hands of the jury, and "as we understood the cases of this Court it has not heretofore gone into the question of the excessiveness or inadequacy of damages."

At 2:33, Nachman thanked the Court and sat down, and the clerk intoned. "The Honorable Court is now adjourned until tomorrow at 10 o'clock."

Both men had done well, neither had made any gaffes, and both had emphasized the key points of his argument. When they left the Court that afternoon neither of them could have had any idea which way the Court would go. Unlike some cases where observers can get a hint of the justices' preferences by the friendliness or hostility of their questions, that had not been the case here. There were no clues whether the Court would strike out and adopt a radically new interpretation of the First Amendment, or adhere to its prior jurisprudence regarding jury findings.

The next morning Nachman returned to the Court to argue *Abernathy v. Sullivan*, the appeal of the four black ministers, now represented by William Rogers, a former attorney general who had written the amicus brief for the *Washington Post*, and Samuel Pierce, a former New York judge associated with Wachtel.

Rogers denounced Sullivan's suit as a "perversion of the judicial process," and said that if the Court upheld the verdict, it would be the greatest threat to a free press in the twentieth century. In a point not made in the *Times* case, Rogers pointed out that Alabama had a maximum penalty of $500 in cases of criminal libel (the malicious publication of durable defamation, intended to provoke the victim to wrath and to deprive him of the benefits of public confidence and social intercourse), a thousandth of the damages awarded Sullivan. In addition to a threat to the press, the suit also attacked other First Amendment freedoms crucial to the civil rights movement — freedom of speech and of assembly. If the Alabama judgment was allowed to stand, there would indeed be dire consequences.

Just as Wachtel had emphasized race in the brief, so Pierce spoke about the racial aspects of the trial. Sullivan and the others who filed suit against the *Times* and the ministers had one purpose, to "suppress and punish the voices for racial equality." Once again noting that the black lawyers for the men were not addressed as "Mr." in the trial, a trial that took place in an atmosphere of "racial bias and passion," Pierce claimed that one could not find the equal protection of the laws in a judicial process where equality of courtesy went missing.

In response Nachman told Justice Harlan that the basic issues he had argued earlier — the inviolability of jury verdicts and respect for Alabama law — were the same here. Some of the justices, however, were upset at how the ministers had been hauled into the case. They had received a letter demanding a retraction when they did not even know about the ad, and Sullivan had filed his suit before they had a chance to learn about it or consult their attorneys.

Justice Black wanted to know what evidence would have been presented to the jury to justify a finding that they were responsible for their names appearing in the ad. The ministers' names were there, Nachman said, and they had failed to respond to Sullivan's demand for retraction. Under Alabama law, a "failure to break silence indicates they did what we say they did."

This prompted Justice Goldberg to note that "I get a lot of mail every day that I don't answer. Without a prior relationship between the parties, I can't conceive of a rule of law that says you must reply." The chief justice said that he got dozens of letters every day accusing him of one thing or another, including making libelous statements. "If he has made no such statements, must he reply or suffer a one-half million dollar libel judgment." The justices seemed astounded when Nachman said that "when it becomes important later in a lawsuit, then we submit his failure to reply may be evidence that he made it."

If Nachman had held his own against the *Times*, he did far worse in the case against the ministers. Clearly the justices sympathized with men who even Nachman admitted had not signed on to the ad, but could be held liable under Alabama law afterward because they had not responded to a letter about which they knew nothing. Conceivably the Court could have distinguished the cases, and dismissed the suits against the ministers while upholding the verdict against the *Times*. Nachman had, however, claimed that the same arguments governed both cases. All he and the other parties could do now was wait.

# "Uninhibited, Robust, and Wide-Open"

Shortly after oral argument, the nine justices gather in the large conference room to discuss the cases heard that week and then to vote. No one else is present, not even clerks, and if some material is needed, or if there is an urgent message for one of the justices, the most junior member goes to the door to receive the note or to ask a page to retrieve the needed folders. After the vote is taken, the chief justice, if he is in the majority, either takes the case for himself or assigns it to one of his like-minded colleagues; if the chief is in the minority, the senior justice in the majority makes the assignment. Those in the minority discuss among themselves who will write a dissent.

Whoever has the assignment then begins work on a draft, usually with the aid of one or more clerks from his or her chambers, and when the justice feels the draft states pretty much what the conference (as the justices call themselves when not sitting) decided, it goes out for comment to the other justices. Their "returns" determine what revisions have to be made, and indicate whether any justice who voted one way at the conference will change his or her mind, either to dissent or to concur only in the results but not the reasoning, or perhaps to approve of certain parts but not others.

Although in the past there have been famous lobbyists, such as Felix Frankfurter, who used to go from chamber to chamber to convince his colleagues to vote with him, a far more accurate portrayal of the court is in Justice Lewis Powell's description of nine separate law offices under one roof. Each justice has clerks, a secretary, and access to the Court's research facilities, including one of the best law libraries in the country. Much of the fine tuning of a written opinion comes from the returns, where a justice can say he or she agrees completely and "joins" the opinion, or may inform the writer of what words, passages, or whole sections are in their present form troubling, or says he or she cannot join as it stands.

The goal is to get what Justice William Brennan once called the most important number in the Court's work — five — the number needed for a majority. In important cases, however — and everyone agreed that *New York Times v. Sullivan* was a very important case — the justices recognized that a 5–4 vote would not do, since it would leave Alabama and other states that wielded libel laws against the press free to go on doing so, on the grounds that the Court had not really foreclosed that option. They also understood that a split decision would be a severe blow to the civil rights movement. There would have to be a large majority, preferably unanimous. The question was whether a case in which both sides appealed to important jurisprudential traditions could garner the votes of all nine justices.

In conference the chief justice speaks first, summarizing the case and indicating how he will vote; then the other justices speak, starting with the most senior of the associate justices and so on down to the newest member; there may be some discussion, and then a vote taken; the chief justice will assign the writing, although this may be done afterward so that he can make sure that the opinion assignments are balanced among the nine.

The justices then return to their chambers, and many of them talk with their clerks about what happened, but since the clerks are under a vow of silence they rarely talk about what they have heard, and usually not until years later. The justices sometimes tell stories about the conference, such as the fact that James McReynolds, a notorious anti-Semite, would often go over to the sofa to read his mail or even leave the room when Louis Brandeis spoke. Felix Frankfurter, a former law school professor, would stand and walk around the room lecturing the brethren, but never more than the forty-five minutes that a class would take. This angered William O. Douglas so much that he, too, would repair to the sofa for mail, and once, when Frankfurter had finished, Douglas announced that he had come into the conference prepared to vote as Felix suggested, but Felix had now talked him out of it! Some of the justices keep notes about the discussion and the votes as *aide-mémoire* to rely on when looking over opinion drafts to make sure they reflect the intent of the conference. William O. Douglas, who had an excellent memory and who could recall discussions and events many years afterward, kept relatively detailed narratives. While the cramped handwriting is at times hard to decipher, it is our best description of the meeting that took place on Friday, January 10, 1964, four days after oral argument.

Earl Warren went first, and immediately said the verdict had to be reversed, but was not sure on what grounds the Court should rule. He disagreed with Wechsler that there could never be libel, even with malice, but he would define "fair comment" rather broadly. Inaccuracies by themselves ought not make criticism of a public official libelous, and Warren listed the alleged factual errors, and dismissed them as inconsequential, so slight "that it can't be called libel." Alabama's rule circumscribed the First Amendment too much.

Hugo Black spoke next, and while he had often argued the absolute nature of First Amendment protection, he had doubts about how this complicated case should be resolved. He condemned the $500,000 award as clearly punitive, and the First Amendment, if nothing else, protected speech on issues of public importance. But it would be hard to reverse, because "if libel laws are at all valid on the press when it talks about public affairs, then this should be affirmed." But he came back to the idea that speech should be free when discussing matters of public affairs.

William O. Douglas spoke briefly, and said he would reverse on First Amendment grounds, and did not go into any other details of the case. In his files there is a two-page single-spaced memorandum that his clerk, Evan Schwab, had prepared for Douglas prior to the decision to grant certiorari. Schwab considered both the verdict and the half-million-dollar damage award "ridiculous"; the judgment had to be reversed because of the chilling effect it would have on the First Amendment if allowed to stand. The results, however, could not be attacked under Alabama law, and somehow or other, "new rules are going to have to be laid down."

Tom Clark questioned whether the amount of the damages could be reached on constitutional grounds, but believed that libel of private individuals might be separated from criticism of public officials, and he would create a much heavier burden of proof for government officers suing for libel. The case could be reversed, possibly because the evidence introduced did not support the charge.

John Marshall Harlan would also reverse, but he did not believe that the First Amendment necessarily prohibited libel laws even when the speech involved public officials. If the Court reversed, then it had to lay down clear rules for state libel laws so that the Court would not be inundated by subsequent suits because the judgment had been vague. He suggested that, first, there should be a high standard of proof, analogous to federal rules in denaturalization cases, and second, while punitive damages should not be outlawed, they should not be imposed without proof of actual malice.

William J. Brennan Jr. also voted to reverse. The First Amendment did not proscribe all libel laws, but it certainly protected criticism of public officials. Like Harlan, he believed there should be clear rules laid down for lower courts to follow, especially on evidence to prove actual malice, a standard that should be "clear, convincing, and unequivocal," a test that he also borrowed from the denaturalization cases.

Potter Stewart said the First Amendment protected the *Times* ad, and agreed with Harlan and Brennan on establishing clear rules. He would reverse, but, he suggested, it should be done so there could be no new trial. He would require clear proof of actual malice for any punitive damages, but he would not strike down all punitive damages, since their purpose is to deter future bad conduct.

Byron White agreed with Harlan, Brennan, and Stewart, and like Stewart thought that the obscenity cases provided a good analogy in terms of a need for conclusive proof to establish the nature of the material. He also thought that even if one followed common law rather than constitutional standards, the judgment could be reversed on evidentiary and procedural grounds, such as the presumption of damages without proof.

Arthur Goldberg, as the most junior member of the Court, spoke last. The case should be reversed, but he disagreed with Harlan's suggestions for rules, which he considered unworkable. Even if they had been in force, the judge in this case could easily have instructed the jury that the evidentiary standard had been met and malice shown. As for the idea that all punitive damages might be "constitutionally infirm," Goldberg argued that that issue should not be addressed in this case. The nature of the ad went straight to the heart of the First Amendment. The ad had not charged Sullivan with adultery, but "what kind of a commissioner you are," a matter of the conduct of public affairs that had to be fully protected under the First Amendment.

All nine justices conceded that the case, as it had been tried, followed existing Alabama law, and that the trial judge and jury, under that law, had been technically correct in finding for Sullivan. But they also agreed, with the possible exception of Black at this point, that the results had to be reversed, although no clear consensus had emerged from the meeting on the grounds for a reversal, other than the broad and rather vague rubric of the First Amendment protecting discussion of public affairs.


The chief justice, given the perceived importance of the case, might have kept the opinion for himself, as he had done in the desegregation and reapportionment cases, but Warren recognized that First Amendment jurisprudence was not his forte. He assigned the case to William Brennan, who since joining the Court had written seven majority or plurality opinions in speech cases, including *Roth*, the obscenity case that several of the justices suggested as a model for establishing rules. There also had to be some new way to protect defendants in libel suits involving public officials, and there were at least four votes to support such an approach.

More importantly, Warren trusted Brennan. Not only did the two men consult together before the Friday conferences, they had an astounding level of agreement, between 92 and 97 percent, from the 1962 term until Warren's retirement, a rate that two other ideologically compatible pairings, Black and Douglas or Frankfurter and Harlan, never achieved during a single term.

Moreover, Brennan had a technique of conceding in principle the government's power to pursue an objective, while at the same time making it extraordinarily difficult to do so. In *Roth v. United States* (1957), the obscenity case that some of the justices referred to, Brennan wrote that obscenity did not enjoy First Amendment protection, thus granting the government the power to censor obscene materials. He then imposed a test, "whether to the average person, applying contemporary community standards, the dominant theme of the material taken as a whole appeals to the prurient interests." This standard made it much harder – but not completely impossible – for local officials to prove obscenity. The concession, that government could regulate obscene speech, deflected criticism of absolutism and judicial activism, while the rules accomplished the task of strictly limiting government censorship.

For Brennan, strict scrutiny (the highest level of judicial review), compelling interests, the chilling effect, and the need for breathing space made up the vocabulary by which he would judge First Amendment questions. He was, according to Lucas Powe, the only member of the liberal majority capable of acting as principal doctrinalist, and he may have been the only one to even care about theory and doctrine at this time. In *New York Times v. Sullivan* – what some scholars call "the" First Amendment case of the era – Brennan wrote one of the great opinions of his career, and did it as Warren had hoped. He conceded the right of a state to have libel laws to protect reputation, then carved out a broad exception – comment on public officials and the conduct of their office – and laid down a rule that made it practically impossible for this group to ever win a libel case.

Following the conference discussion, Brennan had a few guidelines: the case had to be reversed, a standard had to be articulated comparable to those in the obscenity and denaturalization cases, a rule of actual malice had to be included, and comments on public officials and their work had to be distinguished from attacks on private citizens. However, no unity existed on the jurisprudential question. He could no doubt write a minimalist opinion that would apply to the *Times* case, and leave other matters to be resolved on a case-by-case basis later on. That would have been the easiest way to go, and would certainly have garnered the necessary votes. But Brennan sensed, correctly, that the conference wanted to go much further, to embrace a radical change that would breathe new meaning into the First Amendment.

On his return from the conference, Brennan sat down with his clerks and outlined the research and materials he would need from them. He finished his first draft in less than a month, had his clerks critique it, and then circulated it to the conference on February 6. The Court announced the decision a little over a month later, on March 9, but the short time between first and final draft masks the difficulties Brennan faced. Altogether he wrote some seven drafts, working to get as many of the justices to sign on as possible, and the last member did not do so until the morning of the announcement. Yet throughout he managed to keep the basic points of law enunciated in his first draft.

Brennan may have been the greatest judicial politician of his time, and by this I mean his uncanny ability to write and rewrite to take into account his colleagues' comments and objections, finally securing a majority to support his opinion. Long after the Warren Court's liberal majority evaporated in the early seventies, Brennan kept snatching victory away from the conservative majority. While the seeming unanimity of the conference would suggest that he had relatively little to do to win their support, in fact the justices did not share any consistent opinions on this case, and even if they all supported reversal, they differed on why it should be done, how it should be done, and what would be the future of state libel laws. William Brennan had his work cut out for him, and as it turned out, it proved to be one of his enduring achievements as a justice.

Brennan began with a fairly straightforward and judgment-free account of what the advertisement said (with a copy printed in the appendix to the opinion), the implication of the four ministers, the resulting trial and jury verdict, and the decision on review by the Alabama Supreme Court. He then set forth under three headings the holdings of the Court and its reasoning.

In Part I he rejected two arguments made by Sullivan's lawyers: first, that the Fourteenth Amendment is directed against state rather than private action (and this was a private libel action), and second, that the First Amendment did not apply either, since the defamatory material appeared in a paid advertisement. Brennan made short work of both these claims. The *Times* had been tried under and had now challenged a law of the State of Alabama, and nothing could more clearly be state action than a state law. The advertisement communicated information and opinions on a public matter, and this invoked the First Amendment. (The opinion, as finally handed down by the Court, will be discussed more fully later in this chapter.)

In Part II Brennan laid out the reasons why constitutional protection should be extended to defamatory and false statements, arguments that then provide the basis for the actual malice rule. A reader familiar with the final opinion and its powerful rhetoric in defense of First Amendment values will find that missing from this draft, which is a bare-bones explanation of why the Court decided as it did. But one does find some familiar concepts: the need for "breathing space" in expressing unpopular views; the commitment to freedom of expression that the First Amendment embodied, a commitment that cannot be narrowed by the imposition of labels, such as "libel"; the inevitable appearance of error in a lively debate, and therefore the inadequacy of truth as a test. He also brought in the Sedition Act of 1798, and since the damage award was a thousand times greater in this civil case than the law allowed in criminal libel, this clearly amounted to the state enforcing seditious libel. He then noted that many states had a rule protecting public officials or candidates for office from libel charges without proof of falsity or "express malice," a phrase that he used interchangeably with "actual malice."

(Although Brennan treated the phrase "actual malice" as if it had an accepted legal meaning, one scholar who examined cases in all fifty states reported that there were "as many definitions of actual malice as there are states." The common thread that ran through all the definitions related to the motivation behind the publication, and if courts found that the publisher had been motivated by spite, ill will, or a desire to do harm, that would usually suffice. However, William Prosser, the dean of tort scholars, noted that actual malice could be more than this—and also less.)

The third part proved the most difficult, and almost cost Brennan his majority. Alabama law presumed malice to exist for the purpose of awarding general damages, and for that reason the verdict had to be reversed, a point with which most of the conference concurred. He then went on to describe the evidence in this case, and concluded it to be insufficient to support a finding of actual malice. As a result, there could not be a new trial. This, of course, had been the argument that Potter Stewart had made, but a majority of the justices felt uncomfortable with it. In nearly all instances, when the high court reverses a lower appellate court ruling or the results of a trial court, it returns the case to that court for a rehearing "consistent with these findings." In other words, normal procedure would have been to return the case to Alabama for a new trial. But as Arthur Goldberg had pointed out, a trial judge could bend the rules so that a jury might return the same verdict and damages. Brennan wanted to foreclose that option completely.

Only Earl Warren joined this first draft. Brennan reworked it, and sent out a revised draft on February 17, one that secured the votes of Warren and Byron White. In the meantime Goldberg had prepared and circulated a draft concurring in the result but taking a far more absolutist First Amendment position that would have barred any libel suit by a public official and precluded the actual malice test. Black also prepared a concurrence, and Douglas instructed a clerk to start preparing a possible concurring opinion, based on *Barr v. Matteo*, a 1959 case in which the Court had held that public officials had immunity from libel for statements made as part of their official duties. Douglas would have inverted the holding to rule that private citizens and the press had absolute immunity for comments made about public officials.

Brennan had only three votes after two circulations, his own and those of Warren and White. He hoped to get Harlan, who after all had appeared very close to Brennan in the conference discussion, but although the two men exchanged several notes regarding wording, they could not seem to agree on why there should not be a new trial or how far down the line of public officials the new doctrine would go. Harlan in early March issued a draft of a concurring statement that said he would support Parts I and II, and disassociating himself from the evidentiary discussion in Part III. Moreover, he wanted to base his reason for reversal under 28 U.S.C. 2106, a section of the federal code that gave federal appellate courts power to "direct the entry of such appropriate judgment, decree, or order, or require such further proceedings to be had as may be just under the circumstances." But this section had for the most part been used primarily within the federal system, a federal appellate court directing a lower federal court to do something. To extend this reasoning to include state courts would mean the Supreme Court's assuming a vast new power, one that might be unconstitutional.

This bothered Brennan a great deal, and he tried to pull some of Harlan's ideas into another revision of the opinion, even for a time referencing § 2106. The use of the U.S. Code did not bother Tom

Clark, who now joined, giving Brennan four votes. As February ended, Brennan hoped he would soon have a fifth vote, and hoped that the changes he made to Part III would bring Harlan on board.

Then in early March the pot really began to boil, as Harlan not only backed away from earlier suggestions he had made, but thought Brennan should drop Part III entirely. Brennan would not do this, since this section would inform the legal profession that if other states tried to pursue this avenue of attacking individuals or the press the Supreme Court would step in to review the evidence. Harlan expressed disappointment, and on March 3 told Brennan he would join Parts I and II, but not III, because he did not believe it appropriate for the high court to review the evidence since other constitutional reasons existed to reverse the judgment.

That same day Brennan deleted references to § 2106, and circulated another revision, arguing that he believed "an analysis of the evidence to show its insufficiency under the constitutional rule we lay down is essential to the opinion." He reminded the justices that there were other libel suits pending against the *Times* in Birmingham and Montgomery and that fairness required that the Court explain not only the constitutional but the evidentiary rules it adopted. Potter Stewart now joined, giving Brennan his fifth vote.

But he still did not know what Black, Douglas, Harlan, or Goldberg would do. Black and Douglas sent notes saying that they had reservations about the actual malice test, and suggesting that perhaps it might be handled internally, with Brennan acknowledging in the opinion that some members of the Court did not endorse this test. Douglas did not say whether he would join Brennan's opinion, but "I have associated myself with Hugo, as you know, and if Arthur writes the way he talks, I will likely join him also." Then out of the blue, Tom Clark said he would write a concurring opinion, agreeing with Parts I and II but not III.

A troubled Brennan turned to his friend the chief justice, wanting to know what he should do. He still believed Part III necessary for the opinion, and he seemed to agree with the Douglas suggestion that he add a section noting that Black, Douglas, and Goldberg do not reach the evidentiary question of actual malice. Warren wrote back immediately: "I agree with you that III must remain in the opinion if I and II are to have any meaning. Otherwise we will merely be going through a meaningless exercise." A very relieved Brennan said, "That's precisely the argument I've been pressing on Tom [Clark]."

He now, at least for the moment, decided to ignore Harlan and Clark, and began to woo Black, Douglas, and Goldberg. Despite the fact that he intended to write separately, Black did not necessarily disapprove of Brennan's arguments. "You know of course," Black had written, "that despite my position and what I write, I think you are doing a wonderful job in the *Times* case and however it finally comes out it is bound to be a very long step towards preserving the right to communicate ideas."

Goldberg also extended a hand. "I am certainly agreeable to joining your excellent opinion," he told Brennan, "and then writing very briefly that I would go beyond to the extent I have indicated. You can count on my vote for your opinion. It would be very bad if you didn't get a court." Brennan took this for what it was, a note of encouragement, because Goldberg never wavered in his belief that the Constitution afforded an absolute immunity to press and citizens for criticism of official conduct and that there could be no actual malice test open to misuse in state courts.

Apparently Douglas and Goldberg actually wanted Brennan to get his majority, since they each agreed with more than nine-tenths of what he had written. They both then had roughly the same idea. "Why don't you just say in your opinion all justices agree to page 25. All justices agree on your malice test except Black, Douglas and Goldberg. All justices agree on your analysis of the malice evidence except Harlan and Clark. That gives you a majority for your opinion on all issues. Then all of the concurring opinions can be labeled concurring — not just in the results."

Brennan was willing, but he made one more overture to Douglas, who gave in, albeit a bit grudgingly. "If having five for the entire opinion is all important to you," he would join, provided there was a footnote that Mr. Justice Douglas has a different view on the evidence. Then Tom Clark reappeared, and said he would join if there was a minor word change in Part III, one that did not affect Brennan's main point, but meant a great deal to Clark because of his passion for the proper administration of justice.

By now Brennan was on his seventh draft, and he sent it out just before the justices met for their Friday conference on March 6. At the conference, he had a majority. Warren, Clark, Stewart, and White joined him in all three parts. Black, joined by Douglas, changed his opinion to "concurring" from "concurring in the judgment." Only Harlan and Goldberg refused to join. Brennan now set about the final polishing of the opinion, readying it for announcement the following week.

On Monday morning, just as the justices were about to leave their chambers and head for the robbing room, they received a memorandum from Harlan: "I have advised Brother Brennan, and I wish the other Brethren to know, that I am withdrawing my Separate memorandum in this case, and am unreservedly joining the majority opinion." Brennan had a unanimous court for the judgment, and only Goldberg did not join the opinion.

Why did Harlan change his mind? In part, not only Brennan but Chief Justice Warren had lobbied him ceaselessly to join. Anthony Lewis thinks that Harlan, who along with Frankfurter had been the great champions of federalism on the Warren Court, may have been influenced by Wechsler that such a ruling would not be an attack on federalism. Many believed Wechsler to be one of the nation's outstanding scholars on federalism, and Harlan knew that Wechsler would not urge a result on the Court that would be inconsistent with the demands of the federal system.

Harlan's only real complaint had been with one point in Brennan's opinion – holding that the evidence presented had been insufficient to support the constitutional test of actual malice. He believed that the ad in the *Times* was protected by the First Amendment, that the high court had jurisdiction to hear the case, and that public officials suing for libel should have to meet a higher standard of proof than did private citizens. As for the term "actual malice," Harlan had used it himself at the conference on February 6. He might not have agreed with Black's view that the *rationale* for protecting speech is not important, but the *result* is. Harlan was too careful a lawyer and a judge to take that view. Finally, Brennan had tried to accommodate him, and he agreed with so much of the end result that he may well have come to believe that his minor qualms were not worth registering.

At ten o'clock in the morning of March 9, 1964, the marshal of the Court stood and began his ritual chant, "Oyez. Oyez. Oyez." The justices filed in, and Chief Justice Warren announced that the first decision would be in number 39, *New York Times v. Sullivan*, together with number 40, *Abernathy et al. v. Sullivan*. He looked down the bench and nodded to Brennan.

The first paragraph telegraphed the results: "We are required in this case to determine for the first time the extent to which the constitutional protections for speech and press limit a State's power to award damages in a libel action brought by a public official against critics of his official conduct." The Court was not going to "review" or "consider" the question, but "determine" it, and on constitutional grounds.

After reviewing the facts in the two cases in a relatively straightforward manner, Brennan concluded his introductory section by declaring, "We reverse the judgment. We hold that the rule of law applied by the Alabama courts is constitutionally deficient for failure to provide the safeguards for freedom of speech and press that are required by the First and Fourteenth Amendments in a libel action brought by a public official against critics of his official conduct. We further hold that under the proper safeguards the evidence presented in this case is constitutionally insufficient to support the judgment for respondent." Reporters, lawyers, and other in the chamber that day would have understood by now that the decision would be an important one that implicated crucial constitutional principles, and not merely the reversal of the lower courts on technical grounds.

(In a footnote Brennan explained that since the case had been decided on constitutional grounds of freedom of speech and press, other claims presented by the *Times* and the four ministers relating to due process and jurisdiction did not have to be addressed. Moreover, in the debate as to whether the *Times* had made a special or a general appearance, a key question as to whether the Alabama trial court had jurisdiction, "we cannot say that this ruling lacks 'fair or substantial support' in prior Alabama decisions." This was a minor and, in terms of this case, inconsequential victory for Nachman, but it did leave the long-arm statutes of Alabama and the other states intact.)

Parts I and II had enjoyed full support from the beginning. In Part I Brennan quickly disposed of two of Alabama's claims — that the Fourteenth Amendment applied only to state action, not to private libel suits, and that the advertisement lacked First Amendment protection because it was commercial speech. Granted, the lawsuit had been between private parties, but the Court agreed that the manner in which Alabama's laws of libel had been applied imposed invalid restrictions on speech and press. "The test is not the form in which state power has been applied but, whatever the form, whether such power has been exercised." The use of a state law, enforced in state courts, clearly made this "state action" under the Fourteenth Amendment.

The Court had used this argument before, most notably in *Shelley v. Kraemer* (1948), when it had struck down enforcement of restrictive covenants in private housing deeds. Only by going into state court could these covenants, which forbade sale of the house to non-whites, be enforced, and that made it state action. Under this rationale private forms of discrimination, if they required state resources, such as police or courts, to enforce, could be seen as state action and thus implicating the Fourteenth Amendment.

Brennan also made quick work of the claim that the advertisement as commercial speech did not enjoy First Amendment protection. Alabama had relied on *Valentine v. Chrestensen* (1942), in which the Court had upheld a city ordinance forbidding street distribution of commercial and business advertising. In that case a handbill involved in the dispute had a commercial message on one side and a protest against official action on the other. The Court, Brennan claimed, had never intended to outlaw the dissemination of political statements. Rather, an examination of the facts showed that the handbill was "purely commercial advertising," and the protest had been added for the sole purpose of evading the ordinance and not to engage in civil debate.

"Heed Their Rising Voices" was not "commercial" in the sense that the word had been used in *Chrestensen*. The ad in the *Times* "communicated information, expressed opinion, recited grievances, protested claimed abuses, and sought financial support on behalf of a movement whose existence and objectives are matters of the highest public concern." That the *Times* received payment "is as immaterial in this connection as is the fact that newspapers and books are sold." Any other conclusion would discourage newspapers from carrying these "editorial advertisements," and thus shut off an important outlet for groups or persons "who do not themselves have access to publishing facilities — who wish to exercise their freedom of speech even though they are not members of the press." They do not forfeit their constitutional rights simply because they pay to publish their ideas.

Part II also had not caused much debate in the conference, and centered on the question of whether the First Amendment protected libel. It is the heart of the opinion, and contains some of Brennan's best writing. There had been, of course, a number of cases in which the Court had seemingly excluded libel from constitutional protection, most notably *Chaplinsky v. New Hampshire* (1942). Moreover, even while denying judges the power to issue contempt citations for defamatory statements made against them in *Pennekamp v. Florida* (1946), the Court had said that "when the statements amount to defamation, a judge has such remedy in damages for libel as do other public servants." In *Beauharnais v. Illinois* (1952), the Court had sustained a state criminal libel statute that punished defamatory statements made against groups as well as individuals. But the Court in *Beauharnais* also took care to note that "it retains and exercises authority to nullify action which encroaches on freedom of utterance under the guise of punishing libel . . . for public men, are, as it were, public property . . . and discussion cannot be denied and the right, as well as the duty, of criticism must not be stifled."

(The Court had heard only one case regarding constitutional limits on the award of libel for criticism of public officials, and had divided evenly on the matter. This left the lower court award in place but did not reach the constitutional issue. *Schenectady Union Publishing Co. v. Sweeney* [1942].)

The general proposition that the First Amendment protects speech on matters of public import "has long been settled by our decisions." As such, the mere fact that some speech is called "libel" does not matter. The label is unimportant; what counts is the subject of the speech. "It is a prized American privilege to speak one's mind, though not always with perfect good taste, on all public institutions" (*Bridges v. California* [1952]). Brennan also quoted at length from Justice Louis Brandeis's great and eloquent opinion in *Whitney v. California* (1927), which many consider the keystone decision in First Amendment jurisprudence.

> Those who won our independence believed . . . that public discussion is a political duty; and that this should be a fundamental principle of the American government. . . . Believing in the power of reason as applied through public discussion, they eschewed silence coerced by law — the argument of force in its worst form. Recognizing the occasional tyrannies of governing majorities, they amended the Constitution so that free speech and assembly should be guaranteed.

What Brandeis and others recognized, and what Brennan explicated, is that public discussion is not always polite or accurate; it can get nasty and messy and loud, but it still must be protected:

> Thus we consider this case against the background of a profound national commitment to the principle that debate in public issues should be uninhibited, robust, and wide-open, and that it may well include vehement, caustic, and sometimes unpleasantly sharp attacks on government and public officials. The present advertisement, as an expression of grievance and protest on one of the major public issues of our time, would seem clearly to qualify for the constitutional protection.

The free speech tradition, he went on, never included a test for truth, and as James Madison said, "some degree of abuse is inseparable from the proper use of everything; and in no instance is this more true than in that of the press." The erroneous statement, according to Brennan, "is inevitable in a free debate, and it must be protected if the freedoms of expression are to have the 'breathing space' that they need to survive."

Debate over matters of public interest invariably included discussion of public officials and the conduct of their office, and here Brennan, following the suggestion Herbert Wechsler had made, revisited the Sedition Act of 1798, "which first crystallized a national awareness of the central meaning of the First Amendment." Going over the act, as well as the positions taken by Jefferson and Madison, Brennan in effect took the opportunity to declare it unconstitutional 166 years after its enactment. "Although the Sedition Act was never tested in this Court, the attack upon its validity has carried the day in the court of history." After citing numerous sources (including a collection of essays by his colleague William O. Douglas, *The Right of the People*), he concluded that these views "reflect a broad consensus that the Act, because of the restraint it imposed upon criticism of government and public officials, was inconsistent with the First Amendment."

Brennan brushed away Nachman's claim that the First Amendment did not apply to the states, since the process of incorporation had made freedom of speech and of the press applicable through the Fourteenth Amendment. This being the case, "what a State may not constitutionally bring about by means of a criminal statute is likewise beyond the reach of its civil law of libel. The fear of damage award under a rule such as that invoked by the Alabama courts here may be markedly more inhibiting than the fear of prosecution under a criminal statute."

Here again the brilliance of Wechsler's strategy can be seen. Brennan did not, of course, slavishly follow the appellant's brief, but Wechsler believed that a good appellate brief would show the court how to write its opinion. He had compared the Alabama libel law to a sedition act in that it stifled criticism of public officials by the press, and had gone back in history to the Sedition Act of 1798 to prove that Madison and Jefferson had strenuously opposed that law as a violation of a free press. He had carefully drawn the distinction between libel of private citizens and criticism of public officials and their policies, holding the latter fair game under the First Amendment. Wechsler had also pointed out that in such a debate error was unavoidable, and so the supposed complete defense of truth in an Alabama libel suit comprised no real defense at all. Brennan and the Court adopted each and every one of these arguments.

"A rule compelling the critic of official conduct to guarantee the truth of all his factual assertions—and to do so on pain of libel judgments virtually unlimited in amount—leads to a comparable 'self-censorship.'" Government censorship, as well as self-censorship inspired by fear of punishment for the smallest factual error, inhibited the free discussion of public affairs that is the goal of the First Amendment. What did this mean in terms of actual application? The conference

{ *Chapter 9* }

had agreed that if criticism of public officials could not be reached through libel law, then there had to be rules that state courts could follow. "The constitutional guarantee requires, we think, a federal rule that prohibits a public official from recovering damages for a defamatory falsehood relating to his official conduct unless he proves that the statement was made with 'actual malice' — that is, with knowledge that it was false or with reckless disregard of whether it was false or not."

Brennan went on to explain what this mean by referring to an early Kansas case, *Coleman v. MacLennan* (1908), which prevented the state attorney general from suing a newspaper for statements made regarding his official conduct in connection with a school fund. The paper had believed it to be true at the time, and in the debate over public office, errors of fact did not amount to libel if the statements had not been made maliciously and if the paper had believed them true at the time.

Douglas had suggested that the privilege extended in *Barr v. Matteo* (1959), protecting public officials from libel suits for statements made in the official conduct of their office, should be reciprocal — that is, comments made by citizens and the press about these officials should be protected too — and Brennan included that argument as well. It would be unfair to allow public servants an unjustified preference over the public, which would be the case if the citizenry did not have the equivalent of the immunity granted to officials. Brennan concluded this section by quoting Madison, that "the censorial power is in the people over the Government, and not in the Government over the people."

Part III had caused Brennan the most problems, yet when one reads it now it all seems so straightforward. In the second part the Court had announced a new rule, that public officials could not successfully prosecute a libel action for comment on their official conduct or programs under their responsibility without a showing of actual malice. The Alabama law presumed malice for purposes of general damages, and this presumption was clearly inconsistent with the new federal rule. Since the trial judge had not distinguished between general and punitive damages, it was impossible to know if the award had been wholly one or the other, or a mixture. "Because of this uncertainty, the judgment must be reversed and the case remanded."

So far this sounded normal enough: a verdict is overturned, the reasons are explained, and the case is sent back for a new trial to be governed under the new rule. All the justices considered this a bad idea, since they all believed that at a new trial Judge Jones would be able to twist the rule and the results would be the same—a heavy punitive fine against the *Times* and the ministers. Since they assumed that Sullivan would seek a new trial, "considerations of effective judicial administration [the phrase Tom Clark suggested] require us to review the evidence in the present record to determine whether it could constitutionally support a judgment" for Sullivan. This is the point where Harlan had become uncomfortable: the idea of an appellate court, indeed the highest court in the land, reviewing evidence—a task nearly always left to either a jury or a trial judge—and claiming a constitutional reason to do so.

To be sure, the Court had reviewed evidence in the past, and often in connection with civil rights and speech cases. The Court, Brennan explained, not only elaborated constitutional principles; in doing so it had the duty, "in proper cases," to review evidence to make certain that the principles had been constitutionally applied. Normally, the process would have been to give the trial court another chance, and then review the second trial to make sure that judge and jury had in fact followed the Supreme Court's constitutional directives. Harlan until the last minute wanted to follow that procedure, but a majority of the justices expected the Alabama courts to find a way around it. They wanted to make sure not only that there would not be another trial with Sullivan as the plaintiff, but also that the other trials then pending against the *Times* would also be derailed.

To do that, the Court would decide for itself whether sufficient evidence existed to proceed to a second trial, and "we consider that the proof presented to show actual malice lacks the convincing clarity which the constitutional standard demands, and hence that it would not constitutionally sustain the judgment for respondent under the proper rule of law." The case of the four ministers "requires little discussion." Even if somehow it could be shown that they authorized the use of their names, "there was no evidence whatever that they were aware of any erroneous statements or were in any way reckless in that regard." The case against Ralph Abernathy, Fred Shuttlesworth, Solomon Seay, and Joseph Lowery "is thus without constitutional support."

Brennan then detailed the problems of the evidence against the *Times*. Despite the factual errors, the people at the newspaper thought the general allegations "substantially correct," and Brennan indicated that he did too, without quite coming out so directly. Perhaps most damaging, and a point that had been made over and over again at every level — and dismissed in the Alabama courts — was that the evidence "was incapable of supporting the jury's finding that the allegedly libelous statements were made 'of and concerning' respondent."

Finally, he rebutted the Alabama Supreme Court's assertion that people know that if the conduct of the police department, or any other governmental agency, is criticized, that criticism is really directed against the person in charge of that department. That theory had "disquieting implications for criticism of governmental conduct." It had been the rule for decades that one could not prosecute a libel for comments made about governmental operations, but if that could be translated as a matter of course into criticism of the official in charge, then fear of libel suits by individuals would effectively silence legitimate and necessary comment on government. A state cannot create a cause of action that would otherwise be denied by the alchemy of transmuting it into an individual suit. That had been the entire foundation of Sullivan's suit, and it had no constitutional basis.

Ironically, the opinion ended with the traditional formula. "The judgment of the Supreme Court of Alabama is reversed and the case is remanded to that court for further proceedings not inconsistent with this opinion." The justices of the Alabama court, who had defied the nation's highest court in regard to the NAACP, had no choice in this case. Their only option "not inconsistent with this opinion" was to dismiss the case.

Justice Black filed a concurring opinion, in which Justice Douglas joined. Black at the initial conference had questioned whether the Court could reverse the trial results. He now accepted Brennan's opinion and, in accordance with his own view of the absolute nature of the First Amendment, went further. Brennan had written that the Constitution "delimits a State's power to award damages for libels brought by public officials against critics of their official conduct." Relying on the First Amendment, as applied to the states through the Fourteenth, Black believed it did not "delimit" but completely prohibited a state from allowing it for any reason. As for the malice standard set forth by the Court, he described it as "an elusive, abstract concept, hard to prove and hard to disprove."

Black did not base his vote on the grounds that there had been a failure to prove that the individual defendants, the four ministers, signed the advertisement or that they intended the criticism against Sullivan — "for present purposes I assume these things were proved." Similarly, he did not vote to reverse because of the size of the damage award. "I know of no provision in the Federal Constitution which either expressly or impliedly bars the State from fixing the amount of damages." The size of the award, however, gives "dramatic proof that state libel laws threaten the very existence of an American press virile enough to publish unpopular views on public affairs and bold enough to criticize the conduct of public officials."

Then Black said what Brennan had so carefully skirted in his opinion, that the case arose because of the efforts of "many people, including some public officials, to continue state-commanded segregation of races in the public schools and other public places, despite our several holdings that such a state practice is forbidden by the Fourteenth Amendment. Montgomery is one of the localities in which widespread hostility to desegregation has been manifested." This suit, and the others pending against the *Times*, had one purpose and one purpose only, to silence criticism of a government that did not heed a constitutional command. The *Sullivan* case was essentially the tip of the iceberg, because other suits against the *Times* then pending sought $5.6 million, and five suits against the Columbia Broadcasting Company sought $1.7 million.

The Constitution deals with such a deadly danger to a free press in the only way possible — "by granting the press an absolute immunity for criticism of the way public officials do their public duty." There was no question in his mind that the First Amendment applied to the states, and he believed that the Speech and Press Clauses leave "the people and the press free to criticize officials and discuss public affairs with impunity." He regretted "that the Court has stopped short of this holding indispensable to preserve our free press from destruction."

Arthur Goldberg, with whom Douglas also concurred, was the only justice who did not join Brennan's opinion, but concurred only in the result. In essence, he said pretty much what Black did, that the Court had not gone far enough and that citizens and the press should enjoy an "absolute, unconditional privilege to criticize official conduct despite the harm which may flow from excesses and abuses." He then spent several pages delineating this idea, warning that any standard less than total immunity would eventually put governmental critics at risk.

Goldberg did, however, note that even if citizens and the press enjoyed an absolute privilege, the public official is not defenseless against unsubstantiated opinions or even deliberate falsehoods. Under the American system of government, counterargument and education, not abridgment of speech, are the weapons to expose such abuses. As Justice Brandeis had observed, "sunlight is the most powerful of all disinfectants."

# CHAPTER 10

# Libel Law after *Sullivan*

The press and free speech advocates cheered of course, and rightly so. The media had been saved from ruinous damages and believed it had found a champion, the U.S. Supreme Court. Twenty years later Floyd Abrams, one of the leading First Amendment lawyers in the country, described it as "a majestic opinion. It had a command of American history that is rare in a judicial opinion. It reminded us of how young we are as a country." Some lines from Brennan's opinion continue to resonate — "the central meaning of the First Amendment," "a profound national commitment to the principle that debate in public issues should be uninhibited, robust, and wide-open."

But while *Sullivan* profoundly changed the law of libel, and in doing so, relieved the press from some of the restraints associated with it, it was not primarily a Press Clause case. First and foremost it needs to be seen as a civil rights case. Justice Black clearly saw this, and it is even plainer in the companion case of *Abernathy v. Sullivan*. The Reverend Ralph Abernathy identified the libel suits for exactly what they were, "part of a concerted, calculated program to carry out a policy of punishing, intimidating and silencing all who criticize and seek to change Alabama's notorious political system of enforced segregation." Civil rights activists such as Andrew Young cheered the decision as a victory for the movement.

Second, the case dealt with free speech, and stopped just short of declaring seditious libel unconstitutional once and for all, a step the Court finally took five years later in *Brandenburg v. Ohio*. Americans must have, as part of a democratic society, the right to discuss and criticize their government without fear of retribution. Brennan's whole discussion of the 1798 Sedition Act focused on this idea, one that Brandeis, whom he quoted, had explicated so eloquently in *Whitney v. California* (1927).

Third, the case did involve press freedom, but it did not go as far as either its defenders or its detractors claimed.

Although some critics saw *New York Times v. Sullivan* as a radical departure from established jurisprudence — and in some ways this is true — Brennan's opinion built upon the Court's developing protection of free expression. In speech cases dating back to 1920, the Court had routinely looked at the offending statements to see if they met the clear-and-present danger test. Oliver Wendell Holmes Jr. had put forth a theory of free speech that rested on the "marketplace of ideas," while Louis D. Brandeis had argued that an informed citizenry needed free expression in order to perform their civic duty. The Court had also been aware of the writings of academics, such as Zechariah Chafee Jr., Alexander Meiklejohn, and Thomas Emerson.

Chafee's influential book, *Free Speech in the United States* (1920) had been read carefully by both Holmes and Brandeis, and his ideas had played an important role in the 1940s speech cases. Chafee argued for nearly unlimited speech in the political arena, but did not favor expanding the First Amendment to nonpolitical speech, such as the profane, the indecent, or the insulting. Such speech contributed nothing to the analysis of ideas and the search for truth, and it could be restricted in order to serve the greater social values of "order, morality, the training of the young, and the peace of mind for those who see and hear." The Court had unanimously endorsed Chafee's view of the social uselessness and lack of First Amendment protection of obscenity, libel, and fighting words in *Chaplinsky v. New Hampshire* (1942).

One of the most influential theorists of free speech in the twentieth century happened to have been a man who taught Chafee when the latter was an undergraduate at Brown. Alexander Meiklejohn went even further than his former pupil in postulating an absolute protection for political speech, which he like Brandeis saw as essential to self-government. Meiklejohn used the analogy of a New England town meeting, where the voters are made wise by means of vigorous debate. In such a situation, he argued, it is not necessary that each person be heard but instead that "everything worth saying be said." Although there may be procedural rules to allow for orderly debate, there must be no fetters on ideas — "the freedom of ideas shall not be abridged."

The protection of congressional speech in the Constitution (Art. I, Sec. 6) is designed to allow just that type of robust, unfettered discussion, and according to Meiklejohn, it is as essential for the people to enjoy that protection as it is for representatives and senators, for both are engaged in the business of developing public policy. Where Chafee drew a limit on political speech when it created a real and imminent danger, Meiklejohn seemed to believe it totally untouchable, "beyond the reach of legislative limitations, beyond even the due process of law."

Private speech, on the other hand, defined primarily as not involving political matters, enjoys only a limited protection. Chafee criticized Meiklejohn on this bifurcation between public and private speech, asserting that no historical evidence supported the view that the Founders had any such distinction in mind. Moreover, the line is not always sharp, and what may strike one person as "public" may appear to another as "private." Would a novel, for example, be considered a private expression if it dealt fictionally with important social matters? For Chafee, it would be far better to exclude clearly useless speech and protect all other expression, public or private.

The problem of line drawing, or balancing, led Yale law professor Thomas Emerson to attempt a systematic exploration of free speech, in which he proposed the "expression/action" theory, a criterion reminiscent of the belief/action dichotomy utilized by the Court in religion cases. For Emerson, freedom of expression was absolute, no matter what form it took. People may express their views either through traditional speech or writing or by other means, such as music and art. Moreover, the right of free expression includes the right to hear the opinion of others, the right to enquire freely, and the right to associate with others of similar views.

Emerson drew the line between expression of ideas, no matter what form they take, and their manifestation as action, which may be controlled by other constitutional requirements. The problem, as he himself recognized, was that the distinction between expression and action may not always be clear, especially in areas that Chafee delineated as outside First Amendment protection — obscenity, libel, and provocation. While more systematic than either Chafee or Meiklejohn, and while providing judges with greater guidance in determining what is protected, in the end Emerson also required judges to balance, to draw lines.

Chafee's ideas had guided the Court's thinking for two decades, and there are still commentators who share his view that political expression is the only form protected by the First Amendment and that socially useless speech is excluded. Justices Black and Douglas, who opposed balancing and adopted an absolute position, stood closer to Emerson's ideas. The decision in the *Times* case can be described as "Meiklejohnian," as Justice Brennan himself declared. Any speech that in any form involved public policy needed to be protected. In this case Brennan utilized what he termed "the central meaning of the First Amendment" to cut through the confusion of whether libel was "useless" or "private" and saw instead that the speech involved implicated public policy. According to Lucas Powe, "Beyond reflecting Wechsler the advocate, the opinion combined the insights of the philosopher Alexander Meiklejohn on the necessities of political speech with those of William Brennan, lawyer and jurist, on the practical effects of litigation. It was a stunning combination."

When the First Amendment scholar Harry Kalven talked with Meiklejohn, then 92 years old, and asked what he thought of the *Times* decision, the philosopher replied, "It is an occasion for dancing in the streets." But the opinion, breathtaking as it was, did not go as far as either Meiklejohn or James Madison might have done. The decision did not do away with the law of libel. Even in our own time most people believe that a person's reputation ought to be protected against defamation. Judge Harold Leventhal, writing two years after *Sullivan*, declared that "the rule that permits satisfaction of the deep-seated need for vindication of honor is not a mere historic relic, but promotes the law's civilizing function of providing an acceptable substitute for violence in the settlement of disputes." *Sullivan* did carve out a rather wide swath — speech relating to a public official or the conduct of a government program — but even here the official could sue if evidence existed of "actual malice" or if the utterance or publication showed a reckless disregard for the truth or falsity of the statement. Brennan may have saved the *Times*, as everyone on the Court agreed needed to be done, but the justices would soon have to explicate exactly what these tests meant.

The Warren Court demonstrated its commitment to the doctrine it had enunciated in the *Times* case by deciding four other cases in the next few years. In these cases it significantly expanded the class of plaintiffs who would have to meet the new standards to include "public figures." It also policed the action of lower courts and strengthened the rules involved.

The Court had not found actual malice in the inconsequential errors in the *Times* advertisement, but later in the year it had the opportunity to develop this standard in *Garrison v. Louisiana*. James Garrison, the flamboyant district attorney of Orleans Parish, got into a shouting match with eight justices of the criminal district court when they denied him access to the fines and fees fund for money to conduct an investigation of commercial vice. He called a press conference and claimed that the judges' decision "raises interesting questions about the racketeer influence on our eight vacation-minded judges." The judges sued, and a Louisiana court tried and convicted Garrison of libel under the state criminal defamation law. He appealed, and the Supreme Court unanimously reversed on the basis of the *Times* doctrine.

Honest although inaccurate statements always have the potential for furthering the search for truth, Justice Brennan explained, and therefore are to be protected:

> It does not follow that the lie, knowingly and deliberately published about a public official, should enjoy a like immunity. . . . For the use of the known lie as a tool is at once at odds with the premises of democratic government and with the orderly manner in which economic, social, or political change is to be effected. . . . Hence the knowingly false statement and the false statement made with reckless disregard of the truth do not enjoy constitutional protection.

Garrison's charges may have been reckless, but there had been no showing made, nor even required under Louisiana law, that there had been actual malice against the officials.

The first case the justices heard that resembled the *Times* case came in 1966, *Rosenblatt v. Baer*. As Harry Kalven noted, it was a "relatively homely controversy," but illustrated "how deeply the constitutional criticism of libel law now cuts into the handling of routine local disputes." Baer had been the supervisor of a county-operated recreation area in New Hampshire, employed by and responsible to three county commissioners. A local controversy over the way the area operated resulted in a change of administration, and Baer lost his job.

In an opinion column in the local newspaper, Rosenblatt noted the "fantastic" improvement in income from the recreation area under the new management and asked: "What happened to the money last year? And every other year?" Baer sued and charged that Rosenblatt had "greatly exaggerated the facts" as to how much improvement took place, and that even though he had not been mentioned by name, many people in the town understood the column to impute "mismanagement and peculation" to him. A local jury found for Baer and awarded him $31,500.

The case had gone to trial before the *Times* decision, and the jury had been instructed that mere negligent misstatement of fact would defeat Rosenblatt's claim of privilege of comment. Armed with the *Times* doctrine, Rosenblatt launched a constitutional challenge against an apparently routine application of New Hampshire law, and one that clearly did not have the civil rights context that shaped the earlier case.

The justices by an 8–1 vote reversed the reward and sent the case back to New Hampshire for a new trial. Only Justice Fortas (who replaced Goldberg in 1965) dissented, objecting to the fact that the trial had taken place prior to the *Times* decision and therefore neither judge nor jury could have taken that doctrine into account. He would have dismissed the writ of certiorari as improvidently granted, letting the verdict and award stand.

Although the other justices agreed on the result, they wrote six separate opinions. For Justice Brennan, who wrote the opinion of the Court, the case raised two questions. Did the defendant's column sufficiently refer to Baer, and did Baer, as a former manager of a recreation area, come within the "public official" category of the *Times*? The trial judge had instructed the jury that an "imputation of impropriety or crime to one or some of a small group that casts suspicion on all is actionable." Brennan found this in error, because it allowed impersonal criticism of governmental policy to be converted into personal defamation. As to whether Baer qualified as a public official,

Brennan found the record unclear. He remanded the case to the state courts to give Baer a chance to show whether his complaint fell outside the *Times* privilege, either because he was a private person or because he could prove actual malice.

Brennan's opinion stressed to the lower courts that they had to be aware of any public policy implications in even seemingly minor libel cases. "Criticism of government is at the very center of the constitutionally protected area of free discussion. Criticism of those responsible for government operations must be free, lest criticism of government itself be penalized."

Brennan's opinion continued the position he had articulated in the *Times* case, and while he had the votes of Black and Douglas for the result, neither one of them would endorse any restrictions on speech. "This Court should free private critics of public agents from fear of libel judgments for money just as it has freed critics from fear of pains and penalties inflicted by government." Then in a prescient statement, Black declared that the case illustrated "what a short and inadequate step this Court took in the *New York Times* case to guard free press and free speech. . . . The only sure way to protect speech and press against these threats is to recognize that libel laws are abridgements of speech and press and therefore are barred in both federal and state courts."

That step, however, the Court would not take, because the majority of the justices believed there should be a legal remedy to repair a reputation damaged by false or misleading statements, and Potter Stewart's opinion is reflective of this feeling.

> The right of a man to the protection of his reputation from unjustified invasion and wrongful hurt reflects no more than our basic concept of the essential dignity and worth of every human being — a concept at the root of any decent system of ordered liberty. The protection of private personality, like the protection of life itself, is left primarily to the individual States under the Ninth and Tenth Amendments. But this does not mean that the right is entitled to any less recognition by this Court as a basic of our constitutional system.

State laws, therefore, except where they have been converted into seditious libel, as had been in the case in Alabama, should be upheld to provide private citizens "all means of redress for injuries inflicted upon them by careless liars." And, in case any of the Brethren had forgotten recent history, Stewart warned them that "surely if the 1950s taught us anything, they taught us that the poisonous atmosphere of the easy lie can infect and degrade a whole society."

To some it appeared that the Court seemed intent on blurring the distinctions between the public arena and private life, but this proved not to be the case when the justices refined the *Times* test in two cases decided together in 1967, *Curtis Publishing Co. v. Butts* and *Associated Press v. Walker*. The first case came out of a *Saturday Evening Post* article alleging that Wally Butts, a former coach and then University of Georgia athletic director, had given information about the Bulldogs' plays to Bear Bryant, the University of Alabama coach, just prior to a game between the two schools in which Alabama won by a lopsided margin. In the second case, Edwin Walker, a retired army general, sued the Associated Press following a story that he had led a violent crowd in opposing enforcement of a desegregation decree at the University of Mississippi.

Neither plaintiff held public office, and therefore they did not come under the public-official category of the *Times* test. But as Chief Justice Warren explained, "differentiation between 'public figures' and 'public officials' and adoption of separate standards of proof for each have no basis in law, logic, or First Amendment policy." Such public figures, by their reputation, have access to the press through which they may rebut allegations against them, a right enjoyed by public officials as well but denied to private citizens.

Although the Court did extend the *Times* doctrine, it also introduced the ideas of "reckless disregard" and "hot news" into the formula. In the *Butts* case, the magazine based its story on the questionable report of George Burnett, who allegedly overheard a telephone conversation because of an electronic glitch. As Justice Harlan explained in the 5–4 decision that upheld the libel award to Butts, the information provided by Burnett "was in no sense 'hot' news and the editors of the magazine recognized the need for a thorough investigation of the serious charges." They failed to do so, however, and this showed a reckless disregard for the facts and a gross failure to conform to normal standards for investigative journalism.

In the *Walker* case, however, a unanimous Court overturned the libel judgment against the wire service because the news had been reported in the midst of riots on the Ole Miss campus. It was "hot" news that required immediate dissemination, from a reporter on the scene who gave every indication of trustworthiness and reliability. Under the pressure of events, such errors must be considered innocent and not a reckless disregard of the truth.

The *Butts* and *Walker* cases marked the limit to which the Warren Court was willing to expand the *Times* doctrine, and four members of the bench — Clark, Harlan, Stewart, and Fortas — opposed that extension. In fact, only three members of the Court actually supported the "public figure" doctrine (Warren, Brennan, and White), and they prevailed because Black and Douglas supported a broader immunity.

In its speech cases the Warren Court opened a figurative Pandora's box of issues, not the least being the inclusion of obscenity and libel within First Amendment protection. In many areas the Warren Court had the "easy" cases, not in the sense that it did not take courage to resolve issues such as racial segregation, but rather that the answers were obvious and relatively straightforward. Of course it was wrong to isolate children in school on the basis of race, and segregation should be ended. Of course it was wrong to have malapportioned legislatures, and there should be one vote for one person. Of course it was wrong to impose penalties on criticism of government, and the law of seditious libel, in whatever form, had finally to be buried. Once the initial decisions had been handed down, however, lower courts grappled with the complexities of implementation. What did a desegregated school look like, and to what extent could or should courts get involved in setting school policies? How far down did states have to reapportion — county councils, city wards, school boards? How did one determine if a person was "public" or "private"?

Problems inhered in the *Times* opinion from the start — problems that few people noticed in the heady atmosphere of the late sixties. As Justice Brennan explained, the decision rested on a Meiklejohnian view that free expression was bound up with sovereignty and was as part of the "governmental responsibility . . . a public power." The Constitution protected the press so that it could participate in the governing responsibility through reporting and criticism, a view Potter Stewart once described as the "institutional function" of the press.

As Lyle Denniston, the *Baltimore Sun*'s Supreme Court correspondent, suggested, this view proved troublesome for two reasons. First, it established a variable measure for press freedom; more freedom is attached to those press activities that have high social value because they contribute to the political debate. Second, it required public accountability as a regulatory device; otherwise the press could abuse its power and distort the political process. The first prong did not bother the press, because it believed that its normal journalistic endeavors, if unhindered, easily satisfied the criterion of social usefulness. The second prong, that of accountability, also did not seem to bother reporters and columnists, because their professional rhetoric already spoke to the ideal of meeting high standards. They did not expect, and were not prepared to accept, the possibility that other agencies, such as the courts, would judge their social usefulness and impose standards of accountability. As Denniston noted:

> Without bothering to analyze critically what it believed, the press proceeded upon the assumption that it enjoyed its rights as a matter of institutional autonomy for its organizations, and personal autonomy for its individual practitioners. The internal inconsistency of a private industry serving a public right, yet doing so under an ill-defined and probably indefinable code of private ethics, apparently never troubled the press, which failed to appreciate that, in any ultimate constitutional reckoning over its performance, public law would prevail over industry self-restraint. The "public's right to know" would be too important to be left to journalists.

The reckoning actually began with the *Times* case, because in granting the press freedom to criticize, it also imbued that criticism with an element of public accountability. As such, the standards by which criticism would be judged would not be professional ethics taught in journalism schools or adopted by trade groups, but standards of law. The Warren Court had set out the first standard — actual malice — in the *Times* case, and in subsequent decisions added other criteria even as it seemed to expand freedom of the press. The process continued into the early years of the Burger Court, with the justices allowing almost any connection to the *public* interest to justify hitherto restricted press behavior.

The Court upheld a libelous statement about a candidate's personal life, because some people might consider it relevant in determining his fitness for public office (*Monitor Patriot Co. v. Roy* [1971]). A radio station called a subsequently exonerated magazine distributor a "smut peddler," and the Court overturned a libel conviction because the news story had involved a matter of public interest (*Rosenbloom v. Metromedia* [1971]). In *Old Dominion Branch, Letter Carriers v. Austin* (1974), the Court held that federal law, which favored "uninhibited, robust and wide-open debate in labor disputes," superseded state libel law and reversed a judgment against a union for accurately listing a person as a scab.

Then in *Gertz v. Robert Welch, Inc.* (1974), Justice Powell led the Court in shifting its analysis to the difference between public and private figures. Elmer Gertz, a Chicago lawyer, represented the Nelsons, the family of a young boy who had been shot by a police officer; the policeman, Nuccio, was eventually convicted of second-degree murder. In 1969 *American Opinion*, the official magazine of the John Birch Society, falsely accused Gertz of being a "Leninist" and "Communist-fronter" for his role in representing the Nelsons in their civil suit against Nuccio. The magazine also falsely asserted that Gertz had a criminal record, and these and other inaccuracies led Gertz to sue for defamation.

The jury awarded him damages, but the federal district judge overruled the jury, asserting that under the *Times* standard, Gertz would have to prove actual malice on the part of the publisher rather than mere falsity. The *Times* criterion applied to public figures, and although the district court conceded that Gertz was not a public figure, it asserted that the issues were of public interest, and so the *Times* decision would apply. Considering the Court's decision in its earlier cases, the district court judge seemed on solid ground.

But the Court reversed by a 5–4 vote, due in part to the changes that had taken place on the bench. Warren had been replaced as chief justice by Warren Burger. Hugo Black, Tom Clark, John Harlan, and Arthur Goldberg had left, and in their places sat Thurgood Marshall, Harry Blackmun, Lewis Powell, and William Rehnquist. Justice Powell wrote the majority decision, and held that because Gertz was a private person, he had only to prove the publication was false and that there was a "fault" on the part of the publisher.

Brennan, as expected, dissented, arguing that the decision would undermine a "free and robust debate," but the mood of the Court had changed. Byron White, who had joined his opinion in *Sullivan*, dissented, but not because he agreed with Brennan. He thought that even under the current standard the Court had gone too far in protecting the press. He would have reversed the lower court and reinstated the judgment. (On remand for a new trial, Gertz again triumphed, and the jury awarded him $400,000.)

Over the next few years the Court refused to grant exemption to the press in cases involving private persons in a highly publicized divorce proceeding (*Time v. Firestone* [1976]), receiving public funds (*Hutchinson v. Proxmire* [1979]), or even convicted of crime (*Wolston v. Reader's Digest Assn.* [1979]).

Journalists in the 1970s and early 1980s might well be excused if they were hopelessly confused, unable to tell under which circumstances the law would protect them, and when it would not. The Court had seemingly created a shield for the press against libel suits, and while the restraints of actual malice or reckless disregard remained in place, the public nature of the matter pushed even these to one side. The Court refused to expand *New York Times v. Sullivan*, and the journalistic vision of a nation free from libel suits against the media never came to pass. If Alexander Meiklejohn had said that the 1964 decision was cause for "dancing in the streets," twenty years later Richard Epstein, a conservative law professor, declared that "the dancing has stopped." The 1980s saw a significant upsurge in libel suits against the press, with million-dollar verdicts a not unusual occurrence, and another conservative, Judge Robert Bork, said that such awards "threatened to impose a self-censorship on the press."

At the time Judge Bork made this comment in 1984, a jury had just awarded $26.5 million to a former Miss Wyoming, who claimed that a sexually hyperactive character in a fictional story in *Penthouse* magazine resembled and therefore insulted her. The president of the Mobil Corporation won a $2 million jury verdict against the *Washington Post* for a story that he had set up his son in a shipping company that did business with Mobil. Eventually the courts overturned both judgments on appeal, but the litigation placed a heavy financial burden on the magazine and the paper. In the *Post* case several reporters and editors spent weeks preparing for and attending the trial, and legal fees amounted to nearly the amount that had been awarded in the trial.

Libel suits had not been abolished, but the press had better defenses than they had enjoyed in the pre-*Sullivan* era. The barriers of "actual malice" and "reckless disregard," however, were not insurmountable, and a determined plaintiff could, if not always win, make a deep dent in the defendant's pocket. To begin with, how does one prove malice or disregard? The answer, at least in part, is to find out what facts a reporter or a broadcaster had used. Any print article or broadcast program represents a winnowing process; the reporters and researchers dig for anything they can find, put together background materials, and then try to make sense of their notes. It is a selective and subjective process, and while reporters expect their editors to grill them on accuracy and fairness, neither wants a third party, especially a lawyer, nosing into their research materials and second-guessing them on their choice. But how else does a plaintiff prove that malice or reckless disregard existed?

The issue came up in *Herbert v. Lando* (1979). Colonel Anthony Herbert, a veteran of Vietnam, claimed that he had been punished by his superiors for trying to bring to their attention massacres of civilians by American troops. CBS television aired a segment of its acclaimed *60 Minutes* program, entitled "The Selling of Colonel Herbert," that seemed skeptical of the claims. Herbert sued CBS, producer Barry Lando, and others for libel. In discovery, the search for evidence before a trial, Herbert's lawyer asked to see the CBS files as well as film segments that had been edited out of the final show. He wanted to figure out why some things that might have been more favorable to his client had not been used, while other more negative material had been kept. CBS cooperated at first, and then balked, complaining that this type of investigation by an outsider would lead to fear on the part of reporters, editors, and producers, the very type of self-censorship that *Sullivan* intended to prevent.

CBS made this argument to the Supreme Court, which rejected it. Justice White explained that public officials or figures had the burden under the *Times* rule of proving that a publisher or broadcaster knew of a probable falsity. If they could not find out what the publisher knew, they would in effect be barred from any recovery, even if in fact there had been reckless disregard, and the Court had consistently refused to take this step. Libel defendants must therefore provide material such as Colonel Herbert had demanded.

The decision allowed plaintiffs who had the money to go fishing in media files and put reporters through hours of depositions to discover what they thought. The producer, Barry Lando, was questioned at twenty-eight separate deposition sessions that produced 3,000 pages of transcript. CBS lawyers demanded that Herbert turn over materials, and received almost 12,000 pages of documents. The case went on for twelve years until the Court of Appeals for the Second Circuit dismissed Herbert's claims in 1986, and the Supreme Court declined to review the case a second time. Mike Wallace, one of the defendants in the case, estimated that the network had spent $3–4 million in lawyer fees.

The press reacted predictably to the Supreme Court decision, charging that White's opinion was "Orwellian," that it imposed "an intolerably chilling effect," that made it "more hazardous to exercise [press] freedom," and it "almost literally put lawyers into editors' chairs." While scholars believe the Court could have fashioned more temperate rules for discovery, the logic was that of *New York Times v. Sullivan*. Justice Brennan, even though he dissented in part, chided the press for its "bitterness" and "acrimonious criticism." "It would scarcely be fair to say," he commented, "that a plaintiff can only recover if he establishes intentional falsehood and at the same time to say that he cannot inquire into a defendant's intentions."

*Sullivan* had never said that public figures could not sue; it merely made it far more difficult for them to win, especially if the news stories dealt reasonably accurately with issues of legitimate public concern. In the early eighties, though, press reputation slipped badly, and the public was treated to several so-called celebrity lawsuits. Carol Burnett sued the *National Enquirer* over its report that she had had a row with Henry Kissinger in a restaurant and its implication that she was drunk. She won $800,000 by proving reckless or intentional falsehood on the tabloid's part. In 1980 NBC in its *Nightly News* reported that the popular Las Vegas entertainer Wayne Newton had associations with a Mafia figure. A jury awarded him $19 million, but on appeal the Ninth Circuit threw the judgment out, holding there was almost no evidence to support knowing or reckless falsehood on the part of the network. The court's opinion even quoted James Madison's protest against the Sedition Act.

As Anthony Lewis has asked, "What did the *Enquirer* item [about

Carol Burnett] have to do with uninhibited debate on public issues . . . ? Why did she have to meet a constitutional test in order to recover damages for a lie in a sleazy tabloid?" He went to ask, "What did Wayne Newton have to do with James Madison? Why did the First Amendment protect critics of an entertainer as Justice Brennan had said it protected the 'citizen-critic of government'?" By spreading First Amendment protection too broadly, Lewis suggests, it may also be spread too thin, protecting things that do not deserve protection but failing to provide an adequate shield where it is truly needed.

The Supreme Court also seemed to have second thoughts on how far the *Times* rule should go. In *Keeton v. Hustler Magazine, Inc.* (1984), the Court reaffirmed the traditional view that state libel laws served a legitimate function in protecting reputation even of public figures. False stories, the Court said, harm "both the subject of the falsehood and the readers of the statement," a view of value and accountability fully in keeping with *Times.*

From the press point of view the nadir of the Court's treatment of the media came in an obscure case over a relatively unimportant issue. The credit service Dun & Bradstreet had sent routine notices to five of its subscribers that a building company in their area had filed for voluntary bankruptcy. The owner of the company first learned of this totally erroneous report when he went to conduct some business with his banker. Dun & Bradstreet eventually sent out a correction but refused to inform the builder about whom it had issued the false report. He sued for libel and damages, and a Vermont jury awarded him $350,000.

The Court, speaking through Justice Powell, ruled that First Amendment protection, as explicated in *Sullivan*, did not apply in libel suits where the subject matter involved "no issue of public concern." While the false report may not have been issued with either malice or reckless disregard, it could in no way be seen as a matter of public concern. Therefore the libel laws held sway, because "there is no threat to the free and robust debate on public issues; there is no potential interference with a meaningful dialogue of ideas concerning self-government; there is no threat of liability causing a reaction of self-censorship by the press." Even Justice Brennan, who dissented, agreed that in libel cases speech on commercial matters enjoyed a lesser constitutional protection because it did not directly implicate "the central meaning of the First Amendment" and was "not at the essence of self-government" (*Dun & Bradstreet v. Greenmoss Builders* [1985]).

The press, which had so cheered the Court in the 1960s, roundly criticized it twenty years later, and in both instances their ardor seems misplaced. The *Times* decision, while protecting the press against the use of private libel law as a surrogate for seditious libel, did not free the press from all responsibility for what it printed or broadcast. The Burger Court cases did not reverse *Sullivan*, but explicated some of the questions Brennan's opinion had raised but left unanswered. Clearly, the law of private libel had not been jettisoned, but where stories did not involve public officials, matters of concern to the citizen-critic, and had been processed with reasonable honesty and accuracy, where exactly did the press stand? In its last press decision, the Burger Court removed any doubt about the emphasis on subject matter rather than person when they held that media defendants would be entitled to constitutional protection against having to prove the truth of stories when those stories dealt with matters of public concern (*Philadelphia Newspapers v. Hepps* [1986]).

The press cheered when Chief Justice William Rehnquist spoke for a unanimous Court in throwing out a suit by the Reverend Jerry Falwell against *Hustler* magazine. Falwell claimed that a parody of himself in a Campari "first time" advertisement, which implied he had sex with his mother in an outhouse, had caused him emotional distress. Rehnquist wrote a strong opinion regarding *Hustler*'s rights, affirming that satire would have full constitutional protection. The decision, according to some scholars, signaled the end of a period of concern about whether the Court would turn back the clock on libel law to the pre-*Sullivan* days.

The Falwell/Hustler case was the last major libel case decided by the Supreme Court. (In 2005 the Court decided *Tory v. Cochran*, a defamation suit brought by the lawyer Johnnie Cochran in which he had secured an injunction against Ulysses Tory to stop him from picketing Cochran's offices and making allegedly defamatory statements against him. Lower courts granted the injunction, Tory appealed, and after cert had been granted Cochran died. The suit was less about the nature of defamation and prior restraint [one scholar called the

Court's analysis of these issues "garbled"] than that in California an injunction does not end with the life of one party, but must be dissolved by a court. Justice Breyer agreed that the case was not moot but that since Cochran's death the underlying rationale for the injunction had disappeared, and so it now amounted to a prior restraint. The case has had no impact whatsoever on the law of defamation and the *Sullivan* holding.) One might therefore assume that the issues have died down and libel has gone the way of the dodo. That would not be true. Every day in the United States, somewhere a jury is hearing a case of alleged defamation, but the vast majority of these are between individuals, with the press occasionally involved, and all are tried and decided under state law. The key ideas of *New York Times v. Sullivan* have been absorbed into the fabric of the law. Absent actual malice or reckless disregard of the truth, comments on public officials — even if there are some factual errors — are protected, and are part of the "uninhibited, robust, and wide-open" civic discourse that is American political life. Public figures are also to some extent barred from suing, but here the press enjoys a lesser degree of immunity. In all other cases, the key to whether the First Amendment is implicated will be determined by the subject matter.

Although private libel law is not dead, the current revolution in technology will certainly alter its application. It is one thing to pick up a tangible object like a newspaper and read a story there. It is another to watch a report on television or hear one on radio, media that, while less tangible, have by this time been absorbed into our consciousness and are accepted as the means by which we receive news.

What effect will the tens of thousands of people who blog on the Internet have in the larger area of civic discourse and the more limited matter of libel? What about Twitter and other forms of social networking — are people who post comments about others on these transitory forms subject to traditional rules of civility and protection of reputation? We are learning every day that things posted on the Net — pictures taken years earlier, comments on party activities, and the like — can come back to haunt a person and affect his or her chances at getting into a school or being hired for a job, sometime long after the initial posting. This will be one of the issues that the courts will face in the years to come, and it remains to be seen how a sentiment, a very important sentiment, first penned in the latter eighteenth century will be applied in the twenty-first.

We started this story by insisting that as much as it is a question of free speech or of free press, *New York Times v. Sullivan* is a civil rights case. Justice Brennan handed down his opinion on March 9, 1964, while Congress was debating the most significant civil rights legislation since Reconstruction. Four months later Congress enacted and President Lyndon Johnson signed into law the 1964 Civil Rights Act. A year after that, despite strong southern resistance, Congress passed the Voting Rights Act, and gave the Justice Department wide authority to enforce its provisions. The two laws broke the back of southern resistance, and while it took years in some instances before the last vestiges of legally imposed segregation disappeared, the corner had been turned.

More than any other statute, the Voting Rights Act gave blacks real power. Two months after a federal registrar arrived in Selma, the percentage of voting-age blacks on the rolls rose from 10 to 60; within a year after passage of the law, 166,000 blacks registered for the first time in Alabama, and within five years, the total number of registered blacks in the South more than doubled. Between 1964 and 1969, black registration in the Deep South increased from 36 to 65 percent of the black adults in the region. Before long, these figures translated into elected black legislators, sheriffs, and mayors, more than 500 in the lower South alone by 1969. The fact that blacks now had a significant voice in the election of sheriffs significantly affected the way law enforcement officials treated African Americans, who, if mistreated by these officials, could conceivably vote them out of office at the next election.

The changing political climate in Alabama got Eric Embry, once vilified as the defender of the northern press, elected to the Supreme Court of Alabama.

Roland Nachman told the New York Bar Association twenty-five years later that the Supreme Court decision was the best thing that happened to him. Alabama newspapers realized that the First Amendment shield raised by the Supreme Court also covered them, and hired

Nachman to be their attorney. In 1973 his fellow lawyers elected him president of the state bar association.

Herbert Wechsler was in the middle of teaching a course when his secretary walked in and handed him a note that the Court had decided *New York Times v. Sullivan* in his favor. Wechsler continued to teach at Columbia and head the American Law Institute until his retirement in 1984.

William J. Brennan Jr. served on the U.S. Supreme Court thirty-three years until his retirement from ill health in 1990, and his opinions on the central meaning of the First Amendment still resonate and influence our jurisprudence.

The time of people like L. B. Sullivan had passed. He easily won reelection as commissioner in 1963, but lost four years later to Jack Rucker, who actively courted the newly enfranchised black voters in Montgomery. He helped get George Wallace elected governor, and in January 1971 Sullivan became Alabama state prison commissioner. His tenure proved to be an unhappy one, torn between federal courts ordering reform of the overcrowded facilities and a legislature unwilling to appropriate the needed funds, and in July 1975 he resigned, saying he was "worn out with fighting this matter of funds, finances, the legislature's stalling and the general failure of the state" to support the prison system. The following year he became executive assistant to the new attorney general, Bill Baxley, but then he died of a heart attack one year later. Controversy about him, however, continued after his death, and when the legislature wanted to induct him into the Alabama Peace Officer's Hall of Fame, and later name a prison after him, the black community protested against honoring a man they still considered an enemy of equal rights.

The City of Montgomery today considers itself one of the premier urban centers in the South, with modern buildings, good transportation, and opportunities in business and the arts. On its Web site it features as one of the city's most important tourist attractions the Civil Rights Memorial, located around the corner from the church where Martin Luther King Jr. served as pastor during the bus boycott. The memorial is in an open plaza adjacent to the Civil Rights Memorial Center, a museum detailing the history of the civil rights movement in Montgomery.

# CHAPTER II

# Coda

## Civility and Reputation

Justice Brennan's decision in *New York Times v. Sullivan* has over the years achieved something of an iconic stature in the legal lexicon. The case presented the Warren Court with a textbook example of illiberal "blockages" in the political and intellectual marketplace. Through the use of libel suits, a minority of entrenched public officials could disrupt the flow of information, undermine the public welfare, and in this case, continue to keep people of African descent in a form of bondage. These blockages had to be removed, Brennan reasoned, so that the citizenry could know the facts regarding important public policy issues, and then join in an enlightened civic discourse to resolve political controversies.

The actual malice test helped to minimize the chill on political speech and at the same time provided constitutional protection for what had previously been a repugnant form of expression — defamation. Even false statements uttered "from personal spite, ill will or a desire to injure" did not amount to constitutional malice. The decision also broadened the scope of appellate review in political libel cases, since appellate judges could now conduct their own independent review of the facts to ensure that a jury had not encroached on a protected area of speech.

But there is another aspect to the case, one less discussed and certainly not celebrated, the impact that the opinion had on traditional cultural assumptions about libel law. Historically, the sense of community in America drew strength from measured public discourse and deference to public officials. Libel law had protected the so-called best men — elected and appointed officials — from slanderous attacks. Brennan's opinion disrupted this traditional basis for civil discourse by eroding the concept of civic republicanism, in which virtuous persons conducted public affairs in a disinterested manner and almost always at considerable sacrifice to themselves.

Of course, it is difficult if not impossible to consider L. B. Sullivan and Eugene Connor as exemplars of the "best men," and the overt bigotry that governed their conduct clearly removes them from the type of public servant that libel laws had been meant to protect. The history of the era paints as provincial racists the white officials of the South who brought *Sullivan* and other libel actions, men who hypocritically complemented the force and violence they used against the civil rights movement with a cynical invocation of the law's sweet reason. From this perspective, which is most certainly correct, Justice Brennan wisely redrew traditional lines of constitutional understanding in the face of a massive demand by people of color for the equality they had long been denied. This is what makes *Sullivan* above all else a civil rights case.

This interpretation, as this book has argued, is correct, but at the same time it may not be complete. It ignores some of the factors that led to the original case in Montgomery, and also pays scant attention to the cultural milieu that governed not only civil society but the courts as well. This view of the case and the events surrounding it dismisses the possibility that, quite apart from the substantive issues of racial equality, the Southern white vision of civil discourse had some intrinsic worth.

Justice Brennan's opinion must have tasted bitter and ironic to men such as Grover Hall and Walter Jones, supporters of the old Gunter machine (see ch. 1) who liked to think of themselves as models for and agents of manners and habits of civility, as moderating influences on the racism of lower-class Southern whites, and a barrier against what they perceived as the hypocritical egalitarianism preached by the North. This mindset also fought with the most profound tensions in American life after World War II, those caused not only by the demand for civil rights but also by the postwar prosperity that at times seemed to bypass the South. Grover Hall, an otherwise educated and intelligent newspaper editor, displayed an overweening sense of southern inferiority that could not escape the region's history of race relations.

{ *Chapter 11* }

Upper-class Southerners who championed ideas of local control and state sovereignty set in motion, albeit unwillingly and for the most part unwittingly, forces of constitutional nationalization that would open the South to greater outside influence, and that would further erode the social dominance that group hitherto enjoyed in Montgomery. Brennan's opinion gave the Supreme Court—which the upper-class South despised—new powers of review and blasted away the old habits and manners of civility they so prized as the proper guide to public discourse. One virtue in protecting public officials was that doing so created a climate of respect for governmental authority and encouraged the best men to enter public life. That vision not only undergirded the rationale for seditious libel, but by 1960 had been considerably weakened in Montgomery by the collapse of the Gunter machine and the rise of a new elite that had more in common with lower-class whites than with the pillars of society.

The *Sullivan* decision reinforced the prevailing ideology of legal liberalism, which emphasized rights consciousness and justice and which had little use or patience for a social system that denied these values and protected one group of people at the expense of a much larger group suffering from decades of bigotry and oppression. Notions of deference to political authority—the very authority that sustained racial inequality—seemed antique. Yet even conceding that many southern leaders did not measure up to the standards of the "best men," some cultural historians believe that Brennan's opinion in a larger sense degraded public life and invited second-rate figures to govern. By this argument, the most talented persons supposedly refused to risk political careers in a climate where independence mattered less than accountability, where truth took second place to criticism, and where the public did not trust the people they elected to govern.

In this sense, the decision contributed to the decay of community values that the expansion of First Amendment law has fostered since the 1930s. Brennan helped push American public life—at least involving criticism of public officials—away from the ideal of the New England town meeting, in which the quality of what was said was more important than the quantity. Others argue that *Sullivan* also debased the news media that so eagerly applauded it. Initially the case brought a burst of enthusiasm from the media, and an expansion of investigative and regular news reporting. It is difficult to think of the stories in the *Washington Post* that exposed Watergate taking place in a pre-*Sullivan* setting. The press created a milieu in which basic social problems became subjects of intense media and ultimately public concern. However, this development also meant that the chances of reporters stepping on the reputations of important public officials grew accordingly, as did charges of an ever-increasing sleazy journalism.

Brennan's opinion embodied an ideal of professional journalism that stood at odds with that in the South in general and Montgomery in particular. It did not involve a question of accurate reporting since both Grover Hall and the staff at the *Times* accepted that. They differed in their contending views of reputation. Yale law professor Robert Post has reminded us that reputation has historically been defined as property, as honor, and as dignity. Each of these concepts of reputation "presupposes an image of how people are tied together, or should be tied together, in a social setting. As this image varies, so does the nature of the reputation that the law of defamation seeks to protect."

Northern courts had historically defined reputation as a species of property in which individuals were connected to one another through the institution of the market. A merchant depends on his reputation to sustain himself in the market, meaning that his reputation may vary with his or her worth in that marketplace. As a result, northern courts appear to have been far less likely to treat reputation as an absolute; judges approached it as a variable condition that the individual might control through personal initiative. This idea of reputation as property presupposed a degree of equality among all persons in the marketplace, so that one earned a reputation through equal competition, with some faring better than others, and thus earning a better reputation. This judicial view of reputation as property complemented the entrepreneurial and industrial ethos of the free, northern states and explains why judges and the common law in the North tended to be more accommodating of fair comment in political libel cases.

In the South reputation turned more on concepts of honor and dignity than property. The South's historic social stratification and racial inequality anchored the notion of reputation as honor and set the area apart from the North. Reputation as honor offered individual southerners a social order with a fixed base that did not fluctuate with the marketplace. Under such circumstances, individual reputation was unalterably linked to individual identity, so much so that a person's social behavior became conditioned by it, and deference was expected of—and often given by—those below to the honorific roles filled by those above. The preservation of honor in the South's deferential society was not a matter of individual well-being; instead, the South saw honor as a public good, not just a private possession.

Both Northerners and Southerners agreed on the connection between reputation and dignity, but prior to *Sullivan* they gave it different weight. Again, race and market relations help explain the two approaches. The concept of reputation as dignity is premised on the notion that an individual's identity is constantly being formed through social action, and how one feels about oneself and how one is treated by those around one can vary. If an individual is slandered, it is not just that others will view him or her negatively but that the individual may view him- or herself that way as well. Under the concept of reputation as dignity, individuals can claim protection against trauma to their own sense of worth.

Originally honor and dignity were closely linked, but in the twentieth century they separated, more quickly in the North than in the South, where prescriptive social status persisted much longer. As Professor Post suggests, the modern image of society is made possible by this split between honor and dignity, because without it, civilization as we know it would not be possible. A modern, egalitarian scheme of social relations developed much more slowly in the South than in the North, and the South's social system derived from its history of slavery and racial segregation. The white community of Montgomery, like most of the South, struggled among itself as much as it did with blacks. Upper-class whites from the south side of the city sought to tie their identity to habits and manners of civility; lower-class whites from the east side turned to violence, intimidation, and the security of the Ku Klux Klan. In the North, however, the race issue did not interfere with the idea that there were universal rules that encompassed all social classes and roles. The market-based societies of the North made individual reputation a public as well as a private good, a development that reinforced ideas of individualism and egalitarianism.

When reputation is approached as an incident of social organization, therefore, the *Sullivan* case speaks with force equal to, if not greater than, that when it is recounted solely as an episode of the civil rights movement or of free speech and press. The South, of which Montgomery, the former capital of the Confederacy, was the heart, had a long tradition of treating reputation more as honor and dignity than as property. Not only was the South considerably more hierarchical than the North, but it was also far more suspicious of social relations created in the marketplace. Southern political leaders cut from the mold of the Gunter machine conducted public affairs that relied on hierarchy, deference, and paternalism, and invoked race to structure interpersonal relations. Under these circumstances, the Montgomery elite in 1960 confronted a dual threat, from competing segregationists on the east side, lower-class whites who dismissed as pretentious the traditional notion of reputation as honor, and from a northern press schooled to understand political reputation as a species of property, its value determined in a marketplace of ideas. Hence the reaction of Montgomery's leaders to "Heed Their Rising Voices" specifically, and to the civil rights movement in general, involved more than just a mean-spirited racism. It had that to be sure, but it also entailed an understanding that certain benefits of order and harmony flowed from a system of libel law that protected the best men. What was distinctive about events in Montgomery was not that its leaders (either from the old Gunter machine or from the east side) were merely racists, but they departed from their northern counterparts in making sense of political discourse, the social bases of politics, and the purposes of the press.

Justice Brennan's opinion in *New York Times v. Sullivan*, therefore, is notable not just for the legal change that it promoted but for the sectionally bound cultural assumptions that it rejected. The justices adopted a modern, northern conception of libel law that was designed to encourage a robust exchange of ideas, but this formulation rejected the South's most enduring contribution to the body of law, the notion that habits and manners of civility should govern civic discourse. Perhaps those notions might have been more valued by others if they had not rested on a basis of racism and a desire to keep African Americans tied to an inferior status.

# CHRONOLOGY

| | |
|---|---|
| July 26, 1948 | President Truman signs order to desegregate armed forces. |
| May 17, 1954 | Supreme Court decides *Brown v. Board of Education I*. |
| 1955 | Supreme Court issues "all deliberate speed" formula in *Brown v. Board of Education II*. |
| Dec. 1, 1955 | Rosa Parks refuses to give up her seat in front of a segregated bus, triggering the Montgomery (Ala.) bus boycott. |
| Dec. 1956 | Montgomery buses are desegregated following Supreme Court decision in *Gayle v. Browder*. |
| Jan. 1957 | Martin Luther King Jr. and Fred Shuttlesworth found the Southern Christian Leadership Conference. |
| Sept. 1957 | Nine black students barred from entering Little Rock, Arkansas, Central High School, and President Eisenhower sends in federal troops to enforce court order. |
| Feb. 1, 1960 | Black students from North Carolina Agricultural and Technical College begin sit-in at Woolworth's lunch counter; movement spreads across South. |
| Mar. 29, 1960 | "Heed Their Rising Voices" appears in *New York Times*. |
| April 1960 | L. B. Sullivan initiates libel suit against the *Times*. |
| November 1960 | Libel trial, *Sullivan et al. v. New York Times*, in Montgomery Circuit Court. |
| May 4, 1961 | Congress of Racial Equality (CORE) and Student Nonviolent Coordinating Committee (SNCC) sponsor Freedom Rides, triggering riots in several southern cities. |
| Aug. 30, 1962 | Alabama Supreme Court affirms judgment against the *Times*. |
| April 16, 1963 | Martin Luther King Jr. jailed during protest, and writes "Letter from a Birmingham Jail." |
| Aug. 28, 1963 | March on Washington; King delivers "I Have a Dream" speech. |
| Jan. 6, 1964 | Oral argument in Supreme Court in *New York Times v. Sullivan*. |

| | |
|---|---|
| Mar. 9, 1964 | Supreme Court hands down decision in *New York Times v. Sullivan.* |
| July 2, 1964 | President Johnson signs Civil Rights Act of 1964. |
| Aug. 10, 1965 | Congress passes Voting Rights Act of 1965. |
| April 4, 1968 | Martin Luther King Jr. assassinated in Memphis, Tennessee. |

# BIBLIOGRAPHICAL ESSAY

*Note from the Series Editors: The following bibliographical essay contains the major primary and secondary sources the author consulted for this volume. We have asked all authors in the series to omit formal citations in order to make our volumes more readable, inexpensive, and appealing for students and general readers. In adopting this format, Landmark Law Cases and American Society follows the precedent of a number of highly regarded and widely consulted series.*

In the late 1980s Kermit Hall conducted interviews with a number of the participants, including M. Roland Nachman Jr., Thomas Eric Embry, William H. MacDonald, Ray Jenkins, Fred Shuttlesworth, Fred Gray, John Patterson, and William Rogers. The transcripts of these interviews, as well as other typescript items, are in the Kermit L. Hall Papers, Special Collections Division of the Library at the State University of New York at Albany. M. Roland Nachman spoke about the case in "New York Times v. Sullivan: A Retrospective," at the Bar Association of the City of New York on March 30, 1989, and a typescript is available of that talk.

The Record of the Case includes the transcript of the trial in Judge Jones's courtroom, the appeal briefs to the Alabama Supreme Court, the decision of that court in *New York Times v. Sullivan*, 273 Ala. 656, 144 So. 2d 25 (1962), the petitions for certiorari to the United States Supreme Court, and the briefs filed by all sides after the Court had taken the case. The opinions in the case are at 376 U.S. 254 (1964). The transcript of oral argument in the case is available in the Supreme Court Library.

The papers of Earl Warren, William J. Brennan Jr., William O. Douglas, and Hugo L. Black are in the Manuscript Division of the Library of Congress; those of John Marshall Harlan II are in the Seeley G. Mudd Manuscript Library at Princeton University. There is an extensive biographical file on Judge Walter B. Jones in the Alabama Department of History and Archives, Montgomery, Alabama.

Some of the participants have written autobiographies, and these include Fred D. Gray, *Bus Ride to Justice: Changing the System by the System: The Life and Works of Fred D. Gray, Preacher, Attorney, Politician* (Montgomery: Black Belt Press, 1995); Ralph D. Abernathy, *And the Walls Came Tumbling Down: An Autobiography* (New York: Harper & Row, 1989); John Lewis, *Walking with the Wind: A Memoir of the Movement* (New York: Simon & Schuster, 1998); Solomon S. Seay Sr., *I Was There by the Grace of God* (Montgomery: Seay Educational Foundation, 1990); and Solomon S. Seay Jr., *Jim Crow and Me: Stories from My Life as a Civil Rights Lawyer* (Montgomery: New State Books, 2008).

Several biographies have been written about the Reverend Shuttlesworth, including Andrew M. Manis, *A Fire You Can't Put Out: the Civil Rights Life of Birmingham's Reverend Fred Shuttlesworth* (Tuscaloosa: University of Alabama Press, 1999); Andrew M. Manis and Marjorie L. White, eds., *Birmingham Revolutionaries: Fred Shuttlesworth and the Alabama Christian Movement for Human Rights* (Macon: Mercer University Press, 2000); and William A. Nunnelley, *Fred Shuttlesworth: Civil Rights Activist* (Montgomery: Seacoast Publications, 2003). For Ralph Abernathy, see Catherine Reef, *Ralph David Abernathy* (Parsippany: Dillon Press, 1995). Rosa Parks has been the subject of a number of books, including Douglas Brinkley, *Rosa Parks* (New York: Viking, 2000), and Rosa Parks and Jim Haskins, *Rosa Parks: My Story* (New York: Dial Press, 1992). However, recent historians have noted that while Parks is correctly given credit for starting the boycott, other women played a major role in sustaining it. See Jo Ann Robinson, *The Montgomery Bus Boycott and the Women Who Started It*, ed. David J. Garrow (Knoxville: University of Tennessee Press, 1987), and Danielle L. McGuire, *At the Dark End of the Street* (New York: Alfred Knopf, 2010).

Martin Luther King's life has been the subject of several first-rate biographies, among which are Taylor Branch's three volumes of *America in the King Years: Parting the Waters* (New York: Simon & Schuster, 1988), *Pillar of Fire* (1998), and *At Canaan's Edge* (2006); and David J. Garrow, *Bearing the Cross: Martin Luther King, Jr., and the Southern Christian Leadership Conference* (New York: William Morrow, 1986)

The literature on the civil rights movement is enormous. A good place to start are the classic works by Richard Kluger, *Simple Justice: The History of Brown v. Board of Education and Black America's Struggle for Freedom* (New York: Knopf, 1976), and C. Vann Woodward, *The Strange Career of Jim Crow* (New York: Oxford University Press, 1966). Although both studies have been somewhat revised by later historians, their basic descriptions of life in the pre-*Brown* South and the legal battle by the NAACP remain valid. A good supplement is William Chafe et al., eds., *Remembering Jim Crow: African Americans Tell about Life in the Segregated South* (New York: New Press, 2001)

The following books are not meant to be exhaustive, but merely serve as an introduction to the history of the civil rights movement. Rhoda Lois Blumberg, *Civil Rights: The 1960s Freedom Struggle* (Boston: Twayne, 1984); Juan Williams, *Eyes on the Prize: America's Civil Rights Years, 1954–1965* (New York: Viking, 1987); Harvard Sitkoff, *The Struggle for Black Equality*, 25th anniversary ed. (New York: Hill & Wang, 2008); Robert Weisbrot, *Freedom Bound: A History of America's Civil Rights Movement* (New York: Norton, 1990); and Steven F. Lawson, *Running for Freedom: Civil Rights and Black Politics in America since 1941*, 3rd ed. (New York: Wiley-Blackwell, 2009).

Much of the history of the movement can also be found in the stories of the organizations. Unfortunately, there is no good overall history of the NAACP, although much of the struggle can be found in two books by Mark V. Tushnet, *The NAACP's Legal Strategy against Segregated Education, 1925–1950* (Chapel Hill: University of North Carolina Press, 1987), and *Making Civil Rights Law: Thurgood Marshall and the Supreme Court, 1936–1961* (New York: Oxford University Press, 1994). Jack Greenburg, one of the team members for the *Brown* case, has written about the Legal Defense Fund in *Crusaders in the Courts* (New York: Twelve Tables Press, 2004).

See also August Meier and Elliot Rudwick, *CORE: A Study in the Civil Rights Movement, 1942–1968* (Urbana: University of Illinois Press, 1975); Wesley C. Hogan, *Many Minds, One Heart: SNCC's Dream for a New America* (Chapel Hill: University of North Carolina Press, 2007); Cheryl Greenberg, *A Circle of Trust: Remembering SNCC* (New Brunswick: Rutgers University Press, 1998); and Clayborne Carson, *In Struggle: SNCC and the Black Awakening of the 1960s* (Cambridge, Mass.: Harvard University Press, 1981).

Also useful are William H. Chafe, *Civilities and Civil Rights: Greensboro, North Carolina, and the Black Struggle for Freedom* (New York: Oxford University Press, 1986), detailing the start of the sit-in movement, and Michal R. Belknap, *Federal Law and Southern Order: Racial Violence and Constitutional Conflict in the Post-Brown South* (Athens: University of Georgia Press, 1987). Because the KKK played so large a part in the violence of this time, see also David M. Chalmers, *Hooded Americanism: The History of the Ku Klux Klan* (Durham: Duke University Press, 1981).

Historians have seen the Montgomery bus boycott as a seminal event in the civil rights movement, and there have been numerous books about it, including Martin Luther King Jr., *Stride toward Freedom: The Montgomery Story* (New York: Harper & Row, 1958), and the books on Rosa Parks mentioned above. See also David Aretha, *Montgomery Bus Boycott* (Greensboro: Morgan Reynolds, 2009); David J. Garrow, ed., *The Walking City: The Montgomery Bus Boycott, 1955–56* (Brooklyn: Carlson, 1989); Fred D. Gray and Willy S. Leventhal, *The Children Are Coming On: A Retrospective of the Montgomery Bus Boycott.* (Montgomery: Black Belt Press, 1998); Stewart Burns, *Daybreak of Freedom: The Montgomery Bus Boycott* (Chapel Hill: University of North Carolina Press, 1997); J. Mills Thornton III, "Challenge and Response in the Montgomery Bus Boycott of 1955–1956," *Alabama Review* (1980): 163–235; and Robert J. Glennon, "The Role of Law in the Civil Rights Movement: The Montgomery Bus Boycott, 1955–1957," 9 *Law & History Review* 59 (1991). The boycott is put into a wider perspective in Catherine A. Barnes, *Journey from Jim Crow: The Desegregation of Southern Transit* (New York: Columbia University Press, 1983).

Events in Alabama (including Montgomery) are discussed in Frye Gaillard, *Cradle of Freedom: Alabama and the Movement That Changed America*

(Tuscaloosa: University of Alabama Press, 2004); Robert J. Norrell, *The Making of Modern Alabama* (Tuscaloosa: Yellowhammer Press, 1993); Glenn T. Eskew, *But for Birmingham: The Local and National Movements in the Civil Rights Struggle* (Chapel Hill: University of North Carolina Press, 1997); and Thornton J. Mills III, *Dividing Line: Municipal Politics and the Struggle for Civil Rights in Montgomery, Birmingham, and Selma* (Tuscaloosa: University of Alabama Press, 2002).

Much has been written on the First Amendment, but I find Harry Kalven Jr., *A Worthy Tradition: Freedom of Speech in America* (New York: Harper & Row, 1988), to be an excellent introduction to the topic. The origins of the Press Clause are in Leonard W. Levy, *Emergence of a Free Press* (New York: Oxford University Press, 1985) and Harold L. Nelson, ed., *Freedom of the Press from Hamilton to the Warren Court* (Indianapolis: Bobbs-Merrill, 1966). Wechsler relied heavily on James Morton Smith, *Freedom's Fetters: The Alien and Sedition Laws and American Civil Liberties* (Ithaca: Cornell University Press, 1956).

Norman L. Rosenberg, *Protecting the Best Men: An Interpretive History of the Law of Libel* (Chapel Hill: University of North Carolina Press, 1986) is a good popular study of the origins of libel law, but see also the essay review by Robert C. Post, "Defaming Public Officials: On Doctrine and Legal History," 1987 *American Bar Foundation Journal* 539. Any law library will have several shelves devoted to the subject, and again, the following items are not meant to be exhaustive. Rodney A. Smolla, *Law of Defamation* (St. Paul: West Publishing, 1999), and *Suing the Press* (New York: Oxford University Press, 1986); Robert Post, *Constitutional Domains: Democracy, Community, Management* (Cambridge, Mass.: Harvard University Press, 1995), and "The Social Foundations of Defamation Law: Reputation and the Constitution," 74 *California Law Review* 691 (1986).

Philosophies on the First Amendment vary considerably, but three men and their works that have had an impact on its jurisprudence are Zechariah Chafee Jr., *Free Speech in The United States*, rev. ed. (Cambridge, Mass.: Harvard University Press, 1941); Alexander Meiklejohn, *Political Freedom: The Constitutional Powers of the People* (New York: Oxford University Press, 1960), and *Free Speech and Its Relation to Self-Government* (New York: Harper's, 1949); and Thomas Emerson, *Toward a General Theory of the First Amendment* (New York: Random House, 1966), and *The System of Freedom of Expression* (New York: Vintage, 1970). Following the *Sullivan* case, Justice Brennan paid tribute to one philosophy in "The Supreme Court and the Meiklejohn Interpretation of the First Amendment," 79 *Harvard Law Review* 1 (1965).

What exactly "freedom of the press" means remains a subject of lively debate. Among useful works in this area are Lucas A. Powe Jr., *The Fourth Estate and the Constitution* (Berkeley: University of California Press, 1991); John Lofton, *The Press as Guardian of the First Amendment* (Columbia: University of South Carolina Press, 1980); and Pnina Lahav, ed., *Press Law in Modern Democracies* (New York: Longman, 1985).

I have relied on Anthony Lewis, *Make No Law: The Sullivan Case and the First Amendment* (New York: Vintage Books, 1992), but differ with him over his focus on the case as primarily dealing with press freedom.

The best introduction to the Warren Court is Lucas A. Powe Jr., *The Warren Court and American Politics* (Cambridge, Mass.: Harvard University Press, 2000). See also Ronald Rotunda, "The Warren Court and Freedom of the Press," in *The Warren Court: A Retrospective*, ed. Bernard Schwartz (New York: Oxford University Press, 1996); W. Wat Hopkins, "Justice Brennan, Justice Harlan, and New York Times Co. v. Sullivan: A Case Study in Supreme Court Decision Making," 1 *Communications Law & Policy* 469 (1996); and E. E. Dennis et al., *Justice Hugo Black and the First Amendment* (Ames: Iowa State University Press, 1978).

The *Sullivan* case, as could be expected, spawned dozens of law review articles over the next two decades, and these are gathered and discussed in Frank G. Houdek, "Constitutional Limitations on Libel Actions: A Bibliography of *New York Times v. Sullivan* and Its Progeny, 1964–1984," 6 *Communications and Entertainment Law Journal* 447 (1984). W. Wat Hopkins, *Actual Malice: Twenty-Five Years after* Times v. Sullivan (New York: Praeger, 1989), looks at how the new standard actually played out in the courts. George K. Rahdert and David M. Snyder, "Rediscovering Florida's Common Law Defenses to Libel and Slander," 11 *Stetson Law Review* 1 (1981), explores how despite *Sullivan* and its progeny, basic state defamation law as applied to private figures remains relatively unchanged. Harry Kalven Jr., "The New York Times Case: A Note on the 'Central Meaning of the First Amendment,'" 1964 *Supreme Court Review* 191, was one of the earliest examinations of the case and remains one of the most insightful.

Media coverage of civil rights played an important role in transforming protests against segregation and discrimination in the South into a national issue, and a number of books have examined this relationship, of which the most comprehensive is Gene Roberts and Hank Klibanoff, *The Race Beat: The Press, the Civil Rights Struggle, and the Awakening of a Nation* (New York: Alfred A. Knopf, 2006). See also John T. Kneebone, *Southern Liberal Journalists and the Issue of Race, 1920–1944* (Chapel Hill: University of North Carolina Press, 1985); Clayborne Carson et al., *Reporting Civil Rights* (New York: Library of America, 2003); Paul L. Fisher and Ralph L. Lowenstein, *Race and the News Media* (New York: Praeger, 1967); and Carolyn Martindale, *The White Press and Black America* (Westport: Greenwood Press, 1986). A different facet is explored in Harry Kalven Jr., *The Negro and the First Amendment* (Columbus: Ohio State University Press, 1965).

For the *New York Times*, see Gay Talese, *The Kingdom and the Power: Behind the Scenes at the New York Times* (New York: World Publishing, 1969); Harrison E. Salisbury, *Without Fear or Favor: The New York Times and Its Times* (New York: Times Books, 1980), and *A Journey for Our Time* (New York: Harper & Row, 1983); and Turner Catledge, *My Life and The Times* (New York: Harper & Row, 1971).

The question of honor, and how it differed in the North and South, can be explored in Robert Bellah, "The Meaning of Reputation in American Society," 74 *California Law Review* 743 (1986), and Bertram Wyatt-Brown, *Southern Honor: Ethics and Behavior in the Old South* (New York: Oxford University Press, 1982). How the law reflects cultural norms and changes is examined in Sandra F. Van Burkeleo et al., eds., *Constitutionalism and American Culture: Writing the New Constitutional History* (Lawrence: University Press of Kansas, 2002).

Abernathy, Ralph David, 8, 51, 56, 89, 182
  attacked by Edward Davis, 13
  car and property seized, 88
  name added to advertisement, 17
  as witness, 63
*Abington Township v. Schempp* (1963), 145
*Abrams v. United States* (1919), 105
Actual malice test, 186, 191, 201
Adams, Abigail, 116
Adams, John, 36, 107
*Age-Herald Publishing Co. v. Huddleston* (Ala., 1921), 90, 97
Alabama, University of, integration at, 74
Alabama Anti-Boycott Act of 1921, 9
Alabama law on libel, 43
  and sedition, 122–26
Alabama State College, 24
Alabama Supreme Court, 45
Alexander, James, 40
Alfred the Great, Laws of, 37
Alien and Sedition Acts (1798), 106–7
American Civil Liberties Union, amici brief in *Sullivan*, 135
American Law Institute, 121
Amicus curiae briefs in *Sullivan*
  by ACLU, 135
  by *Chicago Tribune*, 134, 136
  by *Washington Post*, 134, 136
Anniston, Ala., and freedom riders, 79
Anti-Saloon League, 6
Aronson, Gershon T., 16, 60
Ascalon series, 29
*Associated Press v. Walker* (1967), 189
*Atlanta Journal*, on trial verdict, 84

"Bad tendency" test, 105
Baker, Ella, organizes SNCC, 75–76
Baldwin, James, 77
Bancroft, Harding, 61–62

Barnett, Ross, 73, 80
*Barr v. Matteo* (1959), 168
Barry, Marion, 75, 76, 77
*Beauharnais v. Illinois* (1952), 94–95, 174
Beddow, Roderick, 46, 47
Bickel, Alexander, 87, 105
Birmingham, Ala.
  and violence captured on television, 81
  bombing of church kills four girls in, 82
  children involved in demonstrations, 82
Birmingham, David, 7–8
Bisher, Furman, 85
Black, Hugo, 95, 129, 140
  concurring opinion in *Sullivan*, 179–80
  in conference, 162
  and hesitation to join opinion, 168–69
Blackstone, Sir William, 104
Blackwell, Arnold, as witness, 54
Blasphemy, 34–35
Bolingbroke, Viscount, 39
Bond, Julian, 75
Bork, Robert, 193
*Boynton v. Virginia* (1960), 78
Brandeis, Louis D., 105, 124, 130, 161, 175
  and free speech, 183
*Brandenburg v. Ohio* (1969), 37, 105, 146, 182
Brennan, William J., Jr., 95, 142–43, 196, 200
  in conference, 163
  delivers opinion, 172
  and fashioning the *Sullivan* opinion, 164 ff.
  first draft, 166–68
  and number five, 161

Brennan, William J., Jr., *continued*
  and *Rosenblatt* decision, 187–88
  second draft, 168
  and seventh draft, 170–71
  and test for obscenity, 164–65
*Bridges v. California* (1941), 112, 125, 174
Briefs, in the Supreme Court, 119–20
*Browder v. Gayle* (1956), 78
Brown, Joe David, 85
Brownell, Herbert, Jr., 100, 109, 121
*Brown v. Board of Education* (1954), 8,
  10, 70, 146
*Brown v. Board of Education II* (1955), 71
Bryant, Paul "Bear," sues *Saturday
  Evening Post*, 85
Burger, Warren, and size of briefs, 120
Burnett, Carol, 195, 196
Burnett, George, 189
*Burton v. Wilmington Parking
  Authority* (1961), 72
Butts, Wallace, 85

Calhoun, John C., 107
Callender, Thomas, 107
*Cantwell v. Connecticut* (1940), 112
Carmichael, Stokely, 75
Catledge, Turner, 18, 30
  and editorial, 18–19
*Cato Letters* (Trenchard and Gordon),
  39–40
Chafee, Zechariah, Jr., 130, 183
  on libel law, 42
*Chaplinsky v. New Hampshire* (1942),
  94–95, 174, 183
Chase, Samuel, 108
*Chicago Tribune*, amici brief of, 134, 136
Christian academies, 70
*City of Chicago v. Tribune Co.* (Ill.,
  1923), 124, 136
Civil disobedience, 18
Civil Rights Act (1964), 72, 87, 199
*Civil Rights Cases* (1883), 71
Civil rights groups, response to
  decisions, 182
Clark, Tom C., 141–42
  in conference, 162–63

Clarke, John H., 120
Coke, Edward, 34
Coleman, James S., 97
*Coleman v. MacLennan* (Kan., 1908), 177
Columbia Broadcasting System, 85
Colvard, Dewey, sues Curtis Pub. Co.,
  85
Commission on Equal Employment
  Opportunity, 73
*Communications Assn. v. Douds* (1950),
  125
Community, effect of *Sullivan* on,
  202–6
Compact theory of union, 107
Congress of Racial Equality (CORE),
  75
Connor, Eugene "Bull," 31, 79, 81, 90,
  202
  files libel suit, 32
Contempt, 125–26
Cook, Tom, 79
*Cooper v. Aaron* (1958), 70, 71
Crawford, Vernon A., 51
Crymes, Theotis, attacked by police,
  86
*Curtis Publishing Co. v. Butts* (1967), 189

Daly, Thomas F., 109, 121
Damron, William, 86
*Davis v. Johnson Pub. Co.*, 49
Davis, Edward, 56
  attacks Ralph Abernathy, 13
*De Libellis Famosis* (1606), 34
*Dennis v. United States* (1951), 105
Denniston, Lyle, 191
*Derrington v. Plummer* (1957), 72
*De Scandalis Magnatum* (1275), 33, 136
Diana, Ronald, helps on brief, 120ff.
Douglas, William O., 35, 117, 140–41,
  161, 162
  agrees to Brennan opinion, 170
  in conference, 162
  and hesitation to join opinion,
  168–69
Dryfoos, Orville, 102–3
  apologizes for ad, 32–33

*Dun & Bradstreet v. Greenmoss Builders* (1985), 196
*Duncan v. Louisiana* (1968), 146

Eastland, James, 80
Eisenhower, Dwight D., 73, 139
Embry, T. Eric, 46, 47, 92, 100, 121, 199
   appeal to Alabama Supreme Court, 93–94
   raises First Amendment issue in Alabama Supreme Court, 111
   summation in trial, 65
Emerson, Thomas, and free speech jurisprudence, 184–85
*Engel v. Vitale* (1962), 145, 146
*Epperson v. Arkansas* (1968), 146
Epstein, Richard, 193
Erikson, Kai, 39
Espionage Act (1917), 36
Evers, Medgar, murdered, 82

Faber, Harold, 50
Falwell, Jerry, 186
Farmer, James, 78
*Farmers Educational & Cooperative Union v. WDAY Inc.* (1959), 135
Faubus, Orval, 70, 73
Faulk, John Henry, 116
*Faulk v. Aware, Inc.* (NY, 1962), 131
*Federal Courts and the Federal System, The* (Wechsler and Hart), 101
Field, Stephen, 95
First Amendment, and Alabama law, 122–26, 127–28
   and expansion after *Sullivan*, 190
   and Nachman brief, 129–31
   and strategy adopted by Wechsler, 103ff.
Fortas, Abe, dissents in *Rosenblatt v. Baer*, 187
Fosdick, Harry Emerson, 16
Frankel, Marvin
   suggests comparison to Sedition Act, 106
   and *Times* briefs, 101, 120ff.
Frankfurter, Felix, 95, 145, 160, 161

*Freedman v. Maryland* (1965), 146
Freedom Rides, 77ff.

Gallion, MacDonald, 32
Galloping presumptions of libel law, 40–43
*Galloway v. United States* (1943), 132
Garrison, James, 186
*Garrison v. Louisiana* (1964), 186
Gayle, William A. "Tackey," 11, 12
*Gayle v. Browder* (1965), 10
Gertz, Elmer, 192
*Gertz v. Robert Welch, Inc.* (1974), 192
*Gideon v. Wainwright* (1963), 145
Goldberg, Arthur, 144–45
   and Brennan opinion, 170
   concurring opinion in *Sullivan*, 181
   in conference, 163–64
*Gomillion v. Lightfoot* (1960), 71
Goodale, James, 84–85
Goodwyn, John L., 97
Gordon, Thomas, 39
Gott, John William, 34
Gray, Fred, 8, 51, 64
*Gray v. Sanders* (1963), 145
*Griswold v. Connecticut* (1965), 146
Grooms, Harlan H., 89–90
Gunter, William A., Jr., 5–6
Gunter machine, 5–6
   decline of, 6
   in disarray, 10, 15
   opponents to, 6
Gunther, John, 139

Hall, Grover C., Jr., 14, 22, 23, 28–29, 31, 43, 202
   editorial on ad, 29–30
   witness in trial, 52–54
Hall, Grover C., Sr., 6
Hamilton, Alexander, 108
Harlan, John Marshall, II, 92, 142
   and *Butts* opinion, 189
   changes mind and joins opinion, 171
   in conference, 163

Harlan, John Marshall, II, *continued*
  reluctance to join opinion, 168–69
  wants to base opinion on code
    section, 168
*Harper v. Virginia Board of Elections*
  (1967), 146
Hart, Henry M., Jr., 101
Harwood, Robert B., and Ala.
  Supreme Court opinion, 96–99
*Heart of Atlanta Motel v. United States*
  (1964), 146
"Heed Their Rising Voices"
  background and composition of, 15ff.
  contents of, 19
  copy of, 20
Hellman, Lillian, 85
Herbert, Anthony, 194
*Herbert v. Lando* (1979), and rules of
  discovery in libel suits, 194–95
Hill, Lister, 6
Holmes, Oliver Wendell, Jr., 36–37,
    119, 124, 130
  and free speech, 183
  in *Patterson*, 103–4
  in *Schenck* and *Abrams*, 105
Hoover, J. Edgar, 79
"Hot news" doctrine, 189
Hughes, Charles Evans, 104, 120
*Hutchinson v. Proxmire* (1979), 193

Injury, in libel law, 42
Intent, in libel law, 41–42
*International Shoe Co. v. Washington*
  (1945), 95–96, 97, 126–27
Iushewitz, Morris, 16

Jackson, Miss., and freedom riders, 80
Jackson, Robert H., 95
James, Earl, 23, 30, 88
  elected mayor of Birmingham, 11
  files libel suit, 31
Jefferson, Thomas, 106, 116, 124, 126
  and Kentucky resolution, 107
  on newspapers, 109
Jenkins, Ray, 23, 28, 44
Johnson, Frank, 89

Johnson, Lyndon B., 74
*Johnson v. Virginia* (1963), 71
Jones, Walter Burgwyn, 10, 47, 92, 202
  charge to jury, 65–68
  connections to Alabama officials,
    48–49
  declares ministers' property forfeit,
    88
  efforts to kill NAACP, 91–92
  opposition to civil rights, 49
  reputation for fairness, 49
  southern viewpoint, 48–49
*Joseph Burstyn v. Wilson* (1952)
Judiciary Act (1789), 95
Jurisdiction of Alabama courts, 126–27
Jury
  finds for Sullivan, 68
  selection of, 51–52
Jury trial, and Seventh Amendment,
    131–32

Kalven, Harry, 185, 186–87
Kaminsky, Harry W., 55
*Katzenbach v. McClung* (1964), 146
*Katz v. United States* (1967), 146
*Keeton v. Hustler Magazine, Inc.* (1984),
    196
Kennedy, John F.
  election of and black leaders'
    response, 72–73
  and Ole Miss, 74
  signs executive order on housing, 73
  and University of Alabama, 74
Kennedy, Robert F., 72–73
Kentucky and Virginia Resolutions
  (1798), 107–8
King, Coretta Scott, 72
King, Martin Luther, Jr.
  charged with income tax evasion, 15
  and demonstrations in
    Birmingham, 81
  home bombed, 9, 23, 27, 56, 72, 75
  "Letter from a Birmingham Jail," 81
  named head of Montgomery
    Improvement Association, 8
King, Martin Luther, Sr., 73

King, Tom, sues *Saturday Evening Post*, 85
Kissinger, Henry, 195
*Knapp v. Schweitzer* (1958), 117, 131
Ku Klux Klan, 6, 18
   attacks sit-in students, 14

Lacy, E. Y., as witness, 55–56
*Lady Chatterly's Lover*, 35
Lando, Barry, 194
Lawrence, D. H., 35
Lawson, James, 75
Lawson, Thomas S., 97
Legal Defense Fund, 74
Lewis, Anthony, 86, 195–96
Lewis, John, 75, 80
   attacked in Rock Hill, 79
   beaten in Montgomery, 80
Libel, law of, 28, 33ff.
   in colonial era, 39
   and "country faction," 39
   tests and assumptions, 40–43
   after *Sullivan*, 190ff., 201
Livingston, J. Ed., 97
Loeb, Louis L., 88–89, 101, 103, 121
   lawyer for the *Times*, 46
   strategy on libel suits, 46
"Long-arm" jurisdiction, 95–96
Lord, Day & Lord, 46
*Loving v. Virginia* (1967), 146
Lowery, Joseph E., 51, 89
   name added to advertisement, 17
   as witness, 63
Lyndhurst, Lord Chancellor, 42
Lyon, Matthew, 36, 107

MacDonald, William H., 22, 28
Madison, James, 124, 175, 195
   and Virginia resolution, 107, 123
*Mapp v. Ohio* (1961), 142
Marshall, Thurgood, 51
   appointed to federal bench, 74
   opposes sit-ins, 76
*Massiah v. United States* (1964), 145
Mathews, Z. T., 87
McCabe, John, 50

McComb, Miss., 77
McCormick, Robert, 104
McDaniel, William A., 85
*McGee v. International Life Insurance Co.* (1957), 96, 97
McReynolds, James C., 161
Meiklejohn, Alexander, 193
   and influence on free speech doctrine, 183–84
   and *Sullivan* case, 185
Meredith, James, 73, 74
Merrill, Pelham J., 97
Migration patterns following World War II, 6
*Miller v. California* (1973), 35
*Miranda v. Arizona* (1968), 145
Mississippi, University of, integration of, 73–74
*Mitchell v. United States* (1941), 78
Mobile Plan, 8, 29
*Monitor Patriot Co. v. Roy* (1971), 192
Montgomery, Alabama
   black voting in, 7
   changing residential and political patterns, 6–7
   in 1960, 5
*Montgomery Advertiser*, on trial verdict, 84
Montgomery Bus Boycott, 8–10
Montgomery Improvement Association, 8
Morgan, James, files libel suit, 32
Morgan, Juliette, 10
*Morgan v. Virginia* (1946), 78
Moses, Robert, 75, 77
*Muir v. Louisiana Park Theatrical Assn.* (1958), 72
Murray, John, 29
   as witness, 60
   and writing of advertisement, 16ff.

NAACP. *See* National Association for the Advancement of Colored People
*NAACP v. Alabama* (1958), 91–92
*NAACP v. Button* (1963), 145

Nachman, Merton Roland, 30, 43, 45, 47, 49, 51, 70, 126, 146, 199–200
background and response to ad, 24–25
brief in Supreme Court, 128–33
burden of proof in trial, 54–55
defense of verdict before Alabama Supreme Court, 93–94
files libel suit, 31
and oral argument in Abernathy case, 158–59
and oral argument in Sullivan case, 153–57
prior experience in libel suits, 25–26
responds to petitions for certiorari, 114–17
Nash, Diane, 75, 80
National Association for the Advancement of Colored People (NAACP)
and attacks by Alabama courts, 91–92
opposes sit-ins, 76
Near, Jay, 104
*Near v. Minnesota* (1931), 104, 130
Newton, Wayne, 195, 196
*New York Times*
and acceptance of advertisement, 16–17
apologized to Gov. Patterson, 32–33
circulation in Alabama, 21, 48
defends itself against other lawsuits, 89–90
national circulation, 21
origins and development, 21
retracts ad, 32
*New York Times v. Connor* (1961), 90
*New York Times v. Sullivan* (1964)
analysis of Brennan opinion, 172–79
concurring opinion by Black, 179–80
concurring opinion by Goldberg, 181
and resulting problems in libel law, 190ff.
*New York Times v. Sullivan* (Ala., 1962), 96–99

Nicholas, John, 123
Nixon, Richard, 72

Obscene Publications Acts (GB, 1959, 1964), 35
Obscenity, 34, 35–36
Ochs, Adolph, 18
*Old Dominion Branch, Letter Carriers v. Austin* (1974), 192
Originalism, 108

Parks, Franklin, 23, 30, 31, 88
Parks, Rosa, 8, 75
Patterson, Albert, murdered, 12
Patterson, John, 14, 15, 88, 89, 91
and clean-up of Phenix City, 12
elected governor, 10
files libel suit, 32
Patterson, L. P., as witness, 59
Patterson, Thomas, 103
*Patterson v. Colorado* (1907), 103
Pennekamp, John D., 125
*Pennekamp v. Florida* (1946), 112, 125
*Pennoyer v. Neff* (1878), 95, 97
Persons, Gordon, 11
Petition for certiorari
by black ministers, 113–14
nature of, 110
by *New York Times*, 109–13
Phenix City, clean-up of, 11–12
*Philadelphia Newspapers v. Hepps* (1986)
Pierce, Samuel, 158
*Plessy v. Ferguson* (1896), 71, 142
Post, Robert, 204
Post-trial maneuverings, 88–89
Powe, Lucas (Scot), 145
Powell, Lewis F., Jr., 160, 196
Press Clause jurisprudence, 105
Press response to *Sullivan* decision, 182
Price, H. M., Sr., 55
Private libel, 34, 37ff.

Randolph, A. Philip, 15, 60, 69
Redding, D. Vincent
accepts advertisement, 16–17
as witness, 60–61

Reed, Stanley, 125
*Regina v. Hicklin* (1868), 35
Rehnquist, William H., 186
Reputation
   in Shakespeare, 37
   after *Sullivan*, 204–5
Riesman, David, on libel law, 42
Rock Hill, SC, and freedom riders, 79
Rogers, William, and oral argument
   in Abernathy case, 158
*Rosenblatt v. Baer* (1966), 186–88
*Roth v. United States* (1957), 35, 95,
   124–25, 130, 164–65
Rowe, Gary, 79
Rushin, Judith, 52
Rustin, Bayard, 15, 69
   and CORE, 15
   and role in writing advertisement,
   15ff.
Rutledge, Wiley, 120

Salisbury, Harison, 48, 84, 90
   reports on the South, 30–31, 32
*Saturday Press*, 104
Schenck, Charles, 36
*Schenck v. United States* (1919), 36, 105
*Schenectady Union Publishing Co. v.*
   *Sweeney* (1942), 174
Schwab, Evan, 162
Scienter, in obscenity cases, 136
Seay, Solomon S., Jr., 51
Seay, Solomon S., Sr., 8, 51, 88, 89
   name added to advertisement, 17
Sedition, 34, 36–37
   Alabama law as a form of, 122–26
   buried in *Brandenburg v. Ohio*
   (1969), 182
Sedition Act (1798), 36, 106, 107, 108,
   111, 113, 116, 123
   and use in opinion, 175
Sedition Act (1918), 36
Sellers, 9, 12, 13
   election as police commissioner, 8
   files suit, 33
*Shelley v. Kraemer* (1948), 71, 141, 173
Shelton, Robert, 85

*Sherbert v. Verner* (1963), 145
Shuttlesworth, Fred L., 51, 79, 81, 89
   name added to advertisement, 17
   as witness, 63
Sillars, Malcolm, 109
*Sillars v. Collier* (Mass. 1890), 109
Simpson, Robert Tennent, 97
Sit-in movement, 75ff.
   origins of, 14
   reach Montgomery, 14
Sitton, Claude, 18, 83, 86, 97
   escapes Montgomery, 83–84
Slander
   changes wrought by mercantilism,
   38–39
   in ecclesiastical courts, 38
   in English common law, 38
   punishment for, 37–38
Smith, Charles Lee, 34
*Smith v. Allwright* (1944), 7
*Smith v. California* (1959), 127, 136
SNCC. *See* Student Nonviolent
   Coordinating Committee
*South Carolina v. Katzenbach* (1966),
   146
Southern Christian Leadership
   Conference, 15, 69
Southern University, 76
*Stanley v. Georgia* (1969), 146
Star Chamber, 34
Steiner, Robert F., III, 51, 134
   summation, 63–64
Stewart, Potter, 35, 143–44
   and concurrence in *Rosenblatt*, 188
   in conference, 163
Stone, Harlan Fiske, 100
Strickland, O. M., 56
Student Nonviolent Coordinating
   Committee (SNCC), 75
Sullivan, Lester B., 23, 27, 29, 30, 43,
   45, 69, 70, 116, 131, 200, 202
   background, 11–12
   and clean-up of Phenix City, 12
   elected commissioner of police
   files libel suit, 31
   as witness, 57–59

*Sullivan v. New York Times*, trial in local Alabama court, 48ff.

Sulzberger, Arthur Hays, 46, 88, 102

Supreme Court of Alabama
efforts to cripple NAACP, 91–92
opinion in *New York Times v. Sullivan*, 96–99
and opposition to civil rights, 90ff.
reversals by U.S. Supreme Court, 91–92

Supreme Court of the United States
argument before, 148ff.
and briefs, 119–20
conference, 160–62
grants certiorari in *New York Times v. Sullivan* and *Abernathy et al. v. Sullivan*, 117–18
and oral argument, 147–48
reverses Alabama Supreme Court in NAACP cases, 91–92

Taft, William Howard, 104

Terrell County, Georgia, 87

Thomas, Rex, 83

Thompson, William Hale, 136

*Time v. Firestone* (1976), 193

*Tinker v. Des Moines Independent School District* (1969), 146

*Tory v. Cochran* (2005), 197–98

Trenchard, John, 39

Truman, Harry S., on Tom Clark, 141

Tuttle, Elbert R., 90

*United Gas Public Service Co. v. Texas* (1938), 129

*United States v. Ballard* (1944), 106

*Valentine v. Christensen* (1942), 95, 173

Virginia Report, 123

Voting Rights Act (1965), 87, 199

Wachtel, I. H.
brief in *Abernathy* case, 133–34
serves as attorney for black ministers, 113–14

Waggoner, J. T., files libel suit, 32

Wagner, Joseph B., 50

Wallace, George C., 10, 200
and integration at University of Alabama, 74

Wallace, Mike, 195

Warren, Earl, 138–39
assigns opinion to Brennan, 164
in conference, 162
support for Brennan opinion, 169–70

*Washington Post*, amici brief, 134, 136

Watergate, 204

Waters, Roger J., 50

Wechsler, Doris, helps on brief, 120ff.

Wechsler, Herbert, 100, 146, 200
and ALI, 121
background, 100–101
files petition for certiorari, 109–13
and First Amendment in argument, 150–52
Holmes Lecture on "Neutral Principles," 101
preparation of brief for certiorari, 101ff.
and oral argument in case, 148–53
and preparation of brief for Supreme Court, 120ff.
and *Times* executive board, 102–3

Wechsler, Nancy F., 135

White, Byron, 163, 194

White, Horace W., 55

White Citizens Council, 10, 14

Whitesell, Calvin, 13, 27, 51
reads ad, 22–23

*Whitney v. California* (1927), 105, 174–75, 182

Wilkins, Roy, 73

*Wolston v. Reader's Digest Assn.* (1979), 193

Zenger, Charles Peter, 40